SOCIAL THOUGHT *in* INDIC CIVILIZATION

SOCIAL THOUGHT *in* INDIC CIVILIZATION

Edited by
Himanshu Roy

SAGE

Los Angeles | London | New Delhi
Singapore | Washington DC | Melbourne

First published in 2022 by

SAGE Publications India Pvt Ltd
B1/I-1 Mohan Cooperative Industrial Area
Mathura Road, New Delhi 110 044, India
www.sagepub.in

SAGE Publications Inc
2455 Teller Road
Thousand Oaks, California 91320, USA

SAGE Publications Ltd
1 Oliver's Yard, 55 City Road
London EC1Y 1SP, United Kingdom

SAGE Publications Asia-Pacific Pte Ltd
18 Cross Street #10-10/11/12
China Square Central
Singapore 048423

Published by Vivek Mehra for SAGE Publications India Pvt Ltd and typeset in 10.5/13 pt Sabon by AG Infographics, Delhi.

Library of Congress Cataloging-in-Publication Data Available

Names: Roy, Himanshu, editor.
Title: Social thought in Indic civilization / edited by Himanshu Roy.
Description: New Delhi; Thousand Oaks, California: SAGE Publications India Pvt Ltd, 2022. | Includes bibliographical references and index.
Identifiers: LCCN 2022005513 | ISBN 9789354794469 (hardback) | ISBN 9789354794476 (epub) | ISBN 9789354794483 (ebook)
Subjects: LCSH: Philosophy, Indic—History. | India—Intellectual life. | India—Civilization.
Classification: LCC B131.S63 2022 | DDC 181/.4—dc23/eng/20220303
LC record available at https://lccn.loc.gov/2022005513

ISBN: 978-93-5479-446-9 (HB)

SAGE Team: Rajesh Dey, Shipra Pant, Somyaa Saswoti and Rajinder Kaur

In memory of Shakti Sinha
Former Director, Nehru Memorial Museum and Library

Contents

Preface

Precolonial Indic civilization was the powerhouse of the global economy with approximately 25 per cent of its GDP. In Hegel's metaphor, it was the 'land of desire' and the 'land of wisdom'[1]; in search of wealth and livelihood, as it was the global hub of trade for centuries, the invaders, traders and immigrants had been coming to this land for their opportunities. The recent excavation in Pattnam, a remote village near Kochi in Kerala, which was once a port town, reflects the presence of people from 30 different countries[2]; it confirms the trade dominance of India. The trade, in its wake, brought in different kinds of people from different lands, which constantly enriched the knowledge of Indic civilization.

The trading hub encouraged the social mobility as well as always kept the different professional (caste) groups upgraded in their skills to remain employed. As the economy and society were in flux, so was the social thought which was reflected in diverse texts as well as in praxis. The dynamics of the three different factors, that is, the economy, the society and the social ideas, kept any pan-Indic radical social transformation in check. The fertility of the land and the opportunity of livelihood were integral parts of it in obstructing any radical rupture. There was, however, a wide gap between the elite and the subaltern, as noted by foreign travellers in different ages,[3] which was not so remarkable in their countries.

[1] Georg Wilhelm Friedrich Hegel, 'Introduction', in *Lecture on the History of Philosophy*, Vol. I (New York: Humanities Press, 1974); Georg Wilhelm Friedrich Hegel, 'Indian Philosophy', in *Lecture on the History of Philosophy*, Vol. I (New York: Humanities Press, 1974).

[2] See *The Times of India*, 'Pattanam Site's Importance Isn't Confined to Kerala or India... It Tells Us the World Was Here 2000 Years Ago', 16 November 2020, New Delhi edition.

[3] Neena Kumari, *Madhya Kalin Bhartiya Samaj Evam Sanskriti* (Indian Society and Culture in Medieval Period) (Hindi; Delhi: Research India Press, 2019), chap. 3.

In the absence of any pan-Indic radical rupture, there was continuity in the social thought on two counts visible in the popular discourses of saint-poets[4] and written in different texts on political economy available to us: One was the theme of better governance and strengthening of the state as advised by the texts, and the other was the reflection of democratic protests expressed by the saint-poets who were organic public intellectuals of the time, suggesting the rulers to function like Ram Rajya. The focus was on social adaptation, accommodation and co-optation of merit, and social marginals in the mainstream society. Both the kinds of thought were a combination of honouring justice and rights to the subjects from the top through the instrumentality of the state and the acceptance of social marginals and individual merit in the society. Both the methods were democratic and substantively self-regulating. This combination of the political and the social, with the dynamics of the economy, kept the Indic civilization vibrant for centuries until the British colonial rule altered it forever.

Social Thought in Indic Civilization weaves together interdisciplinary perspectives on the precolonial social thought of Indic civilization. It draws on the methodologies and research traditions of history, political science and sociology to look at major themes and social processes to provide a comprehensive understanding of the society in the historical setting contextualized in the social and political relations of the time. It retrieves, resurrects and analyses the Indian-ness of its history. It also intends to posit this Indian-ness to become the pivot of academic curriculum and of public discourse. The objective is to engage the academics of different disciplines on different themes derived primarily from the Indic traditions. It weaves their heuristic interpretations into a holistic pedagogical volume. The arguments, facts, themes and interpretations presented here are usually not found in the mainstream academic narratives.

[4] For details, see Himanshu Roy and M. P. Singh, eds., preface to *Indian Political Thought*, 3rd ed. (New Delhi: Pearson, 2020).

The manuscript explores a range of key themes such as non-violence in religious praxis, dharma in Indic social traditions, medicinal concepts and institutions, ideas and praxis of Shastrarth, knowledge traditions and institutions, music traditions and Stritva in texts and praxis. It concludes with a chapter on colonial institutions and orient knowledge formation which argues that colonial rule under a deliberate design altered the interpretation of history of Indic civilization famous for being the 'land of desire' and 'land of wisdom'.

The work was facilitated, to arrive at the standard format of pedagogy, by four workshops held in the past four years at different academic centres of India: Developing Countries Research Centre (DCRC), University of Delhi; Department of Political Science, Goa University; Department of Political Science, DDU College, University of Delhi; and Nehru Memorial Museum and Library (NMML), Teen Murti House, New Delhi. I thank Professor Sunil Chaudhry, Director, DCRC; Professor Rahul Tripathi, Head, Department of Political Science, Goa University; Principal Hemchand Jain, DDU College, University of Delhi; and late Mr Shakti Sinha, then Director NMML for organizing the workshops. I also thank Vikas Kumar, research scholar, Department of Political Science, University of Delhi, for his secretarial assistance and Rajesh Dey, Managing Editor (Commissioning), SAGE, for his unstinted support. Finally, I thank my contributors for their brilliant works.

Introduction

Himanshu Roy

Indic social thought has been in constant flux for centuries incorporating and internalizing diverse new ideas as well as recycling and reinterpreting the old ideas in new forms with new inputs tailored to fit the new social context. These ideas, praxis and ethos have been changing to fit the changing structural, technological, topographical and political requirements of the multilingual localities. From the ideational bliss of Rigveda[1] to the 'land of wisdom' and the 'land of desire',[2] it has been a long civilizational history of ideas, open to the new currents of change, but has refused to be blown over of its Indian-ness. The idea of better governance, reflected in the concept of Ram Rajya, and the idea of justice for all providing opportunities for individual and social mobility through co-optation, accommodation, adaptation and adoption for social marginals and meritorious have remained constant. India, therefore, had remained the 'land of wisdom', which Hegel used to remark about it to his students in the 1820s.

[1] For details, See Himanshu Roy and M. P. Singh, eds., conclusion to *Indian Political Thought*, 3rd ed. (Delhi: Pearson, 2020).

[2] Georg Wilhelm Friedrich Hegel, 'Introduction', in *Lecture on the History of Philosophy*, Vol. 1 (New York: Humanities Press, 1974); Georg Wilhelm Friedrich Hegel, 'Indian Philosophy', in *Lecture on the History of Philosophy*, Vol. 1 (New York: Humanities Press, 1974).

As India was the trading hub of the world until the first half of the 18th century, traders, scholars, invaders and immigrants came from all over the world for its wealth and wisdom and carried back their images of opulence about India. India, therefore, was also known as the 'land of desire'. Its residents learnt from the global diversities and enriched and constantly upgraded their skills, which were reflected in their texts and institutions. The recent archaeological excavations in Pattanam, now a small village near Kochi in Kerala, reflect the presence of people of 30 countries of the world who used to come for the trade, from Jordon to China and from Italy to Greece. It was around 2,000 years back as reflected in the DNA report of human skeletons and the carbon dating of the artefacts.[3] Seventeen hundred years later, an Austrian Carmelite missionary, Paolino Da San Bartolomeo, who was in Malabar from 1776 to 1789, had observed in his book *A Voyage to the East Indies* that the residents had universal education which was simple and inexpensive. They learnt alphabets, language, epics and arithmetic at elementary stage. The average entry level of the child was around five years of age. The teachers received 'two panam from each of his pupils for every two months'[4] or were paid in kind. Many of them did not charge anything from their students. The education was, thus, social, not dependent on the state for funding. Yet it was universal and was available to everyone irrespective of caste and gender; the students attended their schools irrespective of their social and economic status. Those who were pursuing higher education were known as Brahmanas. They had to follow strict codes of discipline which were physical and academic. It was a 'knowledge society' in the historical setting of the time. The pluralism of the knowledge lead to Shastrarth, to the public debates. The castes were skilled labour particularly in the trading zones who were, spatially and socially,

[3] See *Times of India,* 'Pattanam Site's Importance Isn't Confined to Kerala or India… It Tells Us the World Was Here 3000 Years Ago', 15 November 2020, New Delhi Editorial Page.

[4] For details, see Paolino Da San Bartolomeo, *A Voyage to the East Indies*, trans. William Johnston (London: Vernor, 1800), 262–263.

mobile, required for the trading economy which was up to 25 per cent of the global GDP of which India was the powerhouse.[5] In such a society, which remained economic powerhouse for centuries, knowledge traditions were built in to drive the economy. It was equally built in to be non-violent in the cultural tradition of time to focus on the international business which was widely prevalent in coastal India with natal linkages in Southeast Asia, and in many other parts of the world as reflected in Pattanam excavation in Kerala, referred to earlier.

The economy, premised on the agriculture—the lifeline of the state and society—was not an autarkic, disconnected part. It was relatively not so monetized. But it was elementarily connected with the wider world through trade that reflected into the flux of social thought. The social discourse emanating out this setting dominated the broad contours of wisdom and knowledge which were substantively reflected in the thoughts of saints or in the texts written on the theme of political economy. As India was the hub of trade, so was its knowledge domain that incorporated diverse textual knowledge and praxis of the world in its treasure with its own experiences which were, in turn, shared with the foreign travellers, traders, immigrants and invaders. The agriculture provided diverse opportunities of livelihood to people who, in turn, lead to its constant expansion to new areas. The new settlements generated new diversities of thought. Their past memories were equally part of their new existence that guided them in their new settlements. And the existence of fertile cultivable land facilitated their expansion. The shortage of labour which was an acute economic problem provided the labour opportunities for their better wages and freedom. With majority of population becoming cultivators, which has an inbuilt system of being independent required by the profession, it was imperative to have a culture of civic freedom in the society. It was substantively autonomous. This freedom led to, in its turn, local market meetings and cultural gatherings that linked the

[5] William Dalrymple, *The Anarchy* (London: Bloomsbury, 2019), 10–14.

residents to wider world, outside their localities. It facilitated the combination of the universal and the local that enriched the social thought. Shankar Dev, the saint-poet of Assam, travelled all over India for 15 years, imbibed its universal ethos and mixed it up with the requirements of the locality to transform the lives of the millions over five centuries that continues to be in practice. The civic freedom ensured democratic transition or, in other words, it minimized the violent radical rupture. The shortage of labour and availability of cultivable land leading to expansion of agriculture to new areas also ensured the minimization of the rupture through the provision of the opportunities of livelihood for all. In case of any long-term coercion, the labour used to migrate to new areas choking the local economy. This was the democratic method of protest that restrained the oppression.

The regional diversities were in-built in the agricultural economy premised on animal and manpower. Each family and each village had its deity; and each region and subregion had its local gods and goddesses. There was absence of any over-arching, paternal god that swept aside all others. Or in other words, derivatively, there was individual freedom of expression which was partly affected after the arrival of political Islam. The damaging transformation came with the arrival of the British colonial rule that drained out the Indian resources and choked its economy leading to the emergence of social morbidities in the forms of illiteracy, untouchability and gender segregation. In the precolonial India, as there were opportunities of livelihood, social violence and radical rupture were minimal despite wide gap between the elite and the subaltern. The result of it was reflected in the social praxis, texts and religious rituals. The different Indic religions preached non-violence, practised Shastrarth, a dialogical form, for ideological hegemony, celebrated diversities and co-opted democratic dissent. It combined the universal with the regional, which was best reflected in the composition of the gods worshipped by the residents. This character of the Indic society was so ingrained in the residents that it impacted the others who arrived from outside. It moderated them and co-opted them while accepting some of their ideas which fitted into the Indic traditions. While the monarchy existed at the top for millennium, there was grassroots democracy at the bottom which varied in its form and functioning across the regions. South India provides more graphic details of it. In the Lingayat movement, there were nearly 60 women saints, many of them were poets; and interestingly, menstruating women were not considered unclean and could attend all the religious functions.[6] Similarly, in other parts of India, the women and Dalits challenged the social structure and its conventions.

The social structure was hierarchical with opportunity of vertical individual mobility. Urbanization, migration, trade, skill development and arrival of new elite provided opportunities. Hierarchy of skilled labour (castes) was more rigid in agricultural economy in comparison to coastal areas; but it was not frozen. As the new technologies and business opportunities emerged, so did the new castes. Similarly, there was decline of old castes when they became irrelevant. The social interactions of different castes, premised on their everyday existence, were a normal affair; it was not a segregated ghetto existence. Each caste, however, protected its domain in economy and culture as it was linked with their existence. Women were equal partners in the workforce imbued with elementary education of language, script and elementary mathematics. There was a degree of gender segregation in public sphere, which is still visible in rural areas, but it did not obstruct much to the growth of the women beyond a point. The existence of female saint-poets in different regions of India, from Kashmir to Kanyakumari, for centuries reflected social freedom. Or in other words, their acceptance and celebration by society as saints reflected the manifestation of individual social freedom across the diverse regions. It was equally applicable for saints who were part of economic–social marginals.

The gender relations and other cultural praxis among the subaltern were different from the elite. It was more equal and least

[6] For details, see Prakash Desai, 'Idea of Democracy in Lingayata Movement', in *Political Thought in Indic Civilization,* ed. Himanshu Roy (New Delhi: SAGE Publications, 2021).

segregated. As they worked together in the fields, their culture was different. Sati among them was almost absent; moreover, sati was not a mass act, it was more episodic and occasional. Veil was negligible; food was mix of vegetarian and non-vegetarian. Labour was valued, as there was shortage of them. Migration of labour, in their search for better livelihood, or for better working condition, in case of coercive oppression, was bad omen for the local economy. The employer, including the peasant households, therefore, cared for them.

Religious institutions were the centre of social life. It represented the local residents. The temples with patronage from the royalty also represented their sovereignty or their honour. Its size, architecture and importance reflected the social–political strength of its patrons. Some of the architectural designs of the temples and their locations reflect the scientific calibre of the Indic minds who were marvels of science of the time. It ran hospitals, schools, academic research centres and coordinated developmental works in its vicinity. Health and medical care were part of it. In the historical setting, Ayurveda was a developed branch of medicine and surgery with hospitals, doctors and nurses. The recent discovery of inscriptions on the walls of Venkatesa Perumal temple, a Chola temple built in 1069 AD, constructed by Vira Rajendra Chola at Thirumukkoodal near Kanchipuram, Chennai, was a 15-bedded hospital. The inscriptions give details of medical procedures, salary paid to doctors in the form of paddy, proportionate to their work, and 19 herbal drugs used for treating fever, lung diseases and dropsy. It was a medical hospital-cum-college where the students stayed and studied, and the staff of the temple and the public were treated. It was an Ayurvedic-cum-Siddah college–hospital which was then known as Atular Salai. Series of such centres were functioning around such temples, for example, in Thanjavur, Srirangam, etc.[7] Fa Hsien had observed about a functioning hospital in Patliputra and in other parts of India in the 5th

[7] For details, see *The Times of India*, 'Tamil Nadu: This 1,100-year-old Chola Hospital Had Beds, Doctors, Surgeons and a Protocol in Place', 20 May 2021, New Delhi Edition.

century AD where the patients were examined, housed and treated. It resembled the description that Charaka had mentioned about it in his book *Charaka Samhita*.[8] It is equally interesting to note that barbers, gardeners and potters were once professional doctors and surgeons. After their elementary education, those who were interested in research used to opt for medicine in their higher studies; this continued until the 18th century. Subsequently, the entire Indic medicinal concepts and its institutions were demeaned by the colonial rule which began to promote its allopathy through laws, funding, policies and institutions.

As temples were centres of social life, it also encompassed dance and music. Famous for their scientific architectural designs, which used sunlight, sound waves, topography, water and air for its optimum use, and which aesthetically captivated, the temples hosted dance and music festivals, trained the artists and helped them, to an extent, to sustain their livelihood. It reflected the culture of the region and promoted regional forms of dance and music which were in honour of different gods and goddesses. Both men and women were part of it and were experts in their domains. Both music and dance were thematically in sync with each other. Folk dance and music, on the other hand, widely popular in the villages, were based on the crop seasons. Simple musical instruments, with elementary expertise, were used; local songs based on marriages, birth and seasonal festivals were part of this repertoire. Interestingly, across the Indic regions, the themes of the classical dances were broadly similar; only the forms of expression differed. Similarly, the themes of folk songs across the regions were broadly similar; only their language and forms differed. These similarities were the unique expression of cultural bonding of the Indic civilization despite historical limitations of social mobility. Social diversities, reflected in the diverse family deities, had generated diverse social thought. As ownership of cultivable lands was diffused, livelihood and freedom were universal despite many theocratic restrictions imposed by monarchs. The Indic religion had 21 textual versions of Rigveda, more than

[8] For details, see Ca Su 15. 1–7.

300 different Rāmāyaṇas, more than 18 Puranas, 20 Smritis and 18 types of Shastras. These numbers further changed with new discoveries of manuscripts. Many of the manuscripts are still not available in the public domain, as these are yet to be translated into English, Hindi or in regional languages. As the new settlements expanded to new regions, people wrote their new texts or adopted old ones with their own interpretations and requirements which multiplied the numbers of Smritis and Puranas. The only problem with the Hindu texts was the absence of names of the authors and the dates, years and places of their writings. These texts were written on bhojpatra; in poetic form, there is absence of contextualization with social history of the time; and, as explained earlier, in the absence of paper (*kagaz*), it was difficult to write history in prose on bhojpatra and cooper plate. Writing on it was a slow and tedious process. What is, however, puzzling is the absence of years, places and names of the authors of these texts. It makes the texts difficult to situate in their historicalities. But there was no dirth of literary production. The Bhakti movement generated wide range of texts across India. Statecraft and medicine were the other important themes.

The ethical–social narrative in popular discourse and its framework of guidance was dharma, which was holistic, encompassing different facets of social life. Even military wars, on many occasions, were impacted by it. It was similar to *relegere* of Latin-European tradition. While dharma, the noun, is derived from the verbal root *dhr* which means to uphold, sustain, maintain[9] or the virtue of a thing,[10] the *relegere/religare* is a Latin word which means 'to bind'.[11] Tagore, Cicero and Lactantius had used it in that sense in their respective South Asian and Latin-European

[9] Gavin Flood, ed., *The Blackwell Companion to Hinduism* (London: Blackwell Publishing, 2003), 102.

[10] Rabindranath Tagore, *The Religion of Man* (London: George Allen and Unwind, 1958), 143–144, 155.

[11] James Hastings, ed., *Encyclopedia of Religion and Ethics*, Vol. X (New York: T&T Clark, 1963), 662; John Bvowker, ed., *The Oxford Dictionary of World Religions* (Oxford: Oxford University Press, 1997), xvi.

culture. Conceptually, there is no difference between the two words '*relegere*' and 'dharma', since both meant to sustain the then existing social orders by binding people to the land. The meaning becomes unambiguous when the concept is posited in the context of pre-capitalist societies when the land was the primary production unit. In the absence of a theocratic state and episcopal order, the freedom to pursue one's dharma in India was more than that of Europe; for once a state includes several creeds having equal rights, it can no longer be a religious state without being a violation of the rights of the particular creeds.[12] But this freedom was not unhindered. There did exist occasional coercion and allurements for religious conversions; or many times, religious discriminations were practised by the state even in secular matters. Such occurrences and processes, however, did not obfuscate for long the freedom to pursue one's dharma. Colonial capitalism from the mid-18th century unleashed an unconscious force that provided impetus to alter the holistic nature of dharma, the way it was unleashed by capitalism in Britain in the mid-17th century. It delinked the dharma from its theistic wrappings, restricted the other worldliness to an autonomous domain and called it religion; the materialistic base of the dharma was called secular and it was separated. The colonial state became 'secular', ex parte, by expanding the task of capitalism and remained 'neutral' towards the religion. The interference of religion in secular affairs was curtailed, and it was forced to limit itself to the private sphere converting the dharma, which was holistic and communitarian, to private caprice. It was the death of dharma separated from the community, for dharma existed in community. It was the beginning of the era of individualism.

The Indic jurisprudence, reflecting the social diversities, was either textual or more policy oriented, formulated at the top, and then applied for which it was intended, which in course of time,

[12] K. Marx and F. Engels, *Collected Works*, Vol. 3 (Moscow: Progress Publishers, 1975), 199.

subsequently, became customary laws until it was substantively changed by the new colonial rules. These precolonial Indic rules, in sync with their customary praxis, were later codified by the scholars which came to be known as texts or Smritis; the most prominent among these were: Manusmriti, Yajnavalkya Smriti, Narada Smriti, Brihaspati Smriti and Kalyayana Smriti. These texts were more normative than operative. It was not a popular praxis.[13]

The native Indian rulers after their initial fight back against the Muslim invaders accepted their authority and were co-opted into the polity as subordinate partners who played collaborative role in the expansion of the Muslim rule. Fortunately, it did not impact the international trade and the local business, neither did the expansion of the rule lead to the conversion of demographic dominance. The Muslims remained less than 10 per cent of the population until the 19th century despite the local residents' conversion to Islam. In this sense, it was a failure of Islam; despite 1,000 years of Muslim rule, starting from Sindh, it failed to convert the majority of the local Indic population to Islam. It also, derivatively, reflects the degree of social freedom enjoyed by the local natives ingrained in the Indic civilization, where Islam was not required for their emancipation despite wide gaps between the opulence of the rich and conditions of the poor as observed by the foreign travellers.[14]

What India lacked, on many occasions, was a constant upgradation of military technology and of its organizational structure to match the invaders. Despite being the most developed economy, it was conquered, looted or ruled over by economically backward invaders who were militarily and organizationally superior at the time of invasion either in archery or in gunpowder.

[13] For details, see Balaji Ranganathan, 'Jurisprudence in Pre-colonial India', in *Political Thought in Indic Civilisation*, ed. Himanshu Roy (New Delhi: SAGE Publications, 2021).

[14] Neena Kumari, *Madhya Kalin Bhartiya Samaj* (Hindi; Delhi: Research India Press, 2019), 91–92; Ram Vilas Sharma, *Itihas Darshan* (Delhi: Vani Prakashan, 1995), 171.

Their armies, despite being smaller in size, were more cohesive and efficient. One example may explain the comparison of warfare: When the early Muslim invaders came, they were masters of archery, shooting from their running horsebacks either while advancing or retreating. 'By contrast, Indian archers in Mahmud's days were, for the most part, infantrymen, mounted archery not being wide spread.'[15] Horseback-mounted archery included iron stirrups or heavy saddles, siege equipment such as the trebuchet used for hurling large missiles and mortar; and most importantly, they had the best of horses which were imported by India. The internal territorial and social divisions further weakened them. The new set of invaders who began to arrive in India, since the 8th century AD, gradually conquered the whole of India in the next few centuries. They were Muslims in religion, but ethnically were from different groups and regions. It was the arrival of political Islam.

The arrival of the political Islam, from the 8th century onwards, and its constant expansion(demographic, political and cultural) changed India substantively over thousand years.[16] With its power of sword, it became the ruling political elite displacing the local political sovereigns. And it ruled India with its distinct Islamic identity, which was not Indic, without merging itself into the Indic. It rather converted the Indic residents to its religion and culture. A tiny segment of invaders, approximately 3 per cent, welded power; and the Muslim immigrants who came from Arabic–Persian–Central Asian regions became part of this elite structure as per their talents and family backgrounds. Mir Zafar, the general of the Nawab army in the Suba of Bengal in 1757 who became the symbol of treachery in India, was a soldier from Iraq. Khusro's father, a soldier, had immigrated to India from Central Asia. Both of them were co-opted in the ruling structure of the time.

[15] Richard M. Eaton, *India in the Persianate Age* (New Delhi: Allen Lane, 2019), 31.

[16] Ramdhari Singh Dinkar, *Sanskriti Ke Char Adhyaya* (Four Phases of Indian History) (Hindi; Patna: Udyachal, 1990), 263–272.

The arrival of political Islam changed the laws partly. The Muslim laws, mostly affecting the residents, were either the religious taxation or civil–criminal disputes. As the Muslims dominated the top tier of the administration, and as they were familiar with the Islamic laws, many such laws became operative in everyday life. These laws were mostly written in Persian with Arabic scripts and belonged to Hanafi school. The ordinary residents were neither familiar with the laws nor with the script and the language. These laws were mostly imported from the Islamic traditions; it did not originate in India. There were separate Arabic-Persian schools and madrasas to teach them, which were mostly studied by the Muslims. In 1670, Aurangzeb ordered a compilation of extracts from the authoritative works of the Hanifi School of jurisprudence which subsequently resulted into Fatawa-al-Alamgiriya.[17] But long before him, different Muslim rulers had already brought compilation of Hanafi School of laws in India beginning with Sultan Mahmud of Ghazni. Since then, it was estimated that there were already 11 major compilations until Aurangzeb's time.[18] These laws changed the idea of justice and the nature of penalties as the laws were alien to Indic traditions. It overshadowed the Indic laws in many of the disputes and in interpretations. Not only that, gradually, the Indic residents began to shift from Sanskrit and other Indic scripts and languages to Arabic-Persian for jobs in administration which impacted the enrichment and development of Indic language in different proportion in different regions,[19] and it continued until the 1830s, best detailed in the Adam's *Reports on the State of Education in Bengal* (1835 and 1838), which provides the graphic details of the Indic education including the number of Persian schools (694) and the Sanskrit schools (353).

It succeeded in the expansion and popularization of its language, Persian, which became not only the language of

[17] For details, see Ranganathan, 'Jurisprudence in Pre-colonial India'.

[18] Ibid.

[19] For details, see Sheldon Pollock, 'The Death of Sanskrit', *Comparative Studies in Societies and History* 43, no. 2 (2011): 394–395, for impact on Sanskrit.

administration but also gradually percolated into the vocabulary of the urban residents either through maktabs and madrasas or through Quran among the Indian Muslim converts. A section of the Hindus aspiring to be part of the administration, and to secure courtly patronage, learnt the language and the etiquettes. As the years rolled by, and the conversion to Islam expanded to new areas, more people became familiar with it or more Persian words entered into the Indic vocabulary of dialects and languages. New dictionaries and other literary production emerged, and the fusion of Persian and the Indic led to the emergence of a new language, Urdu. But it was much later, in the 18th century. The real problem that obstructed popular expansion of Persian into the villages was the Arabic script. In northern India (Punjab and Kashmir), however, it was more profusely spoken and written. The Muslim elite, comprising of different ethnic groups, better versed in Arabic scripts through Quran and Azan, preferred to write in Arabic script and spoke Persian. Had they shifted to Indic scripts, Persian or even Urdu, Islam would have been more popular.

Apart from the script and the literature, Islam brought in multiple other facets of culture, medicine, architecture, religion and technology of the Arabic-Persian world which were different from the Indic civilization. Al-Biruni wrote that 'they (Hindus) differ from us in everything'[20] which led to the 'increasing ideological and emotional hostility'. Many times, it was sublime; many times, it was open. In fact, the rise and expansion of Islam was premised on the graveyard of idolators which had existed before Islam. In Kaba, Mecca, it has been argued that there were 360 idols which were destroyed by Prophet. One survived. It is of black stone which resembles sivalinga known as Sangue- As bad; and it is touched by every visitor.[21] This premise, and then conversion to Islam, may have led to inbuilt hostility. For, otherwise, the two pre-Islamic civilizations (Indic and Arabic-Iranian) were friendly to each other. While Indic remained idol worshipers,

[20] Al-Biruni, *India* (New Delhi: National Book Trust, 1983), v.
[21] Dinkar, *Sanskriti Ke Char Adhyaya*, 263.

Arabic-Persian changed to idol destroyers. In India, too, they destroyed a large number of temples, apart from looting their wealth; but they could not convert the whole population to Islam like they had done in Saudi Arabia, Iran and in other territories of the world. In fact, contrarily, the Indic social structure gripped Islam that still clings to transforming it into a caste-ridden religion, even among the ruling class, which constituted of different ethnic territorial groups. There was more an insular social life restricted to the groups. Interethnic marriages were few and rare; similarly, among the Indian Muslims, who had converted from Hinduism, marriages remained located in their castes. There was, however, wide impact of Islam on them that percolated over the centuries. They changed their names which became Arabic-Persian. Their god, worship, rituals, food and clothes changed with conversion. Many of the Arabic-Persian customs arising out of their topographical, historical and cultural backdrops continued in India as part of their religion or as administrative policies. Continuation of Arabic script and segregation of Persian language, segregation of women through burqa and application of their administrative model were part of such practices. Also, their own internal ethnic differences between Turks, Iranians, Arabs and Afghans remained intact. And despite their internal sectional-ethnic differences, all of them maintained their social distance with Indian Muslims; conversion, subtle or open, remained one of their agenda. For example, Chisti saints welcomed voluntary conversion, whereas in Kashmir, temples were demolished; in Bengal, Sheikh Jamaluddin Suhrarvardi ordered for forcible conversion and destruction of a Hindu temple near Pandua to construct his Khanqah.[22] The worst part of this conversion was that they tried to create an Arab world in India—from changing their Indic names to Arabic names to changing their gods. Within a short span, the converts became Arabs, imitated to be puritan while overlooking the issue that conversion had separated them from their extended families, neighbours, culture

[22] Aniruddha Ray, *The Sultanate of Delhi: 1206–1526* (New Delhi: Manohar, 2019), 410–411.

and Indic history. It had generated social rupture and tension. Many of the policies such as that of Alauddin Khilji which forbade Muslim slaves to be sold to non-Muslims[23] were communal. From the pluralism of gods and holy scriptures, the conversion had created one god and one book for the converts.

In short, they changed their identity and imitated the Arabic elite. The arrival of the political Islam also opened up opportunities for Muslim immigrants from Central Asia and Arabic-Persian world to come to India in search of livelihood, prosperity and power. The constant political instability in their regions had forced them to look towards India which had remained socially stable despite changing monarch. They were co-opted into the elite structure as they were required for the expansion and stability of the state. Once they settled down, they adopted the elements of the prosperity of Indic culture along with the requirements of the local weather, but they remained committed to Islam with its distinct identity unlike other invaders who had merged themselves with the Indic religion despite being the ruling elite. Political Islam remained separate with its religious identity despite adopting many elements of Indic civilization which were not part of Arabic-Islamic culture.[24] The highest percentage of Hindu elite ever to become part of a Muslim monarch's durbar was during Aurangzeb's time; it was approximately 30 per cent.[25] Muslims were the first preference of the administration. Their shortage compelled the Muslim elite to continue with the Hindus in the administration. Muslims immigrants, therefore, had vast opportunities in India, and they were placed according to their capabilities.

The remarkable part of the political Islam was its written history available in abundance, facilitated by the 'paper-making technology which Persianized Turks had introduced in north India from Central Asia'.[26] *Kagaz* and *qalam* (pen), both Arabic-Persian

[23] Ibid., 357.
[24] Dinkar, *Sanskriti Ke Char Adhyaya*, chap. 3.
[25] Eaton, *India in the Persianate Age*, 166.
[26] Ibid., 136.

words, expanded the sphere and velocity of writing that drew in many people from across the literate segment which was earlier, in pre-paper years, confined to a narrow group. The availability of paper facilitated the velocity of development of vernacular literature, scripts and languages as it was easier to handle the paper than the 'copper plate, palm leaf or stone'. Diverse the writings of larger number of writers, more enriched became the history that covered diverse facets of social life. Plus, the paper provided longer space for writing that changed the style of writing from poetry to prose. Earlier, while writing on palm leaf, one had to minimize the words due to constraints of space that led to the development of writing in poetic style. Preparing palm leaf for writing or writing on cooper plate and stone was difficult. As a result of it, the literature on the pre-Islamic social history of India is not so comprehensively available as it is after the arrival of political Islam. The presence of the scribes, chroniclers and poets in the courts or their constant influx provided graphic details of topography, society and about monarchs. The European travellers were the other who wrote comprehensive account of the Indic society of their times.[27] One of the strangest aspects they observed was how idolators of India, so numerous, have allowed themselves to be subjected by so small a number of Muhammedan princes.[28] French traveller Francois Bernier had repeatedly observed that once gold and silver entered into India, these would not come out.

> With the exception of horses and precious metals, India's import demands were few. In contrast, its capacity to export everything, from cotton and silk textiles to spices, manufactured goods, cut stones to cultural products was almost limitless ... the volume of the world's gold and silver pouring into India steadily increased fuelling monetization and reinforcing economic growth.[29]

[27] Kumari, *Madhya Kalin Bhartiya Samaj*, has provided a vivid description of the precolonial social life in India based on the accounts of foreign travellers.

[28] Paraphrased from Jean Baptiste Tavernier, *Travels in India*, Vol. II (London: Macmillan, 1889), 181.

[29] Vasudha Dalmia and Munis D. Faruqui, *Religion Interaction in Mughal India* (New Delhi: Oxford University Press, 2014), xiv.

As a result, there was rarely any serious long, persisted economic crisis despite constant change in the political dynasties. Zonal, regional trades and kingdoms kept the economic buoyancy intact.

In post-Aurangzeb years, new powers from Europe emerged, who were merchants represented by their companies, that begun to take benefits of the fragmented polity. The seizure of political power in Bengal in 1757 by the East India Company was the beginning of a new era in history that transformed India radically. It not only colonized the resources and the labour of India but also began to reinterpret its history. It was the beginning of the colonization of mind. The famed Indian wisdom and the land of desire, for which the world was coming to India for centuries, was now presented as the 'power of comprehension' as they were, in British view, yet to arrive at the stage of development; its history was interpreted as 'fables', and the Brahmins, who were the scientists, researchers and teachers, were presented as murderers and cheats.[30] India was presented as poor, oppressed and illiterate. This colonial, and subsequently, European interpretation, phrased in Hegelian metaphors, began to haunt the reading public. The Asiatic Society, 1784, had begun the systemic destruction. William Jones, its first president, was a good friend of Hegel. Until then, the British had imitated, and had felt elated, in becoming the Mughal nobles. Now, in order to rule, they began to map India, its population, resources and history. For it, numerous institutions were established and processes were initiated; Census Commission, archaeological survey and such other initiatives were part of it.

The society was classified into tribes, caste, race, linguistic and religious communities and then was labelled as thugs, martial and criminal to suit the administrative needs. The information gathered by the various departments (Census Commission, Botanical Survey, Geological Survey, Archaeological Survey, Great Trigonometrical Survey, Linguistic Survey and, the oldest, the Survey of India) were classified, quantified and catalogued. Agricultural population,

[30] Hegel, *Lecture on the History of Philosophy*.

land, topography, history and flora, everything was surveyed and used for colonial rule. The economy and the society were presented as unchanging. Or it was stated that the changes were brought about by the outsiders who were modernizing agents or civilizing missionaries. The fluidity of economy and dynamics of the society, to which they were witness for 150 years, were not accounted. The loot of the resources was not part of their public discourse. Under the rubric of modernity, scientific son and civilizing mission, their economic and political interests were perpetuated.[31] The expenses of their rule were borne by India. The church, the media, the laws and educational institutions were part of the ideological branch of the colonial apparatus to create consent of the public for their rule. It was equally to subvert the discourse on the nature of colonial rule that led to drain of resource and creation of poverty, illiteracy and mal governance.

The 'democratic nationalism' that began to emerge after 1857 countered many of these colonial distortions. But unfortunately, many of these distortions of colonial history continue to haunt postcolonial India perpetuated by academia, dominated by European-American epistemological frameworks. It is substantively fragmentary, Oriental and Westernized.

Fortunately, the larger subterranean popular praxis of the Indians and their non-bookish discourse have, however, remained Indic and holistic with their distinct diverse local ethos integrated with pan-Indic commonalities. These praxis and ethos have also been changing to fit the changing structural, technological, topographical and political requirements of the multilingual localities. From the ideational bliss of the Rigveda to the pluralism of Dara Shikoh, there has been a long civilizational continuity of dharma and Shakti. To put this Indic discourse rooted in its history, this text, interdisciplinary in perspective, a combination of sociology, history and political theory, explains different facets of social thought through its plural social ethos, texts and institutions.

[31] For details, see Santoshi Kumari's chapter 'Colonial Institutions and Oriental Knowledge Formation' in this book.

It focuses on the frameworks, references and the academic explanatory tools in the contextualized historicalities of the precolonial times which was open to new ideas that arrived through trade, migrations and immigrants. It is equally a deconstruction of the colonial knowledge formation that had begun in an organized form through the Asiatic Society initiated by 38 Europeans who were mostly British military, officers and judges, determining the selection and publication of the 'Hindu texts' after their day's work when they used to meet at 7 PM in the chamber of the chief justice of the Supreme Court in Calcutta and then positing it as dominant universal Indic in scriptures and holy books in the mirror image of Bible and Quran. The pluralism of thought reflected in multiple regional texts, and the absence of any single holy book was not taken note of which reduced the textual plurality to singular monologue and transformed the image of wisdom to the image of barbaric civilization. The printing press facilitated the mass circulation of these few 'discovered' and translated 'Hindu' texts to the European readers as Oriental wisdom that hide the diversities of enriched knowledge for which this 'land of wisdom' was famous in its precolonial history.

1

Dharma in Indic Tradition

Ruchi Tyagi

Dharma, being one of the central themes of indigenous social thought, represents a way of life encompassing code of individual vis-à-vis interpersonal conduct and individual's relationship with society and state, depicting multireligious Indian society based on the attitude of *Sarva Dharma Sama Bhāva*, assuring equal respect for, protection of and opportunities to all forms of worship, promoting accommodation of and respect for diverse religious faiths and exemplifying the absence of any organized state religion while delinking institutional religion from state. Under *Varnāshramadharma*, a network of social duties indicated stratification of society delegating the state for its conservation, whereas *Rājadharma* enshrined a system of reciprocal obligations of ruler and ruled.

The concept of dharma is, perhaps, one of the most inclusive concepts in the Indic tradition with no appropriate translation in any modern language. Its English paraphrase 'religion', originated from the Latin *relegere,* literally means 'to bind', indicating the bond between man and God. As such, it signifies faith in a certain theology and, at the same time, covers certain sacraments, an institutionalized ecclesiastical hierarchy and a sense of common belonging.[1]

[1] V. P. Varma, *Studies in Hindu Political Thought and Its Metaphysical Foundations* (Delhi: Motilal Banarsidass, 1959), 106.

The term 'dharma', on the other hand, is not necessarily restricted to the above. It stands for a way of life rather than for theology and religious institutions. Dharma originated from the root *Dhri*, which means to sustain or uphold. Accordingly, it refers to the principle that can sustain society. The Mahābhārata, accordingly, describes it as the principle which bears or maintains society by establishing order.[2]

In the Vedic literature, *Rita* (*Rta*) was yet another term that had a moral content. *Rita* denotes order, regulation and arrangement. It signifies the fixed or established course of natural objects such as the sun and the moon. In addition to justification of the physical order of the universe and the regular order of the ritualistic sacrificialism, it contained a moral content as well.[3]

Dharma encompassed ethics, morality and virtue. In fact, *Niti* (way of life), *Achar* (behaviour), *Sadāchāra* (code of moral conduct) and dharma were considered mutually complementary, interrelated and interdependent. Accordingly, Manu emphatically declared ethics as the real dharma.[4] To him, the four principle characteristics of dharma comprise the codes of the Vedas, the Smriti, the *Sadāchāra* and the *Ātman* (soul),[5] which collectively generate 10 ingredients of dharma[6]: *dhritih* (resolution), *kshamāh*

[2] *Mahabharata, Kama,* LXIX, 58; idem, *Shanti,* CIX, 11, wherein the relevant verse reads as follows:

Dhārnād dharmaityahu dharmena vidhritah prajāh
Yah syād dharmasamyuktah sa dharmah iti nishchayah.

[3] *Rigveda* (New Delhi: Dayananda Sansthan, 1973), I, 2, 8; idem, I, 68, 3; idem, IV, 3, 4; idem, VII, 36,1.

Yah syad dharmasamyuktah sa dharmah iti nishchayah

[4] Har Govind Shastri, trans., *Manusmriti* (Hindi; Varanasi: Chaukhamba Sanskrit Series Office, 1970), 1, 108, wherein Manu proclaims '*Acharan Parmo Dharmah:*'

[5] See ibid., II, 12 for the verse:

Vedah Smritih Sadāchāran Svasya Cha Priyamātmanah
Aiachchaturoidham Prahuh Sakshaddharmasya Lakshanam.

[6] Ibid., VI, 92; A. C. Burnell, *Hindu Polity: The Ordinances of Manu* (Ludhiana: Kalyani Publishers, 1984), 146, for the verse

Dhritih Kshaman Damoasteyam Shauchamindriuanigrahan
Dheervidya Satyamakrodho Dashakam Dharma lakshanam.

(patience or forgiveness), *damah* (self-restraint), *asteya* (honesty), *shaucha* (purity), *indrianigrah* (control of the organs), *dheeh* (devotion), *vidyā* (knowledge devised in the Vedas), *satya* (truth) and *akrodha* (absence of anger). In fact, the ancient Indian thinkers hardly distinguished between dharma, ethics and law. Dharma, apart from other meanings, also signified law and custom.[7] In the Upanishads, this concept comprehended a qualitatively different meaning by ascertaining it with the social duties of various castes and orders in terms of *Varnashrama* (fourfold division of society and age-bound stages of individual life).[8]

In the Mahābhārata,[9] dharma specified a web of obligations, such as the *Rājadharma* (obligations of the ruler), the *Prajādharma* (obligations of the subjects) and the *Mitradharma* (obligations of the friend). It indicated a code of conduct towards one's country, kin, caste, class and one's own stage of life, that is, the *Deshadharma, Kuladharma, Jatidharma, Varnadharma,* and *Ashramadharma.*[10] While signifying virtue and righteousness, dharma denoted a comprehensive network of socio-ethico-religious ideas.

The Buddhist literature offered a refreshing reinterpretation of dharma. It denoted a threefold submission to 'Buddha' *(Buddham)*, the 'Buddhist ecclesiastical fraternity' (*Dhammam*) and the 'doctrine' (*Samgham*).[11] In its moral aspect, it stood for *Sheel* (humility), *Samadhi* (contemplation and meditation) and *Pragya* (knowledge or wisdom), collectively leading towards *Nirvana* (salvation).[12]

[7] *Rigveda,* 1.22, 18–164.43 and 50; idem, III, 3.1-17, 1-60; idem, V. 26.6-63 and 7.72-2. See also *Atharvaveda* (New Delhi: Dayanand Sansthan, Samvat 2031), XIV, 1.51.

[8] Varma, *Studies in Hindu Political Thought*, n. 4, 112.

[9] *Mahabharata, Shanti* XV, 6; idem, XVI, 15; idem, XVIII, 3; idem, XXXV, 155.

[10] Ibid., *Anu.* XVI. 21; idem, *Shanti,* CXXXIX, 96.

[11] Bhikshu Dharmrakshit, trans., *Dhammpad* (Hindi; Delhi: Motilal Banarsidass, 1977), 62, wherein the appropriate verse reads as under:

Buddham Cha Dharmam Cha Sangham Cha Sharnam Gatah ...'

[12] Varma, *Studies in Hindu Political Thought*, 114–116.

In Kautilya's *Arthashastra*, the term 'dharma' was used differently at various places. At times, it symbolizes the sense of social duty towards oneself (*Swadharma*) and one's society (*Varnadharma*).[13] As the civil law and the moral law based on truth,[14] it was exalted to the status of the supreme principle of human life, which preserves the one who maintains it and ruins the one who violates it.[15]

Instead of a purely religious concept, A. K. Sen considers dharma as 'an admixture of socio-ethico-religious ideas'.[16] Kane and Sinha construe it as a sacred and secular mode of life and code of conduct.[17] Anjaria interprets it as a code which endures the whole universe.[18] Mees projects it as the *Vedic Rita* or the ethical duty, virtue and justice as per the directives of God.[19] In its inclusiveness, it denotes customs, behaviours, common law and interstate or intertribal law. It can be construed as a compromise between real and ideal situations.[20] These elucidations denote the pervasiveness of dharma as an 'overriding code of conduct'.

Dharma, thus, signifies a principle of both individual and communal self-development. For an individual, it is a principle of meritorious development (*Abhudaya* and *Nishreyasa*), in accordance with one's qualities, habituated by one's nature, temperament and proficiency for higher existence. For the community, it indicates attainment of self-rule (*swaraj*) in terms of its own historical identity. Dharma is a principle which leads a balance between four *purushartha* (pursuits), for the quest of *artha* (righteous earning of wealth and resources), *kāma* (satisfaction

[13] Udaya Vir Shastri, trans., *Arthashastra* (Hindi; Delhi: Mehar Chand Lakshman Das, 1970), 1.3; *ibid.*, 1.19.

[14] Ibid., 1II.1.

[15] Shastri, *Manusmriti,* VII, 10, 13 and 15; idem, II, 13; idem, VII, 10 and 13.

[16] A. K. Sen, *Hindu Political Thought* (Calcutta: NA, 1926), 4.

[17] H. N. Sinha, *Sovereignty in Ancient India* (London: NA, 1930), 27; P. V. Kane, *History of Dharmashastras* (Poona: Bhandarkar Oriental Research Institute, 1930–1946), II, 2.

[18] J. J. Anjaria, *Nature and Ground of Political Obligation in the Hindu State* (Calcutta: Longmans Green & Co., 1935), 150.

[19] G. H. Mees, *Dharma and Society* (Delhi: Seema Publications, 1980), 89.

[20] Ibid.

of aesthetic desires) and moksha (final liberation from the cycle of rebirth). A philosophy of balanced harmonious integration for an individual's aspirations is prescribed and, accordingly, fourfold *purusharthas* or pursuits expect an individual to aspire for dharma (the righteous performance of one's duties in accordance with ethical code of conduct), *Artha*, *Kama* and moksha, behind which the fundamental idea is that the human soul (*Atman*/spirit) is central and all social and political involvements, allurements and fears are to be surpassed for its realization *(Ātmārthe Prithvin Tyajet)*.[21]

Further, highlighting the concept of unity of the entire human race, the concept of *Vasudhaiva Kutumbakam*[22] projects mankind as a family writ large, cutting across divisions of race and religion, and expects the individual to adhere to their dharma as a set of duties and code of conduct. While pursuing for wealth and aesthetic desires, for the attainment of the final liberation from the cycle of rebirth (salvation or moksha) through the service of fellow beings, dharma portrays fulfilment of duties or obligations as the immediate objectives of both the State and the individual.[23] In other words, politics and ethics are treated as complementary and interdependent.

Illustrating the customary spheres of dharma, Vedic and post-Vedic literature altogether elucidates the relationship between the man and the maker due to performance of rituals and procedural worship of numerous gods and goddesses. The summary of dharma simultaneously denotes a moral category indicating truth

[21] *Mahabharata* (Poona: Bhandarkar Oriental Research Institute, 1929–1933); *Udyog*, XI, 40. The verse reads as follows

Tyajet Kulartha Purusham Gramasyarthe Kulam Tyajet
Gramam fanapadasyarthe, Atmārthe Prithvim Tyajet.

[22] Shree Shyamcharan Pandey, trans., *Panchatanira* (Hindi; Delhi: Motilal Banarsidass, 1990), Part III (Aparikshit Karak), 37 for the original verse:

Ayam Nijah Paroveti Gadna Laghuchetasam
Udarcharitanantu Vasudhaiva Kuiumbakam.

[23] *Mahabharata,* Shanti, CLXVII, 8; idem, *CXXM*, 15. See also Manorama Jauhari, *Politics and Ethics in Ancient India* (Varanasi: Bhartiya Vidya Prakashan, 1968), 70.

and a general term for representing the social duties of the four Varnas and the four Ashramas. Buddhism highlighted the moral aspect of dharma, and its influence was reflected in the political philosophy of Emperor Ashoka. The defence of 'one's own dharma', signifying one's social duty, is revealed in the Bhagavad Gita. *Dharmasutras* and Kautilya's *Arthashastra* used the word as law, specifically civil law. The term dharma, thus, comprehended a wide range of subjects, practically covering all matters of public behaviour and interpersonal relationships.

The Western notion of freedom of religion has always been respected in India. One could worship God in any form and adopt any form of prayer. As was declared in Rigveda, '*Ekam Sad Viprah Bahudhā Vadanti*'[24] (truth is one, the wise call it by various names). It was, in fact, an explicit acceptance of the fact that all religions are different paths leading to the same goal. Religions provide the broad framework and the psychological motivation within which one can develop the eternal mystery of communion between man and the divine.

It was, thus, an acceptance of the essential unity of all religions, which altogether expected the follower of one faith or religion not only to tolerate but also to respect the other faiths and their followers. It, therefore, was the concept of *Sarva Dharma Sama Bhāva* or equal respect for all religions.

It was during the medieval period that the emphasis on knowledge was substituted by devotion and faith and dharma was replaced by paradoxes, the *Karmakānda* or adherence to the rituals and sacrifices, which in turn was followed by strong reactions, reform movements and renaissance at a later date.

Relationship between Dharma and Politics

Relationship between dharma and politics can be analysed differently in the context of individual, society and polity.

[24] *Rigveda*, n. 1, I, 164, 46.

At the Individual Level

Ancient Indian tradition considered the individual as a living being, who was an integral part of the society, constantly striving to attain moksha, salvation or liberation from the cycle of rebirth by the balanced following of four *purushartha* in social and economic activities and also striving to attain perfection for himself and also in consonance with others. They were perceived as a person who was more conscious of their duties than the one who was simply concerned for their rights. In the process, the individual became a part and parcel of such a social fabric. It was in this overall context that the State was treated as an institution based on a force providing protection to all living beings. The functions of the State were confined to strike a synthesis between dharma, *artha, kāma* and moksha. The two basic functions of this order, individual's potential of 'self-rule' and the supremacy of knowledge, were substituted by *Bhakti* or devotion to God and his vicegerent the king by worshipping deities and accomplishing rituals. Monarchy became the preferred form of governance, where the relationship between the king and his subjects primarily relied on the reciprocity of the duties and the rights.

Unlike its Western counterpart, the Indian thought assigns priority to duties vis-à-vis the rights. In the Western liberal tradition, rights emerged as 'claims' of an individual against others, including the society as well as the State. In the Indian political thought, on the other hand, an individual is considered not only a part of the society and the State but also of numerous voluntary associations. Accordingly, one is expected to perform a wide range of functions concerning these associations while fulfilling duties in accordance with *Swadharma* (oneself), *Varnadharma* (class/*jati*), *Āshramdharma* (stage in life), *Kuladharma* (kin), *Deshadharma* (country/*Rashtra*), *Rājadharma*, *Prajādharma* (subjects) and also the *Mitradharma* (friends). This emphasis on duties ensured that one would earn the corresponding rights by performing their duties willingly and voluntarily, implying that rights are never asked for or given in charity. This entire network of duties altogether expects the individual to remain committed to the welfare (*upkar*) of others' life.

A wide variety of schools of thought and scholars signified considerable freedom of expression, discussion and discourse that evolved a common cohesive sociopolitical framework to settle inter-religious and inter-sectarian rivalries. Freedom of speech, expression, thought, conscience, worship and religion resulted in some kind of catholicity of outlook and disposition in ancient India while protecting from the extremes of fanaticism and exclusivism. It further evolved remarkable opportunities of coexistence, absorption and assimilation.

At the Level of Society

In ancient Indian system, the social order assigned a specific place for each individual and expected due performance of corresponding duties (*Varnadharma*). The Brahmana was to devote themselves to the pursuit of intellectual, religious and philosophical activities. The development of power through Kshatra (coercive authority) and protection of subjects were the main pursuits of *Rājanya* or Kshatriya. Specialization in trade and commerce was the preordained duty of the Vaishyas. To serve these three and also to pursue *Vārta* (agriculture, industry, trade, arts and commerce) were the duties of the Shudras. Therefore, performance of one's duties (*Swadharma*) was an essential feature of dharma.

A study of the Vedic literature depicts that the early Rigveda society represented a tribal society based on the functional division. The king presented the symbol of regal authority and Kshatriya power. *Purohita, Senāni* and *Grāmani* were noteworthy administrative officials. The post-Rigveda era indicates stratification of society signifying the importance of the four Varnas in the order of Brahmana, Kshatriya, Vaishya and Shudra. The Brahmanical scriptures proclaimed the supremacy of the Brahmans while assigning prominence to the performance of rituals and indicated the declining status of Vaishyas and the inferior status of the Shudras, which resulted in the predominance of Brahmanas and decline of popular institutions of *Sabhā, Samiti* and *Vidath*. The alienation of the Vaishyas and Shudras from the political sphere entailed the preponderance of the rest of the two Varnas. A struggle for supremacy between these two Varnas was later resonated in the Upanishads. Both the epics, Rāmāyana and Mahābhārata, bestowed the same order of precedence. While Rāmāyana indicated a cordial relationship among all the Varnas, the Mahābhārata approved the embracing of the professions of a class other than one's own under *Āpaddharma*. The epics indeed indicated a 'regal' concern for perseverance and maintenance of the Varna system. *Dharmasutras* specified a clear, more or less rigid, division of society with pre-eminence of the Brahmans, lower position of the Shudras, distrust for *Varna-Sankara* and penalties/punishments in accordance with the Varna. The Buddhist scriptures voiced against *Brahmanic* superiority and supported the hegemony of royal temporal Kshatriya power.

While accepting the traditional Varna system, Kautilya expected the ruler to protect, preserve and conserve the societal Varna system and execute a system of law, *Danda* (justice and punishment) and *Bala* (armed forces) based on the Varna system. The Manusmriti enunciated the predominance of the Brahmanas and dispensed strictures against the Shudras.

Thus, the Varna system intertwined the social structure with the polity, resulting in the tug of war between the Brahmanas and the Kshatriyas for supremacy. Evolution during the later period reflected that while the latter held the royal authority, the former remained contented with reverence and significance. This system involved certain inbuilt mechanism of checks and balances. The trivial position of Vaishyas and Shudras, however, resulted in their isolation from the political process, decline of the popular Vedic institutions and legal–judicial system based on Varna system. Efforts to restrain inter-Varna relationship entailed a more rigid and conservative caste system. The Brahmanic social legislation, defining the administration and social obligations of the State, promoted the predominance of spiritual and regal authority, and paved the way for interference of the State in individual's personal and social spheres. However, denominational–ecclesiastical aspect of dharma continued under the

Brahmanic control and supervision, while the supremacy of royal/regal authority symbolized the separation of institutional/ denominational religion from politics.

The equations of power inter se among the *Dvij* (twice-born castes) changed from time to time. A few ancient monarchies as well as republics symbolized caste coalitions, but the primacy of the elective as well as hereditary temporal power was unassailable in the plutocratic, monarchical, dyarchical and republican forms of government during the ancient period. It seems that the secular and temporal power was strengthened by the teachings of the preceptors, the *āchāryas* on ethical and public policy considerations. There was, however, no subservience or subordination of the temporal to the religious authority.

By assuming the preservation of the class system under its purview, the State interacted with the individual and used its machinery to conserve the organizational structure of the society. Subsequently, social legislation of temporal sovereignty and supremacy of the royal/regal authority was also outlined. The ritualistic religion was entirely under the control of the Brahman priests, leading to the separation of institutional religion from politics and preventing the possibility of theocratic rule. The informal network of checks and balances between the spiritual and the temporal power emerged as a characteristic feature of the system. However, caste rigidities later resulted in the appalling condition of the Shudras and raised controversies concerning the birth-oriented rather than function or merit-based social system.

At the Level of Polity

The influence of dharma or moral order on polity was a definite attribute of ancient Indian polity. A close relationship between dharma and politics is reflected through the concept of *Dhritavrata* that acknowledged the king as the *Dharma Pravartak* or 'promulgator of dharma' (expecting the king to lead the duty-bound life); the doctrine of karma and *Rājadharma* apprehended the concept of functions and duties of the king; the gospel of

Aparigraha placed the ideal of self-denial before the king; and special honour was accorded to Brahmana priests. Yet dharma remained only a moral category influencing political life. There was complete absence of any legal agency to control the transgressions of dharma by a king. Dharma was never identified with divine law having any supreme political authority. At best, it was presented as a moral as well as philosophical code for action.

The Concept of *Rājadharma*

Rājadharma comprehended the relationship between dharma and politics, where dharma signified the authority of State, regulated its jurisdiction, generated ethical code of conduct and demarcated the personal premise and interpersonal relationship of the king and the subjects. Dharma altogether defined the virtues, duties, obligations and objectives of the kings. Accordingly, the king was portrayed as the wielder and the sceptre of punishment and was expected to compensate for the loss or to perform penance in case of miscarriage of justice. Extrapolitical sanctions could be imposed on the king for his failure in protecting the fourfold social order.

While narrating dharma of the Kshatriya, the Mahābhārata[25] comprehends self-abnegation, universal compassion, security and social service by curing the diseased and the affected. A king practising dharma has been approximated to the God, while doing the reverse estimated to hell. Manu[26] wants the king to take cognizance of dharmas of castes, countries, guilds and families, thus advocating the moral foundations of political power. The *Rājadharma* monarchical in its connotation comprises the totality of all social, political as well as individual obligations and functions of the king.

The Indian *āchāryas*, in general, and Kautilya, in particular, believed that political order was responsible for and conducive to the attainment of all-round progress and prosperity and helped society to achieve and scale new heights, conserve its achievements,

[25] *Mahabharata,* Shanti, 55–57, 70, 76, 94, 96, 120.
[26] Shastri, *Manusmriti,* VII, 10; idem, VIll, 41.

maximize its gains and promote proper and equitable distribution of social gains. Kautilya[27] defines four branches of knowledge as *Trayeee* (the knowledge contained in Rig, Yajur and Sama Vedas), *Anvikshiki* (the dualistic philosophies of *Sāmkhya* and *Yoga* and the materialistic philosophy of *Lokāyata*), *Vārta* (comprising agriculture, cattle-breeding, trade and commerce) and *Dandaniti* (the 'state' authority striving for *Yogakshema* or the welfare of all). Here, *Dandaniti* is directed towards (a) acquisition of unattained, (b) preservation of acquired, (c) accentuation of already preserved and righteous and (d) due apportionment of *Anvikshiki, Trayee* and *Vārtā*. In other words, *Rājadharma* expected the *Dandadhara* (the promulgator of *Danda*) to acquire, preserve and conserve dialectics. Prosperous treasury (*Kosha*) and a well-knit system of *Danda* (punishment) were considered necessary for the control of one's own kingdom and those of the enemies. *Dandaniti* or the art of government depended on the progress of the other branches of knowledge as well as of the world.

The Indian *āchāryas* have also proclaimed the philosophy of balanced and harmonious approximation of dharma, *artha, kāma* and moksha or the fourfold *purusharthas* for *Dandadhara*[28] while advocating for the expansion of wealth and territory, a prosperous treasury and authority of punishment to control one's own people in pursuance of dharma, *artha, kāma* and moksha and also for conquering the enemy.

Danda and the Notion of Law

In Indic tradition, *Danda* (coercive authority) is used in the context of statehood. The king, also known as *Dandadhara*, is, accordingly, deliberated as the protector of dharma, justice, law,

[27] Shastri, *Arthashastra,* I. 4. The original verse says,

Ānvikshiki Trayeevārtanām Yogakshemsadhano Dandah Tasya Nitirdandanitih
Alabdhalabhartha Labdhaparirakshini Rakshitvivardhani Vriddhasya Tirtheshu Pratipadini.

[28] Ibid., I.7.

order, *Swadharma, Varnāshramadharma* and duty. He persuades the subjects to follow dharma, virtuous civil life and the fulfilment of righteousness. *Danda* becomes instrumental in ensuring a well-regulated society substituting *Arājaka* or anarchical State. Here, dharma can be equated with law or *Danda*. Kautilya is convinced that all the subjects are kept in their designated spheres of activities through an exemplary exercise of *Danda* or the weapon of sovereignty. In case of its absence, the State loses its raison d'être and gets practically extinct.

The king, having projected as *Dandadharabhawe*,[29] ensures that all his subjects follow their *Swadharma* and cooperate with each other in realization of happiness for all. Emphasizing the transcendental feature of *Nyāya* (edicts of kings) and the enacted law, Kautilya projects the king as the source of justice. Considering dharma (sacred law), *vyavahāra* (evidence), *samsthā* (history) and *rājashāsana* (edicts of kings) as the four sources of law, Kautilya has presented the latter as being superior to the one named earlier. When circumstances warrant, the king is acknowledged as the promulgator of new laws, though rooted in the Shastras. Here, Kautilya holds reason to be superior.[30] U. N. Ghoshal[31] realizes judicial sovereignty of the king in all judicial processes. Kautilya seems to be convinced that justice administered in accordance with dharma, *vyavahāra*, *samsthā* and *rājashāsana* will ensure king's suzerainty over all four quarters of the world (*Chaturantam Mahim*).[32] Here, *rājshāsana* is identical with king's decree. In case of conflict between these four, each item in the list overruled those mentioned before. Hence, the overriding authority of king's decree enumerated the principle of the king's judicial sovereignty.

[29] Ibid., I.IV.17.

[30] Ibid., III.1.57. Here, Kautilya has stated that 'whenever Sacred Law (shastra) is in conflict with the rational law (*Dharma Nyāya* in king's law), then reason shall be held authoritative'.

[31] U. N. Ghoshal, *A History of Indian Political Ideas* (London: Oxford University Press, 1966), 62.

[32] Shastri, *Arthashastra*, III.1.55.

Dharma and Political Ethics

The social aspect of dharma and the relative moral and ethical orientations indicate a close relationship between dharma and political ethics.

The sociology of *Varnāshrama* heavily relied on the notion of *Swadharma* instead of any political and constitutional differences. While Aristotle's *Politics* signifies dissimilarity between the virtues of a good man and a good citizen, Kautilya's *Arthashastra* emphasizes on due performance of one's own duties. Kshatriya duties were to be a prime concern for a Kshatriya; *Brahmachāris* were expected to fulfil their own *Swadharma*. Observance to the *Swadharma*, based on *Varnāshramadharma*, was a socio-economic task for Kautilya. It was believed that due performance of one's own dharma would lead to mundane prosperity and spiritual good leading to divine realization.[33]

As prescribed by the Vedas and elaborated by the *Shrotriyas*, the king, a Kshatriya householder, was expected to perform a set of duties and aspire for mundane prosperity. Closer to retirement, he could give up political duties and concentrate on austerities, meditation and God realization. While illustrating the duties or dharmas of the King, Kautilya defines ways and means for an ambitious king to conquer the world.[34] While endorsing the indigenous view, Kautilya considered the duty of a Kshatriya king to expand his territories and conquer the enemies. He prescribed four ways of conquering the earth and advised the king to ascertain *dharmavijaya* (victory of the religion) to win over the conquered subjects and territories.

Instead of a theocratic state, Kautilya envisaged an all-India territorial state from the Himalayas to the sea. To execute his vision, he offered a theory of *maṇḍala* (circle of states), *shadgunya*

[33] Ibid., I.III.16–17

[34] Ibid., III.1.53–55 Kautilya says 'The King who administers (the kingdom) according to *Dharma*, evidence, history, institutional practices and royal edicts, will be able to conquer the whole world bound by four quarters.'

(sixfold policy of interstate relations), system of *duta* (envoys) and *guptachara* (espionage), rules of war and *dharmavijaya*. He visualized an all-powerful all-India State to attain unity in the subcontinent and be able to defend itself from foreign aggression. He was altogether curious to promote local governments nurturing their own language, literature, traditions and culture.

The ethical and moral discourse further highlighted personal as well as sociopolitical connotations.

Personal Ethics

Dharma as *rita* (order, regulation and arrangement) inspired the king towards truth, wisdom, justice and *yajña* (rite) in Rigveda.[35] Rāmāyana, the great epic,[36] announced the king as the *Lokasatkritam* and sketched his highest moral virtues while expecting him to rule for the welfare of his people as per their will.[37]

Buddhism, too, highlighted a close relationship between politics and *Dhamma* (dharma), the absence of which was defined as *Rativijjā* (the antithesis of ethics); it considered *sheel* (modesty) and *sadāchāra* (good conduct) as the basis of politics and projected the king as the *Mahāsammat* (the great elect), who was expected to protect his subjects in accordance with *Dhamma*.[38]

While insisting that an accomplished king must be dedicated to dharma, Kautilya emerges as an emphatic proponent of the moral philosophy of kingship. Hereby, addressed as the *Dharma Pravartak* and utilizing punishment as a deterrent, the king was to restrain mendicants and ascetics engaged in improper proceedings. Subscribing to the dictum '[a]s the king so the people' (*Yathā Rājā Tathā Prajā*),[39] the king and his ministers were supposed

[35] *Rigveda,* 77.1; idem, IV. 3.4; idem, IV.23.8-10; idem, IX. 7.6.

[36] Shrinivasa Katti Mudholakara Shastri, ed., *Valmiki Ramayana* (New Delhi: Mehar Chand Lachhmandas, 1983), Bal, 1.12–1.15.

[37] Ibid., Ayodhya, C. 23.

[38] Ghoshal, *A History of Indian Political Ideas*, 62–66.

[39] Shastri, *Arthashastra*, I.7.2; see also idem, VIII, 1.16.

to be the upholders of highest virtues and role models for the subjects. The king was also portrayed as the possessor of *Trayee* and the protector of his *Prajā* (subjects).

Exemplifying the moral philosophy of kingship, Kautilya moves closer to the 'enlightened royal idealism' and offers a comprehensive list of the following qualities that are expected from a king[40]:

1. *Abhigāmik Guna* (qualities of an inviting nature);
2. *Pragyā Guna* (qualities of intellect and intuition);
3. *Utsāha Guna* (qualities of enthusiasm); and
4. *Ātmasampad* (qualities of self-restraint and spirit).

In addition, the king was expected to refrain from passions such as *kāma* (lust), *krodha* (anger), *lobha* (greed) and *moha* (attachment). The *Shatru-Shadvarga*, the six enemies comprising sex, anger, greed, vanity, haughtiness and overjoy, on the one hand, and four special temptations inclusive of hunting, gambling, drinking and women, on the other hand, were to be conquered by the king. While insisting on control of the senses, Kautilya was of the view that king's overindulgence would incite his own *Prajā*; implicating weakness of policy and thereby instigating enemies. Sensuality and impoliteness were projected as species of demonic actions.[41] While asserting the control of passion and senses, V. P. Varma finds Kautilya's king as a guardian of his subjects.[42] On the same lines, Manu, Yājnavalkya and Shukra also expected the king to observe the highest ethical virtues in their public dealings.[43]

[40] Ibid., VI, 1.21.6.

[41] Ibid., VI, 1.17. Kautilya says that if the 'king of unrighteous character and vicious habits' fails, through these weaknesses or otherwise, to protect people's welfare; he would 'fall a prey either to the fury of his own subjects or that of his enemies'.

[42] Varma, *Studies in Hindu Political Thought*, n. 4, 204. To V. P. Varma, Kautilya's king appears 'to be a despot exercising power through sheer military force, but was to rule his subjects through affection'.

[43] Shastri, *Manusmriti,* X, 85–94, 102–104; Vijnaneshwar, trans., *Yajnavalkyasmriti* (Hindi; Varanasi: Chaukhamba Sanskrit Series Office, n.d.), I. 20; and *Shukraniti,* I. 70–76, 151 and 156.

This moral bias of kingship can be considered as a great contribution of our *āchāryas* to political thought. In the West, scholars such as Plato, Aristotle, Cicero and Kant have signified the moral factors in politics. For example, Plato projected his philosopher king to be wise, courageous and temperate. However, a comparative illustration of Indian and Western political thought reflects a more pronounced emphasis on moral factors in Indian ethos. Kautilya, widely accepted as a theorist of political power and conquest, was strikingly concerned with the control of unregenerate passions and exalted spiritual truths.

Sociopolitical Ethics

Under the concept of *Rājadharma,* the king was expected to perform protective as well as developmental functions. Under the category of protective functions, his duties included protection of the life and property of people, maintenance of law and order, evasion of dangers, punishment of criminals/wrongdoers and administration of justice impartially. On the other hand, on developmental context, he was expected to promote moral and material happiness, preserve and conserve education through *Trayee* and *Anvikshiki*, encourage economy or *Vārtā* and regulate the means of livelihood. The limits to the authority of the king were imposed by the social and religious customs of his State in the form of dharma, *vyavahār, samsthā* and *rājashāsan*, which have existed from times immemorial and with which he was required not to interfere.

Provision for *Āpaddharma*

While striving for the preservation, expansion, accentuation and acquisition of material resources along with territories, Kautilya allowed his king to deviate from the acknowledged path of dharma, transgress its injunctions in times of acute *āpatti* (crisis),[44] and

[44] Shastri, *Arthashastra*, IX.7.

adopt relentless and ruthless techniques of conquest. The use of deception and immoral means was acknowledged to create despair in the enemy camps at interstate level. After having indulged in all such immoral activities, he was expected to project himself as an innocent person: to express sympathy for many events while holding others responsible for the same. Kautilya deals with at least five circumstances, when deviation from ethical means is acknowledged: (a) to collect revenue for royal treasure at the time of crisis; (b) to identify and arrest corrupt and disloyal officials of the State; (c) to identify and arrest offenders and criminals; (d) to vanish any probable conspiracy or rebellion either by princes, nobles, officials or by ordinary subjects; and (e) to pursue expansionist politics in the enemy state or to punish a king who is against dharma.

On the same lines, the Mahābhārata also advised the king to appear as a perfect gentleman, irrespective of his motives. It seems that the emphasis was more on the public appearance instead of the real content of his character.[45] The king, however, was allowed to deviate from the path of dharma and transgress its injunctions in times of acute crisis.[46]

The advocacy of cruel political diplomacy, however, does not denote that Kautilya separates politics from ethics. He, instead, encourages virtues of self-restraint and propagates the dominant moral concepts of the Indian tradition. The fifth, sixth and seventh chapters of the first book of *Arthashastra* portray Kautilya as an essential proponent of the virtues of moral restraints. Support for ruthless and relentless diplomacy and techniques were only provisional, realistic and calculated. The territorial conquest was essentially to be followed by *dharmavijaya*.

In fact, politics was broadly conceived as *Rājaniti* or the ethics of politics or political ethics. In accordance with the political compulsions, some deviations and departures from the fundamental norms of politics were acknowledged. Subsequently, this departure

[45] *Mahabharata*, Shanti, CXL, 13, 17–18.
[46] Ibid., LXXXVIIl, 32; CXXX, 25; CXLIl, 8.

presented politics as a matter of convenience and expedience. Most of the earthly misdeeds were because of the deplorable fall of politics from its original pedestal. Kautilya's *Arthashastra* was primarily concerned with the complex political situations and offered solutions to the various problems of politics.

Concept of *Dharmavijaya* (Religious Victory)

Recommending various rituals and sacrifices, Kautilya suggested for a mission of conquest. He, however, strove to humanize it to the maximum. Subscribing to the notion of *dharmavijaya*, Kautilya advised his king to remain contented with the formal recognition of his suzerainty and the payment of a tribute by the conquered king; he was not to annex his kingdom or disturb its administration. Kautilya even disapproved the extortion of tribute in *dharmavijaya*.[47] In the event of death of the defeated king in war or unwilling occupant of throne, an appropriate successor was to be placed. In case of annexation being inevitable, the prevailing laws and customs were to be honoured and the new subjects were to be dealt with gently. In spite of paucity of historical evidence and authentic information about the internal condition of the Mauryan Empire, it is more likely that the autonomy of the powerful republic of Punjab and Rajputana continued. It seems that, in general, annexation after conquest was to be avoided due to wide resemblance of culture and religion that prevailed in the states. Religious or cultural divergences or animosities were never a cause of bitterness in relations or an attempt for utter destruction of each other. With the result, internal autonomy was easily conceded.

Religious Sacrifices and the *Purohitas*

The king's dharma was believed to radiate into all sphere of activities. Here, the king, a public person and by virtue of his

[47] Shastri, *Arthashastra*, XIII.5.15.

high office, is dedicated to the service of his State. His conduct is believed to influence the subjects. Even divine manifestations such as fire, floods, epidemics, famine, rats, tigers, serpents and demons are supposed to indicate their displeasure of the king. Here, the king is expected to offer religious ceremonies and prayers to avert dangers. In general, disasters were considered as a failure on the part of the king to protect his subjects and were interpreted as the consequence of his intended or otherwise sinful conduct. In case an innocent man is punished, a fine equal to 30 times the unjust impositions is expected to be thrown into water, dedicating it to the Varuna, the lord of waters and moral and the ruler of sinners among men. Later, the amount was to be distributed among the Brahmanas. As a part of his *Rājadharma*/ duties, the king is expected to offer rituals/sacrifice and evade the kingdom of evil and natural disasters. In other words, the king was expected to study Vedas, perform sacrifice, observe righteous living and gain *tapas* or spiritual energy for the protection of his kingdom. To 'acquire', 'preserve' and 'accentuate' the territory, various political sacrifices such as *Rājasuya, Agnihstobha, Somavikraya, Madhamopasadha, Pravamyovasana* and *Maya* have been advocated by ancient *āchāryas.*

Advocacy for numerous sacrifices entailed the predominance of the class of *Purohitas* or Brahmanas resulting in the success of the sacerdotal order. The institution of *Purohitas* altogether applied a powerful constraint on the authorities of the king. The *Purohitas* gradually grabbed ascendancy in the palace hierarchy. While describing the qualities and creation of the councillors and priests, Kautilya holds 'that *Kshatriya* breed which is brought up by *Brahmanas* ... and faithfully knows the precepts of the *Shastras* became invincible ....' The performance of rituals, in accordance with the Shastras, implied the king's appointment of a domestic *Purohita*, obedience of his injunctions and resulted dependence on the Brahmanas and *Purohitas*. In Kautilya's protocol, the royal *Purohita* occupied the first rank along with the Crown Prince, the Queen Mother, the Chief Queen and the Chief Minister.

Absence of Any Organized State Religion: The Spirit of Inherent Unity of Religions

Indian political economy and statecraft was not divorced from religion and morality, nor was it the handmaid of any religious order or denomination. There was a multitude of diverse viewpoints in religious thought and practices in ancient India. There was often fierce competition among them to claim the allegiance of kings, commoners, soldiers, priests, merchants and cultivators. The post-Vedic period in Indian history particularly abounds in religious polemics and dialectal warfare. It appears that there was a fairly free debate in the marketplace of ideas when different schools of thought and different protest movements surcharged the Indian intellectual milieu. There appears to have been no continuously organized religious persecution or crusades even when there was a measure of state patronage for a particular religion or sect owing to the personal productivities of the ruling prince or his clan. The reason for this appears to be that there was a high degree of tolerance and accommodation. There was considerable freedom of expression, discussion and discourse, and there was a common cohesive sociopolitical framework within which inter-religious and intersect rivalries could work themselves out. Freedom of thought and conscience, freedom of worship and religion, and freedom of speech and expression bred a certain catholicity of outlook and temperament in ancient India, and this protected the Indian society from the excesses of fanaticism and exclusivism. For centuries, it gave the Indian society a remarkable power and frequent opportunities of assimilation and absorption.

The Vedic view of life attached higher importance to the impending evolution of man, to the final immersion of human soul in the absolute; gave lower prominence to individual religious beliefs; and inspired toleration of various religions. It believed in the possibility of multiple ways of spiritual liberation of a man,[48] resulting

[48] Shankar Dayal Sharma, *Secularism in the Indian Ethos* (New Delhi: Ministry of Information and Broadcasting, Directorate of Advertising and Visual Publicity, Government of India, 1989), 4.

in the total absence of imposition of a particular religion upon its people; allowing practice, preach and propagation of diverse faiths; construction of the places of worship and following of varied ways of life and processes of worship. This aspect of Hinduism subsequently evolved into the notion of *Sarva Dharma Sama Bhāva* or tolerance towards and respect for all religions.[49]

The Rigveda asserts that 'truth is one', even though 'the learned may describe it variously'.[50] The Bhagavad Gita personalizes this summation in Lord Krishna.[51] This spirit of coexistence, tolerance of and mutual respect for all faiths is the fundamental spirit of ancient Indian thought. Accordingly, the Rigveda unequivocally pronounces that irrespective of their religious faiths, 'All human beings are of one-race.'[52] Accordingly, it inspires all human beings to consider each other as their friend and as part of universal soul.[53] A significant manifestation of diversity of faith and belief is

[49] Donald Eugene Smith, *India as a Secular State* (Princeton: Princeton University Press, 1963), 61–62.

Here, the following is stated,

> It is an undoubted fact that, in India, religious and philosophical thinkers were able to enjoy perfect, nearly absolute, freedom for a long period, with a spirit of 'Sarva Dharma Sambhāv, i.e. an approach of tolerance towards, equality of and respect for all religions. The freedom of thought in ancient India was so considerable as to find no parallel in the West before the most recent age.

[50] *Rigveda* (New Delhi: Dayananda Sansthan, 1973), I. 164.46, wherein it is observed *Ekam Sad Viprah Bahudha Vadanti.*

[51] Satyapal Vidyalankar, trans., *Bhagavad Gita* (Hindi; Delhi: Govindram Hasanand, 1981), IV. II, wherein Lord Krishna makes this observation by stating, 'In whatever way men identify with Me, in the same way do I carry out their desires; men pursue my path, in all ways.'

[52] *Rigveda,* X. 191. 2.

[53] Ibid., X, 191.2 wherein the appropriate verse reads as follows:

> *Sangachhadhvam Samvadadhvam Sam Vo Manaansi Jaanataam*
> *Devaa Bhaagam Yatha Poorve Sanjaanaana Upasate.*

It enjoins to

> Behave with others as you would with yourself. Look upon all the living beings as your friends, for in all of them there resides one soul. All are but a part of that universal soul. A person who believes that all are his soulmates and loves them all alike, never feels lonely.

contained in the *Prithvi Sūkta* of the Atharva Veda while revering Mother Earth for sustaining all human beings.[54] In another reference, Mother Earth is also invoked to inculcate the capacity to interact harmoniously.[55] On similar lines, Yajurveda also inspires for friendly relationship among co-living beings.[56] In short, the ancient Indian thought provided philosophical and ethnological composite and inculcated the liberal outlook of *Sarva Dharma Sama Bhāva*.

During Precolonial Period

In the later period, the process of enhancement of the secular outlook continued and was further enhanced by Shankaracharya through the establishment of the four *Mathas* in the four corners of the subcontinent and his belief in *Advaita*: the philosophy of non-dualism, recognition of the equality of all human beings and rejection of ritualism and superstition.

The indigenous process of merger and fusion continued with the growing interaction between the earlier religious movements of the East and the ones which came from the West. Statesmen like Akbar realized the value of this fusion and initiated the movement of Din-i-Ilahi (divine faith or divine monotheism).[57] The process continued and was further enriched by the efforts

[54] *Atharva Veda* (New Delhi: Dayananda Sansthan, Samvat 2031), XII. 1.45 wherein the appropriate verse reads as follows: *Janam Vibhratee Bahudhaa Vivaachasam Nanaadharmaanam Prithvee Yathoukasam*, which means the following: 'This earth, which accommodates people of different persuasions and languages, as in a peaceful home, may it benefit all of us'.

[55] *Ibid.*, XII. 1.16, wherein the appropriate verse reads as follows:

> *Taa Nah Prajaah Sam Duhataam Samagraa Vaacho Madhu Prithivi Dhehi Mahyam.*

[56] *Yajurveda* (New Delhi: Dayananda Sansthan, Samvat, 2030), XXXVI, 18. The verse says, 'May all beings look on me with the eyes of a friend. May I look on all beings with the eyes of a friend. May we look on all beings with the eyes of a friend'.

[57] Vincent A. Smith, *Akbar: The Great Mugal, 1542–1605* (Delhi: S. Chand & Co., 1962), 150, 154.

of Abdul Rahim Khan-e-Khanan, Dara Shikoh, Kabir and Guru Nanak, just to name a few.

Cultural osmosis and synthesis of the indigenous Hindu and Islamic ways of life and thought sustained in a considerable measure in the realm of music, dance, painting, architecture, literature, philosophy, spiritualism and in the cores, mannerisms and daily lives of the people. The stamp of India's composite culture can be comprehended in Mughal, Kangra and Rajput miniature paintings; Kathak nritya; Hindustani music; new developments in music refinements of calligraphy; efflorescence of architecture; and the growth of handicrafts and interior decoration aesthetics. The languages and literatures of India emerged as natural vehicles for the new synthesis. Philosophies of Amir Khusro, Abdul Rahim Khan-e-Khanan, Malik Muhammad Jayasi, Raskhan and Dara Shikoh, to name only a few of the most prominent, readily adopted gastronomical and sartorial changes while augmenting mutual empathy and interchange. Sufi and Vaishnava saints created liberal attitudes among all sections of Indians. Kabir, Guru Nanak, Dadu, Charan Das, Ramcharan, Sahajanand, Bhiku and others in northern India, Namdev and Tukaram in Maharashtra and Chaitanya in Bengal blazed new traits of thought and illumined the ethical spiritual rational path of mutual coherence, thus providing fruitful and harmonious avenues of synthesis, rising above the pettiness and the parochialism of the sectarian establishment.

The comprehensive approach of coexistence of and respect for all living organized religions summarize the concept of dharma. Denoting all human beings as one race, a philosophical and anthological composite was provided by the ancient Indian thought. Rising above the parochialism of sectarian formations, the concept of dharma provided the harmonious avenues of synthesis in multireligious indigenous society.

However, reference is also necessitated to the later tendencies of societal stratification, institutionalization of religion, dogmatic ritualism and conservative superstitions entailing reform movements within Vedantic fold or Upanishad literature and the harmonious pluralism propagated by *āchāryas,* such as Shankara, Ramanuja, Vallabha and Madhava. However, the social and cultural traditions of the Hindus were not sound enough to integrate the non-Muslims into a single nation.

The Colonial Period and Beyond

The colonial period witnessed religious strife of Hindus with Muslims, on the one hand, and with Christian missionaries, on the other hand. The impact of religious factor ranged from the 'divide and rule policy', forces of communalism and separatism, separate communal electorates perpetuated by the British, and the revivalist trends and Hindu overtones within the socio-religious reform movements. Cultural revivalism fed on the political romanticization of the past and the future; historiography and theology aided and abetted by literature; and the pan-Islamic thrust of revivalism led to a deeper correlation of religion with culture and politics. At the time of the 'Mutiny' of 1857, the Hindus and the Muslims collectively fought the British. The Indian National Congress, formed in 1885, was overtly a non-communal organization, and its membership was not determined by one's religion.

The extremists, at the beginning of the 20th century, brought religion into play as an important factor for mass mobilization against the British and introduced the idea of Hindus as a separate political entity and promoted solidarity among the Hindus. The fear of domination by Hindus kept the Muslims away from the Congress.

The nexus between religion and politics got a new turn with the advent of Gandhi, as he asserted that 'those who say that religion has nothing to do with politics do not know what religion means'.[58] Such a conviction was, however, rooted in his belief in

[58] The Publications Division, Ministry of Information and Broadcasting, *The Collected Works of Mahatma Gandhi* (New Delhi: Government of India, 1958–1984), XXXIX, 401. The statement is in his partial autobiography subtitled, *The Story of My Experiments with Truth*.

the underlying truth and unity of all religions. While asserting for *Sarva Dharma Sama Bhāva* or equal respect for all religions, he too, however, used religious symbols to give the national movement a mass base. The use of religious symbols and slogans, no doubt, enthused the masses, and it also led to the identification of Hindu revivalism with Indian nationalism. The Khilafat movement further legitimized the intrusion of religion into the political sphere. A short-lived historic Hindu–Muslim unity was followed by frequent clashes among Hindus and Muslims after the sudden suspension of Non-Cooperation Movement. Two simultaneous trends were noteworthy, one of communalism and the other of intermingling of the common people. Spontaneous support and cooperation by all sections and communities of the Indian society during the Civil Disobedience Movement was another evidence of this momentum.

The successive decade, however, witnessed the gradually increasing communalization, which, in turn, resulted in the emergence of the Two-Nation Theory and held that the Hindus and Muslims constitute two nations. The concept of universal Islam and of Koranic or Muslim State began to gain ground side by side with the growth of the national movement. The idea of the Partition was first mooted by Choudhry Rahamat Ali in 1931, and this demand was adopted by the Muslim League in 1940 on the basis of the 'Two-Nation Theory' at the behest of Muhammad Ali Jinnah. The 1946 elections, based on separate electorates and limited franchise, were held in a communally surcharged atmosphere.

Significantly, it is to be noted that during the initial stages, the nationalist could not organize a consistent and principled fight against the communalism and separatist tendencies. The Indian national movement, thus, coincided with religious vocabulary, politics of appeasement and compromise, religious exhibitionism, and failure to separate institutional religion from ethical religion and also from politics. Separatism in politics, politicization of religious communities, communal divisions and dissentions formed the raison d'être of India's Partition.

The nexus between electoral process and communal considerations is often an open secret. In the minority–majority dilemma, political parties have sought to convert religious communities into political communities. In fact, the spirit of nationalism has waved so precipitously under the impact of competitive politics of elections that all kinds of pluralistic trends are on the rise, and nationalism, without denominational labels, is becoming a disappearing species. Religion has got communalized, internalizing the values of aggressive pursuit of self-interest of the individual, on the one hand, and the strategic factors of political pressure groups, on the other hand.

An analysis of Indian politics during the post-Independence era reflects a notable upsurge in religious affairs. Apart from being a private affair, religion has emerged as a social force, making communalism and casteism as the most challenging and intractable problems of modern India, manifested through religious processions, hate campaigns, communal riots, politics of religious conversions and re-conversions, and electoral exigencies of 'vote bank' politics. The communal tendencies of both the majority and the minority communities are seen to be on the ascendance putting the ancient notion of dharma in grave peril.

2

Strītva in *Ṛgveda*

Kaustubh Gaurh and Abhishek Parashar

The role of women in the Vedic tradition has been a major point of study and engagement amongst scholars while studying the early Indian societies. The contemporary Indian perspective on women traces its history to the times of the Rigvedic traditions and much before that to draw inferences.[1] In the study herein, after scanning through the trends in Indian historiography on the question of women, we first try and understand the significance of an ancient text like Ṛgveda in terms of its relationship with the question of women in Indian history. Thereafter, the proposed chapter attempts to look at the position of women in the Vedic traditions by evaluating the 'feminine' aspects of the society. These feminine aspects incorporate gendered language, symbolisms, zoomorphic elements, concerns and authority of women, and the relative position of female deities in the societies. The chapter carefully studies these aspects to make observations on the general attitude of the societies towards women in Rigvedic traditions. For this purpose, the entire chapter is divided into

[1] Romila Thapar, *History of Early India: From the Origins to AD 1300* (Gurugram: Penguin Books India, 2002), 118. Also, see Upinder Singh, *A History of Ancient and Early Medieval India: From the Stone Age to the 12th Century* (Gurugram: Pearson Publications, 2008), 233, 333.

three sections. The first section covers the insentient aspects such as language and symbolisms; the second section deals specifically with the role of women, the sentient beings of the societies; and the third section covers the spiritual element devoted to the female deities during the Vedic period. The primary source of the study has been the Rigvedic corpus as it is the first written text to historicize the gender roles in the societies in early India.

Ṛgveda: The Text and the Context

For an Indologist, it is perhaps an easier task to know what Ṛgveda is not than what it actually is. This is because there are so many contrived assumptions that have been circulating among scholars and lay readers who take interest in the text. Notable Indologist Frits Staal enumerates some of these common assumptions. He observes that the Ṛgveda is commonly regarded as a set of 10 books, mysterious and sacred. But it is interesting to note that the Vedas were not books in a conventional sense. They were oral compositions memorized in an extremely precise manner for centuries. These oral compositions were composed in a language that was popular during the time of their composition, and, thereafter, they were transmitted orally for generations. It must be noted that the 10 *maṇḍalas* are referred to as the 10 books of Ṛgveda. *Maṇḍala* means circle of states, and it has nothing to do with books. It is due to the superimpositions of the colonial thought on Indic thought that the Vedas were understood simply as books. The term 'book' is more appropriate for literary texts such as Quran or Bible which are believed to have a central authority. But the Vedas did not have a central authority, and the thought imbibed in the Vedic tradition is different from how the colonial authorities perceived it to be.[2]

There are more such myths that Staal attempts to clear. One of the most common adjectives attributed to Vedas is *apauruṣeya* (that which is not written by humans), but nowhere such an adjective

[2] Frits Staal, *Discovering the Vedas: Origins, Mantras, Rituals, Insights* (Gurugram: Penguin Books India, 2008), 12.

is attributed to Ṛgveda in its hymns. Rather, there are names of different sages and families who composed the hymns. It is only from *Pūrva Mīmāṃsā*, a philosophical system that developed much later, that the idea came from. The Vedas have been called śruti, or 'what is heard'; this is again true to only a very limited manner. They were heard to facilitate the dissemination, or the transmission from father to son. Therefore, the Vedas exhibit a decentralized tendency of composition and dissemination. The Vedas, and especially Ṛgveda, had no supreme authority. It did not concern with a single Pope, and it was not a subject of a centralizing agency as grand as a Church, but it dealt with the rishis and their concerns. The rishis, in return, were reflecting the concerns of the societies around them. Therefore, Ṛgveda enriched the Indic thought that existed in early Indian societies. Frits Staal is not wrong to say that Vedas embody a civilization.[3]

It is, therefore, to be used by a historian meticulously. The date of Ṛgveda's composition can help a student of history know the exact period that the Ṛgveda could be an authoritative representative of. But a precise and a satisfactory answer to this is still awaited. Scholars such as Jamison and Staal, who have worked extensively on the Vedas, placed the Ṛgvedic hymns between 1500 BCE and 1000 BCE. But it should be noted that Jamison has suggested that the poetic conventions that developed during the period of composition of the hymns evolved over a wider period of time. At most, the agreed dates are congruous; the surviving portions of Ṛgveda were conceived and composed much earlier. And most of the scholars trace the antecedents of Ṛgveda to an old Indian heritage. If that is the case, then the dating would go back even further. Jamison very aptly argues that what we know as Ṛgveda indeed presents us the surface of a long tradition in the past.[4]

The responsibility to preserve, transmit and disseminate the hymns of Ṛgveda was taken up by different schools, popularly known as the śākhās (branches). These schools specialized in

[3] Ibid.

[4] Stephanie Jamison and Joel Brereton, *Guides to Sacred Texts: The Ṛgveda, A Guide* (New York: Oxford University Press, 2020), 14.

different Vedas, and the texts that they composed were employed in their own ways to perform rituals. What we know as śruti texts, which were transmitted through oral traditions, comprised the Veda. The principal text for each school is the saṃhitās that formed the collection of hymns and chants. These Vedic saṃhitās further evolved with the extension of supplementary literature such as the Brāmaṇas and the Āraṇyakas. While the different śākhās shared common texts, they differed mainly with different saṃhitā recensions. For example, the Yajurveda had wider variations in recensions. But Ṛgveda relatively had only a few differences among the saṃhitā recensions that existed. Caraṇavyūha, a Yajurvedic text giving us a fair knowledge about the Vedic śākhās, presented a list of five śākhās of Ṛgveda: the Śākala, Bāṣkala, Āśvalāyana, Śāṅkhāyana and Māṇḍūkāyana (elsewhere called the Māṇḍūkeya or Māṇḍukeya). However, there are more sources that cite different numbers of such branches of Ṛgveda. There are two kinds of recensions of the Ṛgveda that have survived from an early period. One is Śākāla Saṃhitā and the other is Bāṣkala Saṃhitā.[5]

The text which we are dealing here belongs to Śākala School which was established by a great linguist called Śākalya. Although we find other schools, but it has been observed that they do not differ to a large extent in terms of content. Śākalya is credited to the *padapātha* style of Ṛgveda, wherein the *saṃdhi* rules are carefully broken down, and this monumental task deems Śākalya the accolade of first great linguist in history. Śākalya very earnestly preserved the early forms of the language that may have evolved during his time. It is to his credit that he did not view them as 'early', but he credited them to various regions that they came from. Śākalya did not know that he was creating new dimensions in the history writing of the Indian subcontinent, and his analysis was forming the very core of almost the final stage of formation and compilation of what we today know as Ṛgveda. Frits Staal aptly credits 'Śākalya's perspective as historical, systematic and analytical'. He goes on to call Śākala the 'first linguist'.[6]

[5] Ibid., 197–198.
[6] Staal, *Discovering the Vedas*, 88.

One might just ask that what can a text from the past tell us about the societies which shaped it. How does a text like this attempt to answer the question of women in Indic thought? Wendy Doniger tries to answer this question, but with a skewed perspective. She says as follows: 'The Ṛgveda is a book by men about male concerns in a world dominated by men; one of these concerns is women, who appear throughout the hymns as objects, though seldom as subjects.'[7] Perhaps she again answers what Ṛgveda is not. While reading her work to gain a historical understanding, one should not forget that Doniger specializes in philology and though she has interesting conclusions on religion and mythology, it becomes imperative for a reader to put her observations under the lens of history. It has been argued elsewhere that she takes selective narratives to fit cultural blocks in Indian context.[8] Therefore, to say that Ṛgveda reflects on the concerns of only one class, one gender, one social group or just one thin slice of temporal bread is a myopic view. A composition like Ṛgveda holds a significant position in the realm of both historical and literary worlds as it was developing during a very defining phase of the subcontinent. Jamison calls it 'an old monument in the world literature and world religion, echoing a voice, or indeed many voices reflecting an exemplary sophistication and complexity of a culture that it was a product of'.[9]

Strītva

This section discusses exclusively the position of women as deities. Ṛgveda also presents an insight to the feminine aspects through its language that imbibes a strong sense of gender. It has been suggested that the language of Ṛgveda is an archaic form of

[7] Wendy Doniger, *The Ṛgveda: An Anthology—One Hundred and Eight Hymns* (London: Penguin Books, 1981), 232.

[8] Kaustubh Gaurh and Abhishek Parashar, *Perspectives on Love and Longing from the Works of Kālidāsa in Ancient India*, Shodhpragya (Haridwar: Uttarakhand Sanskrit University), 178–187.

[9] Jamison and Brereton, *Guides to Sacred Texts*, 6.

Sanskrit, from a broader family of Indo-Aryan language.[10] It was eventually that the language of Ṛgveda was reduced to a certain uniform linguistic level.[11] Therefore, the attitude exhibited in language used in the Ṛgveda could be our window to see the general attitude for the 'female'. It is interesting that when we embark on our investigation through the language of the text, the text itself emphasizes on language. The authors held the notions of speech with utmost reverence.[12] Speech was seen as the mediating bridge that connected the people(s) with their deities which they identified as Vāc.[13] The absence of the 'masculine' and the emphasis on the 'feminine' here are acknowledgments of feminine thought as the harbinger of knowledge.

Similarly, even the references to male deities are made with the help of feminine adjectives. This has added grandeur and prominence to the imagery of a male deity which has been invoked. For example, while invoking the god of fire, Agni, he is attributed with the features of that of an energy giver. In this regard, energy has been the medium, and the word used for it is *śuci* which has feminine gender.[14] Another example that the most defining features of the prominent male deities were perceived in feminine form is found in the context of Viśvadevas or all gods. Viśvadevas have been compared not with the Sun god, but with his feature of luminosity. Luminosity is called *ustra* here. It is striking to note that sun is revered because of its luminosity. And that feature is seen as a feminine entity in the text.[15] Another important aspect in this regard is knowledge. The terms used for knowledge are *dhī* and *medhā*, and these are in feminine imagery as a gender.[16]

[10] Thapar, *History of Early India*, 104.

[11] Keshav Raj Chalise, *Female Values in the Ṛgveda*, 1.

[12] Staal, *Discovering the Vedas*, i.

[13] Staphenie W. Jamison and Joel P. Brereton, trans., *The Ṛgveda: Earliest Religious Poetry of India* (Oxford: Oxford University Press, 2014), 1208.

[14] T. H. Griffith, trans., *The Hymns of the Ṛgveda* (henceforth RV), II.1.14 (Kotagiri [Nilgiri], 1896).

[15] RV. I.3.8.

[16] See RV. 1.35.5, 1 and RV. 1.3.5 for *dhī*; RV. I.18.6 for *medhā*.

Even the fulfilment in terms of welfare is called *svasti*, which is perceived as a feminine feature.[17] It is notable that the process from thought to speech and, finally, to fulfilment is represented through feminine symbolisms.

A significant feature of the hymns of Ṛgveda are the imageries used in the text. These imageries reflect the position of women in terms of how they were received and venerated by the societies, and especially men. The cow that gave milk has been revered in Ṛgveda. And the gender subscribed to cow is that of a female.[18] Similarly, the imagery of earth has also been conceived as feminine and as a provider.[19] At some instances, two imageries have been used together in a romantic sense to fathom the gravity of emotive aspects of the feminine. An analogy has been drawn where rivers such as Beas and Satluj have been compared to cows which go to meet the sea as their calves.[20] This imagery of feminine as the provider has been a recurring motif in Ṛgveda. At one point, rivers have been projected as feeding the ocean.[21] The last hymn of the sixth *maṇḍalas* presents an interesting case. It deals with the weapons, and Jamison notes that 'particularly striking are the verses in which the subject is described as a seductive woman or tender mother, a characterization that contrasts sharply with the violence of battle'.[22]

But what about the living beings which were not women? To simplify it further, what about animals? It is not surprising that this subject has appeared on the landscape of Indian scholarship time and again. To see the treatment of females among animals in various traditions enables us to delve deeper with the feminine element in the societies. Such a treatment in Rigvedic traditions has been a widely discussed subject among scholars from across the fields and even political activists. It is a different issue that the

[17] RV. I.2.9.
[18] RV. I.4.1.
[19] RV. I.22.13.
[20] RV. III.33.1.
[21] RV. II.13.2.
[22] Jamison and Brereton, *The Ṛgveda*, 876.

study of zoomorphic figures in the Rigvedic tradition is studied mainly in terms of cow. But the studies on cow have yielded an interesting case study on the scholarship on the subject. The most controversial element around the entire discussion has been D. N. Jha's work on dietary habits in early India with respect to cow's meat. While there are references in Ṛgveda as to how cow symbolized motherhood and compassion, it is rather unfortunate to see how Jha has not been able to establish what he intended to, at least with regard to the Ṛgveda. He does not give a clear indication if cow's meat was a popular part of the diet in the Vedic traditions. As a result, this is how he concludes and shifts the focus of the debate about consumption of cow in the age of the Vedas: 'Whether or not the Vedic Aryans ate consecrated, or sacrificed beef or other animal flesh, the heart of the matter is that the milch cattle including the cow was not sacred during the Vedic and post-Vedic centuries.'[23]

It is interesting to note that Keith cites one of the main verses which may invite a reader's attention over the usage of cow's flesh at the funeral (RV. 6.75.).[24] He specifically mentions that the term 'go' is very rarely applied for the flesh of a cow. And in this case, the fat of the cow gives a sense of slathering the body with the fat prepared from cow milk. Besides, he goes on to cite verses where the strings and slings are made of different body parts of the cow, but fresh perspectives on those verses give us a different way of seeing.[25]

As far as the sacred attribution to cow are concerned, there are umpteen references in the Rigvedic saṃhitā where cow has been compared to a mother who sustains life.[26] Ūṣā is a prominent

[23] D. N. Jha, *The Myth of the Holy Cow* (New Delhi: Navyana Publishing, 2009), 38.

[24] Arthur Anthony Macdonell and Arthur Berriedale Keith, *Vedic Index & Names and Subjects*, Vol. I (London: John Murray, published for the Government of India, 1912), 234.

[25] An inquisitive reader may take a look at the following verses: RV. VI.75.2, X.27.22, and RV. I.121.9 from Jamison and Brereton, *The Ṛgveda*.

[26] RV. II.2.2; II,24,14; III.33.4.

goddess in Ṛgveda. Eventually, we shall see how this figure was an emblem of *strītva* in Ṛgveda: She has been compared with cow, not just once, but twice. For example, a verse in the fourth *maṇḍala* says thus, 'Dappled bright and ruddy like a mare, the mother of cows, follower of truth, Dawn has become the companion of the Aśvins.'[27]

Similarly, there is a reference to Indra where he is compared to cow.[28] These instances add to our discussion on the subject. The theme encompassing the dietary patterns still needs a dedicated discussion as it is important to see the conditioning of the elements which were equated with the symbolism of *strītva* in the early Indian societies.

The sentient aspect of feminine deals with women, across different domains of society and in different spheres such as family and politics. The Ṛgveda emphasizes on the institution of family, so much so that it further makes a woman the centre of a household, the wife is the home.[29] In the domestic spaces, women have been represented as daughters, wives and mothers. Nationalist viewpoints have tried to argue for the period of Ṛgveda as the golden age for women.[30] But to call the period a golden age for women would be an exaggeration as there are other factors that influenced the status of women in different ways.[31] The birth of the sons, it is claimed, has been wished for at several instances.[32] But it should be noted that the birth of a girl child is not unwelcomed in Rigvedic tradition. To locate the subtle aspects of the lives of women during the composition of Ṛgveda, it is important to note that there were different social categories of women. There were daughters, there were wives and there were women who either chose to stay out of

[27] RV. IV.52.2; also see RV. VII.77.2.

[28] RV. II.16. 8.

[29] RV. III.53.4.

[30] J. B. Chaudhury, *Position of Women in the Vedic Ritual*, Thesis approved for PhD (London: University of London, 1956), 2.

[31] Bhagwati Saran Upadhyay, *Women in Ṛgveda* (Benaras: Nand Kishore & Bros, 1941), 5.

[32] RV. I.1.3.

marriage or remain as widows. A closer inspection to the conditions of each of these categories would give us a better idea.

Let us examine the first category, the daughter. A daughter, in Rigvedic societies, was engaged in various activities. But it would be fascinating to know how the Rigvedic societies looked at the girl child. It has been argued by the scholars that the birth of the daughters was not sought during the concerned time period.[33] However, there is no reference in Ṛgveda depreciating the birth of a daughter. Also, painstaking work of J. B. Chaudhury is worth citing here who dedicated a significant extent of scholarship to prove that gender-neutral terms in the text were used. He cited several instances to prove this; for example, when it is said *maraṇadharmā mānavaḥ* to say man is mortal, it implies equally for women too.[34]

Shakuntala Rao Shastri marks an interesting observation where she tries to observe various names by which a daughter was assigned different roles in the society. *Kanyā* and *duhitā* are two of these names that are still very popular in many Indian societies. But the word *kanyā* has other variants too which eventually became obsolete in literature.[35] These terms are *kaninakā*, *kanyāna* and, later even in a more mutated form, *kanyāla*.[36] Shastri cites different commentators who broadly infer the meaning of *kanyā* and its variants to be a young attractive girl. Therefore, we see that girls of different age groups were defined distinctly. But it is striking to notice that the *Smritis* had reduced the age of a *kanyā* and fixed it to be 10. The daughter was engaged in household works like looking after the cattle and was called *duhitṛ*.[37] If the Vedic economy was a pastoral one, then the term *duhitṛ* suggests the role that women played in the economy.

[33] Romila Thapar, *The Past before Us: Historical Traditions of Early North India* (London: Harvard University Press, 2013), 122, 131.

[34] Jatindra Bimal Chaudhary, *Position of Women in the Vedic Ritual* (Calcutta: Calcutta Oriental Press, 1956), 10.

[35] RV. I.123.10; Ūṣā is compared to an attractive Kanyā.

[36] See RV. IV.32.23; RV. X.40.9; AV5, 3.

[37] RV. III.31.1,2; also see Upadhyay, *Women in Ṛgveda*, 34.

The freedom that was enjoyed by the women in the Rigvedic societies is inferred from the description of *Samana*, which as a ceremony is mentioned in the hymns of Ṛgveda very frequently. However, the actual meaning of *Samana* has been understood by different scholars in different ways, ranging from sacrificial ceremonies to a kind of social gathering.[38] Young women have been described as engaging with strangers. The ceremony or the gathering called *Samana* was attended by women of various age groups, as words such as *yoṣā* and *agru* have also been used in these contexts to describe different women. Griffith calls *Samana* a 'festal meeting', and it has not been suggested that this was a meeting of a religious kind.[39] If it was a social gathering, it invited different kinds of competition as well, for the sixth *maṇḍala* suggests so.[40] Keith in his Vedic index cites different activities and a wider composition of people that comprised a *Samana*.[41] Therefore, young women seemed to have enjoyed freedom in social systems, in terms of exercising their choice to consort with a man of their choice. However, it is surprising that in the 10th *maṇḍala*, the system was seen out of date.[42] As the 10th *maṇḍala* is a result of later interpolation, it seems that the social systems too became more rigid.

Marriage has been an important institution in Ṛgveda. And it seems that women exercised choices in the matrimonial affairs. For example, women entered into the matrimonial alliances after having attained a considerable age. Keith after having carefully studied the Vedic terms suggests that Vedic tradition saw a considerable freedom on the part of both men and women in choosing a suitable wife or husband.[43] With regard to a suitable

[38] Shakuntala Rao Shastri, *Women in the Vedic Age* (Bombay: Bharatiya Vidya Bhavan, 1954), 6. Shastri cites a wide range of scholars, from Saṃkara to Pischel to describe *Samana*.

[39] RV. tr. Griffith I.124.8.

[40] RV. XI.75.3.

[41] Macdonell and Keith, *Vedic Index & Names and Subjects*, Vol. II, 429.

[42] RV. X.86.10.

[43] Macdonell and Keith, *Vedic Index & Names and Subjects*, Vol. I, 482.

age of marriage, Keith suggests that parents did not control the choice of a matrimonial alliance to adult children.[44] Girls were married when they were physically prepared to procreate. The hymn about Sūryā's bridal marks that the bride was fit to procreate when she was married.[45] It has been observed that the basic characters of the three kinds of marriages, that is, *Rākśasa*, *Svayamvara* and *Prajāpati*, are referred to in Ṛgveda. And among these three, the only instance of the first one is seen where Purumitra's daughter was taken away.[46] Shastri notes that Vimada, who carried away Purumitra's daughter, was reluctant to do it in the first place.[47]

Proceeding to the second category, woman's position in the household was strong as observed, as she was the axis of the household. She is attributed with bliss with lofty adjectives such as *kalyāṇi* and *śivātmā*.[48] Woman after marriage were seen to have had three different roles to play, as she has been called *jāyā*, *janī* and *patni*.[49] *Jāyā* as a consort of the husband, *janī* as the mother of children and *patni* as a partner in the rituals.[50] She was supposed to take an active participation in the sacrificial ceremonies along with her husband.[51] While she was sharing the household responsibilities and exercising the political authority through sacrificial ceremonies, women were engaged in the expression of sexuality. Woman's image as a romantic consort has been well defined, and love sports between the married couples were appreciated.[52] The conjugal activities were encouraged on spiritual level as the husband and wife offered oblations in pairs, and even the gods were imagined in pairs to take the

[44] Ibid.
[45] RV. X.85.27, 36.
[46] RV. I.116.1, I.117.20, X.39.7.
[47] Shastri, *Women in the Vedic* Age, 11–12.
[48] RV. III.53.4; X.85.37.
[49] Shastri, *Women in the Vedic* Age, 18.
[50] Ibid.
[51] RV. II.39.2; also see RV. VIII.31.9.
[52] RV. X.86.6.

offerings.[53] The norm of procreation for wives was so important that Upadhyay argues that it gave wives a political authority.[54]

The imagery of a mother was very powerful in Ṛgveda. One of the main motifs that occur in the text is that of fertility. For example, wood has been referred to as the progenitor of Agni.[55] Just as the prominent features of deities had feminine genders, fertility and motherhood have been credited with the existence of those deities. The deities like Agni were not born out of nowhere; they were conceived by female deities. For example, Ūṣā gave birth to Agni.[56] Similar examples and reference to similar amplification of women's character have been arduously quoted by Upadhyay.[57] Their contributions to the economy were immensely productive.

The daughters depend on their parents for their livelihood in young age.[58] Upadhyay notes it carefully that a daughter could remain unmarried and stay at her home even in old age.[59] It must be noted that a daughter was expected to have strong affinities with her brother as well.[60] It is worth observing that single daughters with no brothers were free to choose their consort without any interference from parents or brother(s).[61] And the community supported such women, as the scandalizing acts against the modesty of such women are abhorred.[62] As far as the legal rights of a daughter are concerned, Upadhyay calls a reference to the sum given to a daughter as *strīdhana* (woman's wealth). He also points that the brother inherits the ancestral property, but in the absence of a brother, the daughter gets the share. However, a grandson inherits his maternal property. So it could

[53] RV. III.6.9.
[54] Upadhyay, *Women in Ṛgveda*, 137.
[55] RV. V.9.3; also see RV. V.2.1.
[56] RV. II.38.5.
[57] Upadhyay, *Women in Ṛgveda*, 145.
[58] RV. II.17.7.
[59] Upadhyay, *Women in Ṛgveda*, 34.
[60] RV. IV.5.5; also see Upadhyay, *Women in Ṛgveda*, 36.
[61] RV. I.124.7.
[62] Macdonell and Keith, *Vedic Index & Names and Subjects*, Vol. I, 486.

be concluded that single women were stronger. An interesting case of *Putrikā* presents a situation where single daughters were to carry forward the lineage.[63] And if a man was around, their position became weak in the inheritance of property. Upadhyay also asks an important question with respect to the legal status of a mother. He questions the inheritance of a mother in the property transferred by the father.

But as we discussed in the beginning, the domestic and political spheres of women are two different categories. While we have discussed the domestic roles of women in the Rigvedic collection of hymns, political domain yields interesting observations too. The sociopolitical institutions such as Vidatha, Sabhā and Samīti find references in Ṛgveda, but R. S. Sharma points that the Vidatha was the earliest common collective organization of the Rigvedic people.[64] The institution is suggested to have been of a military character which had the distributive functions or common consumption of the produce.[65] Sharma emphasizes that in the more early stages of the Rigvedic polity, women were perhaps more important than men, especially in the pre-plough stage; and, hence, women took active participation in Vidatha.[66] The Ṛgveda mentions that the *yoṣā* and that Sūryā were asked to participate in the assembly of Vidatha.[67] A wish to be able to speak up at Vidatha is also expressed in marriage ceremony.[68] Similarly, Sabha was another social institution and women attended it in the Rigvedic phase as women were called *sabhāvatī*.[69] Sabha was also an association for amusement which engaged in dancing and music.[70] This reflects an active engagements of women in the political concerns of the times. However, in the later Vedic phase,

[63] Ibid., Vol. II, 537.

[64] Ram Sharan Sharma, *Aspects of Political Ideas and Institutions in Ancient India* (Delhi: Motilal Banarsidass, 2009), 103.

[65] Ibid., 102.

[66] Ibid., 103, 88–89.

[67] RV. I.167-3; also see RV. X.85.26.

[68] RV. X.85.26.

[69] RV. I.167.3.

[70] RV. X.34.6.

with the changing character of these institutions, the participation of women declined too. Prasad concludes that there have been varying shades of the role and authority of women in the Rigvedic and post-Rigvedic polity. While women enjoyed a good status in the Rigvedic tradition, the post-Rigvedic polity saw a diminishing trend in terms of their authority and power.[71]

The Transcendental

The third category of feminine emanates from the Rigvedic transcendental or mythological cosmos. With different rituals and sacrificial ceremonies at the very core, it can be inferred that gods are the focus of religious activities in Ṛgveda. The Rigvedic gods are very engaging as they are seen as participating eagerly in the rituals; some of them mediate between the humans offering the sacrificial oblations and the higher gods, while others are receivers of the offerings, granting health and wealth to the hosts. A remarkable text with more than a thousand hymns dedicated to one or more gods, in persuasion to make them do the mortals' bidding, presents a good opportunity to assess the position of women. Stephanie Jamison points out an interesting characteristic feature of the Rigvedic gods: they were unified by the Vedic ritual, whereas the Greek gods, or even the later Puranic gods, were held together by an internal social structure, resulting as a unified pantheon.[72] Adding to our perspective on women, it would be a good exercise if we drew a comparison between the various kinds of powers that the different Vedic gods exercised, particularly the goddesses.

There are different categories of gods that are listed in Ṛgveda. But the most celebrated ones are Indra, Agni and Soma. While Indra has the maximum number of hymns dedicated to him, nearly a quarter, he represents neither natural forces nor social elements like his counterparts whose names give us a good idea

[71] R. U. S. Prasad, *The Ṛgvedic and Post Ṛgvedic Polity: 1500 BCE–500 BCE* (Wilmington: Vernon Press, 2015), 153.

[72] Jamison and Brereton, *Guides to Sacred Texts*, 63.

about their existence (e.g., Sūrya, Vāyu, Ūṣā and others). He is also the god, whose mythology was well developed by the time of the composition of Ṛgveda. Agni became significant as the Rigvedic ceremonies centred around the ritual fire. And Soma represented the substance from the ritual which was one of the manifestations of the consequences of the ritual.[73] Before beginning with the female goddesses in Ṛgveda, it should be pointed out that Indra as the most prominent deity has a defined parentage. Although the identity of Indra's mother is not clearly revealed, the fact that he was born from a womb is well pronounced in the birth hymn.[74] He was even assured by his mother that he would emerge victorious against all his enemies.[75] It is worth noting that as the most important god, he needed the assurance of his mother. It is not uncommon to observe that the gods constantly needed a validation of a female deity.

There are hymns devoted to goddesses in Ṛgveda. Some of these goddesses were Aditi, Indrāṇī, Urvaśī, Yamī, Yamī Vaivasvatī, Saramā Devaśunī, Sārparājñī, Sūryā and Sāvitrī.[76] With a close inspection of the text, one observes that the women goddesses were associated with specific strengths and cults. An interesting observation is made by Upadhyay where he gives an etymological reference to Aditi's name which meant 'unbinding', 'freedom' or 'boundlessness'.[77] Jamison concurs and mentions that Aditi signifies freedom from punitive actions resulting against the acts committed against gods. Upadhyay opines that different gods are approached for the sins to be forgiven, but the jurisdiction of amnesty lies exclusively in the mother goddess Aditi. Max Muller has also expressed that Aditi was the earliest expression for infinite.[78] Some scholars have argued that Aditi

[73] Ibid., 65.

[74] RV. IV.18.

[75] RV. VIII.45.4–6.

[76] Michael Witzel, 'Female Rishis and Philosophers in the Veda?' *Journal of South Asia Women Studies* 11, no. 1 (2002): 3.

[77] Upadhyay, *Women in Ṛgveda*, 5.

[78] Ibid., 6.

could also mean nourishing earth as the earth represents space. In an interesting inference made by Jamison, Aditi is not subjugated to the norms of good behaviour, and rather she codified the right behaviour that her sons, the Ādityas, represented.[79] However, it should be noted that in the later Vedic traditions, the motherhood of Aditi emerges as a defining feature of her identity, and, therefore, she came to be revered as a mother to several deities.[80] It seems that gods in the Rigvedic traditions were validated if they had a certain parentage and specially with reference to their maternal lineage.

Ūṣā, the goddess representing dawn, is one of the most prominent female divinities in the Ṛgveda. As an important figure in the Rigvedic mythological cosmos, she presents an interesting case. She is often cited as dressed up in a varied multitude of colours, exhibiting her charm and employing dance as her medium of expression.[81] Dawn's rise from the eastern ocean is compared to a woman emerging from her bath.[82] This suggests how the sexuality of women was explored and not kept askance in the Rigvedic tradition. And if a divinity who was associated with nature and was attributed anthropomorphic features was presented in the light of her sexuality, it is suggestive that sexuality was not to be abhorred in the Rigvedic societies. Another interesting feature that defines Ūṣā is her ability to be born and reborn every day, thus reminding the humankind of the passage of time perpetually. We come across a hymn that suggests some kind of animosity between Indra and Ūṣā, so much that he once smashed her cart and she had to run away.[83] Jamison asks a crucial question that what was the need for Indra to target this emblem of benevolent femininity.[84] It remains to be investigated if Indra as a male god was validated by making an attempt to

[79] Jamison and Brereton, *Guides to Sacred Texts*, 87.
[80] Ibid., 87.
[81] Shastri, *Women in the Vedic* Age, 35.
[82] RV. V.80.5.
[83] RV. IV.30.8-11.
[84] Jamison and Brereton, *Guides to Sacred Texts*, 94.

subjugate the feminine goddess Ūṣā. Also, we have to see if it could see this instance as a direct confrontation between masculine and feminine domains, as Ūṣā has not been described as a goddess representing women.

The Rigvedic deities engaged in anthropic rituals like marriage. Pṛthvi, the female Earth, has been frequently referred to as mother, and she has been imagined as a consort of the Heaven God.[85] Jamison marks that the couple's children do not find many references, but generally most of the gods have been seen as their progeny. Pṛthvi has been referred as the mother of Agni, an important male god in Ṛgveda. But in some verses, both Heaven and Earth have been referred to as mothers, and to complicate it even further, both have been referred to as sisters as they were born together. This suggests some kind of gender fluidity.[86] However, Jamison attributes this gender fluidity to grammar as the word *dyaus* could be used for both masculine and feminine gender. Further on gender fluidity, while dealing with the mythological cosmic sphere of the Rigvedic societies, it must be noted that the genders were not seen in binaries. They were very fluid in imageries, even in case of gods and goddesses. For example, the Aśvins were compared with beautiful women.[87] Another instance of such imageries is found in case of God Agni where he has been compared with the goddesses such as Ida, Aditi and Sarasvati.[88] Similarly, even if male deities have represented ownership and authority, one cannot deny that they derive their authority from the feminine aspect of life. For example, Indra was breastfed before embarking upon the slaying of demons.[89] Therefore, we can say that even if we see that the number of hymns devoted to male gods in Ṛgveda are more than those for their female counterparts, it should also be noted that the male deities derived their power from the female goddesses.

[85] RV. III.1.7.
[86] Jamison and Brereton, *Guides to Sacred Texts*, 96.
[87] RV. II.39.2.
[88] RV. II.1.11.
[89] RV. III.47.3.

While Doniger sees Aditi as the most prominent goddess in Ṛgveda, she also says that there are several immortal and quasi-immortal women mentioned in Ṛgveda who are not typical goddesses.[90] Some of these are Sītā, Uṣā, Rātri, Sūryā, Vāc, Ila, Sarasvati, Bharati, Sinivālī, Rākā, Śradhhā and Anumati. Upadhyay notes that the role and authority of a woman was reflected in the mythological pantheon of goddesses mentioned in Ṛgveda, as it gives us a certain idea about how the authors view the feminine powers that seemed to be controlling their households.[91]

Denouement

A section of scholars has argued that the women may not have been engaged with the composition of Ṛgveda, as the authors may have been men[92] which is to reduce the presence of women in the literary arena merely to a couple of references citing their names. But a historian should view the broader question of how a corpus of literature perceived women, womanhood and received their engagement in the societies. Scholars like Witzel completely negate the role of women in Ṛgveda, but this approach does not take account of any capacity in which women are engaged in societies. It is also interpreted to emphasize the preference of a male child in the text, but it does not focus on how the daughter was brought up. The gender relations have to be considered comprehensively by looking at the gender of the language, prescribed roles for men and women, and the dynamics between the male deities and their female counterparts. Also, while looking at the representations of women in the Rigvedic tradition, it is important to see the representation of men in this regard. This is seen in many ways, especially with respect to the legal rights of property. This could be true for both insentient and transcendental aspects of the societies, where the presence of both the genders had a vital role to play in the overall dynamics.

[90] Doniger, *The Ṛgveda,* 232.
[91] Upadhyay, *Women in Ṛgveda,* 3.
[92] Witzel, 'Female Rishis', 11.

There are certain aspects that need further investigation. One of the points of discussion is whether the women were subjected to self-immolation or burial after the death of their husbands.[93] This idea is largely based on a verse which reads as follows: 'Arise, woman, to the world of the living. You lie beside him whose life is gone. Come here! You have come into existence now as wife of a husband who has grasped your hand and wishes to have you.'[94] It is important to raise this point as it could be held as a preliminary to the practice of the sati system in the succeeding times. Jamison holds that while the practice of sati cannot be attributed to Ṛgveda, the ritual could have provided for a literal enactment in the later times.[95] This verse suggests the wife of the deceased person to not find any affinities for the deceased body and proceed to the house to find life in kinsmen and children. She was even given a chance to be remarried to her deceased husband's brother, but Shastri suggests that it was up to her choice to enter into a marriage again.[96] Interestingly enough, Shastri is doubtful if the Rigvedic tradition saw cremation as an option for the last rites. She is of the opinion that the bodies were burned.[97] Therefore, it is difficult to argue that Ṛgveda provided for the idea of sati practice.

When we speak of the engagement of women with the composition of Ṛgveda, it becomes imperative to discuss their role in it. Their role in the composition of hymns suggests their political participation, concerns and literary status. There are only a few hymns that are entirely attributed to women, while there are others that are partly credited to women or some with dubious credits with regard to the authorship. The hymns that are attributed entirely to women are from Viśvavara and Apāla

[93] Shastri, *Women in the Vedic Age*, 22–23. Shastri quotes Hildebrandt and Delbruck who are of the opinion that certain hymns in Ṛgveda suggest a *Puruṣamedha* ritual with respect to women.

[94] Ṛgveda X.18.8.

[95] Jamison and Brereton, *Guides to Sacred Texts*, 60.

[96] RV. X.40.2. Also see Shastri, *Women in the Vedic Age*, 22–23.

[97] Shastri, *Women in the Vedic Age*, 24.

from the fifth and eighth *maṇḍalas*, respectively. Apāla seems to gather Soma to use its juice for the sacrifice. The second group has portions of the hymns attributed to them. These women are Lopamudrā and Śaśiyasī. Their names appear in the course of dialogues. The third and the largest group consists of women ascetics such as Ghoṣā Kakhivati, Surya-Sāvitri, Sarparajni and Urvashi. The presence of women and their hymns reflects the *strītva* in Ṛgveda.

Bibliography

Altekar, A. S. *The Position of Women in Hindu Civilisation*. Benaras: The Culture Publication House, Benaras Hindu University, 1938.

Aurobindo, Sri, trans. *Hymns to the Mystic Fire*. Pondicherry: Offset at All India Press, 1991.

Kashyap, R. L., ed. *Ṛgveda Samhita*. Bengaluru: Sri Aurobindo Kapali Sastry Institute of Vedic Culture, 1998.

Mill, James. *The History of British India (With Notes by H. H. Wilson)*. London: James Madden, 1840.

Sangari, Kumkum, and Sudesh Vaid. *Recasting Women: Essays in Indian Colonial History*. New Brunswick: Rutgers University Press, 1999.

Sharma, Ram Sharan. *India's Ancient Past*. New Delhi: Oxford University Press, 2010.

Shiva, Vandana. *Staying Alive: Women, Ecology and Survival in India*. London: Zen Books, 1998.

Thapar, Romila. *Śakuntalā: Texts, Readings, Histories*. New York: Columbia University Press, 2011.

3

Music and Musical Thought in Rāmāyaṇa and Mahābhārata

Kaustubh Gaurh

Epics and Music

The two epics, the Rāmāyaṇa and the Mahābhārata, are the main sources for this study.[1] The temporal spread of the evolution of these two literary texts has been broad. Along with a wide range of subjects, their content also consists of specific references to music. For a historian, these traces of music become specimens of a musical culture which existed during the time of

[1] Romila Thapar observes, 'These are not histories per se, but they incorporate fragments of narratives pertaining to what was believed to have happened....' Romila Thapar, 'The Mahābhārata', in *The Past Before Us: Historical Traditions of Early North India* (Cambridge: Harvard University Press, 2013), 144.

Therefore, the attempt here is not to legitimize the surreal elements pertaining to performing arts, or the historicity of the two epics, but to trace the references of music and to expose them to various kinds of inferences to reconstruct the perceptions of a society in a certain period about music as an art form.

their composition. The accretion of multiple narratives in them helps us view the idea of music from various angles. These two texts were developed out of a context, and such literary items, for example, a narrative, when retold a few times, time and again, are redefined. A historian can treat this repetition as a prism to view the points of historical change.[2]

Not only the central themes of the two epics were framed at two different points in a temporal spread but even the societies projected in the two epics are different. The Mahābhārata accentuates the juxtaposition between the lineage-based societies and the chiefships, while the Rāmāyaṇa projects a strong sense of monarchical order in the form of an incipient kingdom.[3] Scholars like Kane have argued that the Mahābhārata is older by centuries than the story of the Rāmāyaṇa.[4] James L. Fitzgerald agrees with an earlier view that the Mahābhārata has traces or 'antecedents' of some kind in older Indo-Aryan, oral bardic literature and perhaps even more ancient Indo-European bardic songs about warriors and wars.[5]

[2] Romila Thapar, *Śakuntalā: Texts, Readings, Histories* (New York: Columbia University Press, 2011), 1.

[3] Kumkum Roy, 'The Emergence of Monarchy in North India (c. 8th–4th centuries BCE) as Reflected in the Brahmanical Tradition' (PhD thesis, School of Social Sciences, Jawaharlal Nehru University, 1991), 2; for the Mahābhārata, Thapar, 'The Mahābhārata', 144, states the following:

> Historical consciousness in these epics is expressed in the representation of two socio-political forms: a society of past times and the society of the present—although earlier one in some places survives as parallel to the later. The two are not starkly distinct, there is considerable fluidity between them. Nevertheless, the difference is recognizable.

[4] P. V. Kane, 'The Two Epics', *Annals of the Bhandarkar Oriental Research Institute* 47, no. ¼ (1966): 31.

[5] James L. Fitzgerald, 'Mahābhārata', in *The Hindu World*, eds. Sushil Mittal and Gene R. Thursby (Routledge, Taylor & Francis e-Library, 2005), 52.

The Rāmāyaṇa, the monumental epic poem in Sanskrit, is attributed to the legendary poet-sage Vālmīki.[6] The epic poem is believed to have been largely composed during the first millennium BCE, but on the issue of a specific date, scholars have varied arguments. But there seems a possibility that certain portions of the text, as they are arranged today, were composed later than the others.[7] The core story of the Mahābhārata focuses on the Gaṅgā–Yamunā doab and its vicinity, more particularly the upper doab, while the Rāmāyaṇa revolves around the middle Gaṅgā valley.

A specific metrical composition known for its succinctness, easy pace and cheerful spirit could be attributed to the portions of both the epics that makes them easy to recite. The origins of epic poetry have been traced to the *dāna-stuti* hymns, *gāthās*, *nārāśaṃsīs* and *ākhyānas* of the Vedic corpus.[8] And the compositions from the epic poetry were recited at the *yajñas*, where the ritual was central, or when bards recited hero-lauds in the *sabhās* (the assembly halls) of clan chiefs.[9] Not only in the narrative do we see a strong sense of dissemination of various ideas through music but the narrative itself was initially carried by the bards in the form of oral tradition. The oral composition was taken out of the hands of its original authors, the Sūtas, and ascribed to a *ṛṣi*, putting it into a Brahmanical framework.[10] The compositions by the Sūtas bore strong affinities to a musical culture. The inclusion of the Bhāgavata cult dates to the rise of Bhagavatism towards the end of the first millennium BCE.[11] However, even within a Brahmanical framework, the Bhāgavata cult in the Mahābhārata bore the elements of musical tradition, for example, Gītā[12] and

[6] R. P. Goldman and Sutherland S. J Goldman, 'Rāmāyaṇa', in *The Hindu World*, eds. Sushil Mittal and Gene R. Thursby (Routledge, Taylor & Francis e-Library, 2005), 75.

[7] Ibid., 76.

[8] Thapar, 'The Mahābhārata', 145.

[9] Ibid., 146.

[10] Ibid., 158.

[11] Ibid., 162.

[12] The *phalaśruti* of the Gītā prescribes it to be sung. *Mahābhārata (Mbh.)*, *Bhīṣma-parvan*, *Bhīṣma*vadha-*parvan*, 43.1

recitation of thousand names of Vishnu.[13] The idea of *phalaśruti* in these two portions of the epic hints to their prescribed regular chanting for the households. The content of music has pushed different ideologies at different times. Music as a source to study history cannot be studied in vacuum. The ideology behind it helps in identifying its role in a social context.

It must be understood that one cannot succeed in getting a precise answer to what kind of music was practised in early India by merely looking at these two texts. This question must be dealt to investigate what constituted music in these texts for the people from early India. What defined music in the concerned space and time? But to answer this, we must answer if music can be defined. Or has music been defined in early India? Defining Indian music, T. M. Krishna puts it very eloquently that music does not have to be defined but understood. It has to be understood because by understanding something so vital to us, we understand ourselves.[14] Therefore, these texts help us understand which elements formed music for the communities in early India by pointing out the sounds which were 'vital' to their existence.

In the Rāmāyaṇa and the Mahābhārata, the sounds of vocal music, that is, *saṁgīta*, are expressed by the terms such as *gā*,[15]

[13] Mbh. *Anuśāsana-parvan, Dānadharma-parvan*, 148.121–122.

Two terms have been used to codify the chanting of Viṣṇu Sahasranāmastotraṁ: *śru* and *kīrtanaṁ*. This seems to imply that both listening and chanting of the *stotram* were prescribed, in an order, which focused on singing. Ananda Lal observes that '[w]ith roots in the Vedic anukirtana tradition, a Kirtana is a call-and-response style song or chant, set to music, wherein multiple singers recite or describe a legend, or express loving devotion to a deity, or discuss spiritual ideas' (Ananda Lal, *Theatres of India: A Concise Companion* [Oxford: Oxford University Press, 2009), 422–424.

[14] T. M. Krishna, *A Southern Music: The Karnataka Story* (Noida: HarperCollins Publishers India, 2013), 3.

[15] Mbh. *Vana-parvan*, 43.7 (This *parvan* is also called *Āraṇyaka-parvan* in the critical edition provided by Bhandarkar Oriental Research Institute, Pune).

gītaṁ,[16] *ghoṣaṁ*,[17] *ninādaṁ*,[18] *nādaṁ*[19] and *vādayan*.[20] The foundation of these two epics seems to have seen romance between sound and its meaning in terms of the vocal music. Both the epics have been predominantly written using *anuṣṭup* metre which has eight syllables in each line of a verse. This implies that though the focus was given on the way of recitation for the epics, each verse carried a very strong meaning with it. The authors tried to portray these epics as poetries which gave the foundation to vocal music.[21] This is further supported by the case of the Rāmāyaṇa; Vālmīki supposedly comes up with a verse, counts the syllables in it and decides to write the entire Rāmāyaṇa in *anuṣṭup* metre, which, interestingly, he wished to accompany with *vīṇā*.[22] While the Mahābhārata was written in the same metre, yet the text uses Brahmā's word to legitimize Vyāsa's composition as a poem.[23] However, the Mahābhārata also has the other kind of metre: the *triṣṭubh*, which makes up about 11 per cent of the almost 160,500 lines of the verses in the epic.[24] These ideas of a composition were derived from the Vedic tradition where there seems to have been a constant friction between syntax, semantics and phonology.

The tradition of chanting and recitation of the Vedic mantras seems to have been very much alive in the educational institutions as is evident from the description of Duṣyanta's entrance in the Kaṇva's hermitage where chanting of the Vedic mantras was made in a synchronized manner[25] or even when the wisdom of king Geya is defined by the rituals that he performed; a *yajña* performed by Geya is described where chanting of the Vedic mantras has been described as very auspicious, consisting of a

[16] Mbh. *Ādi-parvan, Sambhava-parvan*, 70.39.
[17] Mbh. *Vana-parvan, Tīrthayātra-parvan*, 95.22.
[18] Rmṇ. *(Rāmāyaṇa), Sundarakāṇḍa*, 4.12.
[19] Mbh. *Ādi-parvan, Āstīka-parvan*, 21.18.
[20] Rmṇ. *Bālakāṇḍa*, 32.13.
[21] Mbh. *Ādi-paravan, Anukramaṇikā-parvan*, 1,72.
[22] Rmṇ. *Bālakāṇḍa*, 2.15–19.
[23] Mbh. *Ādi-paravan, Anukramaṇikā-parvan*, 1.72.
[24] Fitzgerald, 'Mahābhārata', 52.
[25] Mbh. *Ādi-parvan, Sambhava-parvan*, 70.39–40.

synchronized high pitch.[26] Therefore, to Krishna, who considers the vitality of an element as something intrinsic to music, it could be said that chanting has been a 'vital' aspect of music. During the time period of the epics, there seems to have been a transition between chanting and singing, as clearly expressed in case of the Gītā and Viṣṇu Sahasranāmastotraṁ, which were associated with singing in the form of *kīrtanaṁ*.[27]

Further, there are several references in both the Rāmāyaṇa and the Mahābhārata where the perception of various sounds has been described as either mellifluous or cacophonic. For example, the chirping of birds, which is just a collection of various sounds produced by the birds at a given point of time, has been described as singing.[28] The birds do not actually sing, but they were imagined to be singing. Not only this but onomatopoeia has been used multiple times to ascribe a particular sound to a particular situation. For example, the thundering of clouds is ascribed to the scene in the battlefield.[29] Sounds made by the fountains have been discussed as something adding to the scenic beauty,[30] and the echoes in the valleys have been compared to the sound of the *mṛdaṅgam*.[31] In the Rāmāyaṇa, the voices of the reverend personalities have been compared to the beating of the drums.[32]

The onomatopoeic ideas helped to bring together the two forms of music: vocal and instrumental. They became seeds for both vocal and instrumental forms of music by the way in which they evoked certain memories and then the human tendencies to replicate those memories through sounds.

Krishna argues that in terms of feelings and memory, music triggers images and emotions that establish our relationship

[26] Mbh. *Vana-parvan, Tīrthayātra-parvan*, 95.22
[27] Mbh. *Anuśāsana-parvan, Dānadharma-parvan*, 148.121–122.
[28] Mbh. *Ādi-parvan, Sambhava-parvan*, 70.5.
[29] Mbh. *Vana-parvan, Kairāta-parvan*, 38.15.
[30] Rmṇ. *Ayodhyākāṇḍa*, 28.7.
[31] Ibid., 103.49.
[32] Ibid., 2.2.

with it.[33] But does the 'Indian' musical sound induce a particular memory? If so, he says, then the sound must be very peculiar in itself. One may then ask why the 'sound' from certain frameworks is so different, as apparent from some of the classical dance forms of India. Venkatasubramanian indirectly answers this question, and somewhere he also hints to what defines music. He points out that a sound with a definite pitch is a 'musical sound' and such sounds predate the human race. Western scholars argue that music is originated with a particular effort by a man to evoke desired feelings in the listeners. But Venkatasubramanian cites the Tamil work *Tolkāppiyam* which mentions that the soul desiring to speak out its intention ignites the mind, the mind operates in the vital heat of the body and sets the air in motion, and the air thus stimulated produces the sound. Tamil literary works portray how the Tamils enjoyed music in the ripples of water, the roar of thunder, the waves of the sea, the splash of waterfalls, the hum of the bees, and the chuckle and chirp of birds. These may be taken as the regional idioms according to him. But he argues that to understand the content of art, the individuality of the regional language is to be understood in a deeper sense.[34]

This is a glimpse of how the conceptions about the sounds have been present in an amorphous form in the epics. The tradition of the chanting of the Vedic mantras with the amalgamation of ideas pertaining to sound and music provided a prelude to the musical ideas that existed at a time of composition of the epics.

Instruments: Carriers of Musical Thought

The idea of vocal music was not evolving in vacuum, but it was complemented with its material dimension that manifested in the form of musical instruments. The musical instruments in India have been undergoing a continuous process of accretion,

[33] Krishna, *A Southern Music*, 8.

[34] T. K. Venkatasubramanian, *Music as History in Tamil Nadu* (New Delhi: Primus Books, 2010), 14.

evolution, extinction and formation for over 2,000 years. In the epics, a single instrument played multiple roles depending on the time, space and the context. Not much of difference is seen in the instruments used in both the Rāmāyaṇa and the Mahābhārata. For example, Arjuna's entrance in a forest is seen as something that induced the sound of drums and conches, which signified bliss,[35] and Daśaratha's entrance to Ayodhyā was also marked by these two instruments.[36] In the Rāmāyaṇa, the *Bālakāṇḍa*, the *Ayodhyākāṇḍa* and the *Sundarakāṇḍa* presented the imagination of a city with a stronger musical culture. The instruments such as *dundubhi* (drums), *vīṇā* and *paṇava* were played to keep the city alive.[37] In the Mahābhārata, the city culture has not been described as such, but the transcendental spaces like the courts of gods and the utopian state (*swarga*) in the imagination of people are described as spaces with a strong musical culture. However, interestingly, the *Arthashastra*, the kernel of which is ascribed between 400 BCE and 150 CE,[38] a time period which partially coincides with the composition of the epics, had been in consonance with the excerpts from the Rāmāyaṇa in this case. According to the *Arthashastra*, the city had a variety of musicians to entertain the city dwellers.[39]

The improvisation with the instruments probably gave birth to the point of rendezvous for music and dance. *Urvaśī* is represented with the dancing anklets, which would signify that the importance of beats must have been recognized by the artists.[40] Another instance of dance based on beats is found in the Rāmāyaṇa where a particular *tāla* or beat called *śamyā* accompanied the steps of dance.[41]

[35] Mbh. *Vana-parvan, Kairāta-parvan*, 38.16.

[36] Rmṇ. *Bālakāṇḍa*, 11.26.

[37] Ibid., 5.18.

[38] L. N. Rangarajan, *Kautilya: The Arthashastra* (New Delhi: Penguin Books India, 1992), 20–21.

[39] Ibid., 97.

[40] Mbh. *Vana-parvan, Indralokābhigamana-parvan*, 46.12.

[41] Rmṇ. *Ayodhyākāṇḍa*, 91.49.

The instruments conveyed multiple feelings. There are various kinds of musical instruments which are mentioned in both the Rāmāyaṇa and the Mahābhārata, and they can be classified in the way in which they were played. Table 3.1 shows the classification in a detailed manner.[42] The categorization of the instruments from the epics satisfies their classification made in the Natyashastra. The pioneer treatise codified the aspects of performing arts while the epics were evolving. The dating of the *Natyashastra* is ascribed between 200 BCE and 200 CE.[43] According to the *Natyashastra*, the instruments were of four kinds: *tata*, *avanaddha*, *ghana* and *suṣira*. *Tata vādya* were the stringed instruments, *avanaddha* were the membranophonic instruments, *ghana* were the idiophonic instruments and *suṣira* were the wind instruments.[44]

A closer look at the role of the instruments draws an interesting observation. The instruments in the epics have been used effectively to give a variety of shades to the context in various episodes. At some points, the instruments take the control of the scene, while at certain instances, the context painted the role of the instruments. For example, *dundubhi* were beaten when Kṛṣṇa was born[45]; this suggests that drum was an important and a common musical instrument that was used for the delightful occasions and auspicious ceremonies. As mentioned above, the instruments such as *dundubhi*, *vīṇā* and *paṇava* were played to keep the city alive. After Daśaratha's demise when Bharata reached Ayodhyā, he noticed that there was no music being played around and sensed the undesirable circumstances.[46] These instances convey that situations were governed by music, even if in the texts, to create an orchestrated effect for a reader.

[42] Dimpy, 'Experimentation in Instrumental Music in India' (PhD thesis, University of Delhi, 2012), 27. (The Table has been modified further.)

[43] Tarla Mehta, *Sanskrit Play Production in Ancient India* (New Delhi: Motilal Banarsidass, 1995), xxiv, 19–20.

[44] Adya Rangacharya, trans., *Nāṭyaśāstra* (New Delhi: Munshiram Manoharlal Publishers, 1996), 218; Dimpy, *Experimentation in Instrumental Music*, 58.

[45] Mbh. *Sabhā-parvan, Arghābhiharaṇa-parvan*, 38.11.

[46] Rmṇ. *Ayodhyākāṇḍa*, 71.29.

Table 3.1 *Classification of the Instruments That Were Used in the Rāmāyaṇa and the Mahābhārata*

Wind Instruments (*Suṣira Vādya*)	**Instruments with Sound When Struck against One Another (*Ghana Vādya*)**	**String Instruments (*Tata Vādya*)**	**Instruments Covered with a Membrane (*Avanaddha Vādya*)**
1. *Veṇu*	1. *Ghantā*	1. *Yantra*	1. *Paṇava*
2. *Gomukha*	2. *Maṇi*	2. *Vallaki*	2. *Mridangaṁ*
3. *Goviśana*	3. *Kiddiki*	3. *Vīṇa*	3. *Bherī*
4. *Śaṁkha*	4. *Kanchī*	4. *Tumba Vīṇā*	4. *Peśī*
	5. *Parivahatak*	5. *Kachhapi Vīṇā*	5. *Turya*
	6. *Bhekhla*	6. *Mahāti Vīṇā*	6. *Ādambra*
	7. *Kalāpa*		7. *Dignidam*
	8. *Nūpur*		8. *Mardal*
			9. *Muraja*
			10. *Puşkara*
			11. *Alingya*
			12. *Jharjhara*
			13. *Dundubhi*

In the following instances, we will see how the situations governed music, contrasting to the observation made above. An interesting case of conch or the *Śaṁkha* enables an observer to see how an instrument that produced sound served the occasion as per the need of the context and lost its identity as an instrument used in musical tradition. Viṣṇu has been shown holding conch in the Mahābhārata as one of his *āyudhapuruṣas*.[47] It was also blown during Yudhiṣṭhira's coronation[48]; it finds its description as an instrument that was used to welcome the guests. For example, Arjuna was welcomed in a forest and then at Amarāvatī with the sounds of conch and drums.[49] But conches and drums were used at the battlefield as well. This signifies the extent to which the role of a musical instrument could be accentuated by the scene. So much so that the imagination of people of a battlefield or warfare seems to be incomplete without the musical dimensions. For example, before the war, when Sañjaya and Yudhiṣṭhira exchanged their thoughts about the situation, Sañjaya began talking about war with a brief discussion on the drums and conches in the battlefield.[50] In the Mahābhārata, the war between the Pāṇḍavas and the Kauravas started with the blows and beats of the conches and drums, respectively, to induce a sense of terror in the field.[51] An analogy has been made where warfare has been compared to a sacrificial ritual where the actions of a warrior have been compared to chanting and recitations.[52] Music and musical instruments found their prominent space in the warfare in the epics.

Here, when it is pointed out that the music was contextualized in war, the instruments would give the context such different shades that even their role could be seen in a different colour. They seem to have transcended the boundaries of what was

[47] Mbh. *Sabhā-parvan, Arghābhiharaṇa-parvan*, 38.

[48] Ibid., *Dyuta-parvan*, 53, 17–18.

[49] Mbh. *Vana-parvan, Kairāta-parvan*, 38.16; Mbh. *Vana-parvan, Indralokābhigamana-parvan*, 43.11.

[50] Mbh. *Udyoga-parvan, Sañjayayāna-parvan*, 24.5.

[51] Ibid., 191.71.

[52] Mbh. *Udyoga-parvan, Bhagvadyāna-parvan*, 141.31.

considered a conventional form of music and got involved in warfare as weapons. The case of conch from the Mahābhārata is a classic example of how the context of music was changed to serve warfare.

I have discussed above how the relevance of conch shell was located in various spaces. It experiences transition in its role as a prominent feature of a deity and a significant marker of warfare. It was used to welcome prosperity at households and to warn the humankind in the battlefield about the death that was lurking around at the battlefield. It was not just an instrument, rather it became an extension to the code of conduct of warfare. The significant warriors have been shown with their own conches in the battlefield of the Mahābhārata. Kṛṣṇa, Arjuna, Yudhiṣṭhira, Bhīma, Nakula and Sahadeva blew Pāñcajanya, Devadatta, Anantavijaya, Poṇḍra, Sughoṣa and Maṇipuṣpaka, respectively.[53] It is also mentioned that the king of Kāśī, Śikhandi, Driṣṭadyumna, Virāṭa, Ajeya, Satyaki, Drupada, the Upapāṇḍavas and Abhimanyu blew their respective conch shells.[54] This signifies that the prominent personalities of the state used their own conch shells to signify some kind of stature. When Jayadratha killed Arjuna's son Abhimanyu in the war, Arjuna took vow to kill Jayadratha, and his vow was followed by the roar of Kṛṣṇa's Pāñcajanya.[55] The conch as a means of war etiquette was played before the attacks too; an individual would blow conch before making an attack on another individual or a group. For example, Abhimanyu blew his conch shell and then went on to attack a battalion of the Kauravas.[56] Also, these conches carried personal messages on the battlefield. This is suggested from the order that Kṛṣṇa gave Dārūka in the battlefield where he asked Dārūka to be around him at the blow of his Pāñcajanya.[57] In the same verse, Kṛṣṇa also mentions that he

[53] Mbh. *Bhīṣma-parvan, Bhagvadgītā-parvan*, 1.15.
[54] Ibid., 1.16–1.18.
[55] Mbh. *Droṇa-parvan, Pratigyā-parvan*, 73.51.
[56] Ibid., *Abhimanyuvadha-parvan*, 41.11.
[57] Ibid., *Pratigyā-parvan*, 19.39.

would blow his Pāñcajanya in the *Riṣabha swara*. This signifies two things. First, that each time a conch shell was blown in the battlefield, it marked an impact over the battle. Second, the conch shells must have been incorporated into the royal educational curriculum for warfare that could teach the princes the usage of conch with an appropriate pitch and its significance. Similarly, in the *Droṇa Parvan*, the drums and conch shells find umpteen references to mark multiple significant points in the war.

Social Context of Music

To trace the social context of music in early India, it is required to understand how the various communities interacted with each other through the means of music as central to occupation. Prominent of these for our study are the communities of Sūta and Māgadha which are mentioned in both the epics. It could be observed that along with the Brāhmaṇas, these communities were the officials to solemnize a ritual by complementing it with the musical instruments. For an instance, while the mantras were chanted in Draupadi's *svayaṁvara*, they were accompanied by the acoustics as well.[58] The communities of the Sūta and the Māgadha have been considered of greater importance as the emergence of the two communities has been described as something that happened prior to the rise of Pṛthu.[59] These two communities have been described as the Bandis who were assigned the duty to recite the praises for the dynasties. Pṛthu has also been shown giving land grants to the two communities.[60] This hints that these communities were given patronage by the state and were entitled to huge benefits from the royal authority. Also, it is interesting to note that these communities did not descend in the regions out of nowhere, but that there were laws that governed the basis of the existence of these communities. These communities seem to have come into existence as a result of the contact among the various

[58] Mbh. *Ādi-parvan, Svayamvara-parvan*, 183.32.
[59] Mbh. *Śānti-parvan, Rājadharma-parvan*, 59.112.
[60] Ibid., 59.112.

Varṇas. For example, in the Mahābhārata, it is mentioned that the union of a Śūdra man with a Kśatriya Brāhmaṇa woman gave rise to a Sūta, who was assigned either the job to sing the eulogies for the prominent personalities or was given the duty to deal with the chariots.[61] It is also indicated that these communities were kept out of the Varṇa system; perhaps, the vicinity of these communities to the royal authorities gave them an edge over the other communities that rose as a result of the inter-Varṇa unions.

One prominent difference in the Rāmāyaṇa and the Mahābhārata is that in the Rāmāyaṇa, even the *gaṇikās* were seen to be involved in the musical tradition,[62] while in the Mahābhārata, this feature is absent. According to the *Arthashastra*, a *gaṇikā* was to learn music at the state expense.[63]

One of the jobs carried out by these communities was to implant a historical conscience through the musical tradition (however, the historicity may be often romanticized, as the narratives served an ideology). The prominent example would be the music from Luva and Kuśa who disseminated a popular narrative among the people.[64] Music had been devised as something that was deeply political. The Sūta and the Māgadha communities were paid to recite the history of the lineages in a glorified form during the time of the composition of the Rāmāyaṇa.[65] Another example is when Arjuna went to Amarāvatī, the Gandharvas sang the praises (*stuti*) of his lineage,[66] and a Gandharva called Tambrū especially began to sing eulogies for Arjuna.[67] This seems to have been a very common way to welcome a guest from a state even in the Rāmāyaṇa. This is why it was inferred in the beginning of this study that a strong sense of transmission was seen through the Sūtas in the epics. Our focus is now shifting from

[61] Mbh. *Anuśāsana-parvan, Dānadharma-parvan*, 48.10.
[62] Rmṇ. *Bālakāṇḍa*, 10.26.
[63] Rangarajan, *Kautilya*, 63.
[64] Rmṇ. *Bālakāṇḍa*, 4.8–10.
[65] Ibid., 5.11.
[66] Mbh. *Vana-parvan, Indralokābhigamana-parvan*, 43.9.
[67] Ibid., 43.28.

the communities to the role that music played in the society. The musical eulogies performed by the communities could not be spontaneous and erroneous on the grounds which the patrons wanted to emphasize. Thus, it must have required the musicians to keep in touch with the clerics of the chief authority who could tell them about the 'desired facts' and the expected arrival of the guests. This also suggests that the musicians spent a fair amount of time in the palace. The *Arthashastra* mentions that the musical instruments were to be kept inside the palace for security purposes. The musicians were on a check on regular basis to avoid any possession of arms and poison.[68]

By historical conscience here, it is meant that the ability of music and the musicians could take people in the past through the narratives which were created and redefined with times. Having looked at the historical conscience implanted by these musical communities through their performance for the royal authority in a certain way, it is also important to look at how the royal authorities engaged these communities with the masses through the means of music. For instance, one of the music festivals is described in the Mahābhārata. Kṛṣṇa and Arjuna have been seen attending a music festival at Raivataka mountain.[69] The festival was organized by Vṛṣṇī and Andhaka communities.[70] It is seen that many dancing and singing communities took part in it.[71] Similarly, a music and dance festival has been referred to in the Rāmāyaṇa as well where different art forms were showcased, and the dancers and singers have been seen performing in it.[72]

As mentioned in the beginning, the chapter aims to look at an art form to understand the fertile social ground that was provided for its cultivation. With a better understanding of the history of an art form, one can understand the musical thought that was carried and preserved by a society. One aspect of the societal norms are the

[68] Rangarajan, Kautilya, 153.
[69] Mbh. *Ādi-parvan, Arjunavanvāsa-parvan*, 217.1.
[70] Ibid., 217.2.
[71] Ibid., 217.4–8.
[72] Rmṇ. *Bālakāṇḍa,* 17.24.

gender relations. Let us see how music shaped the gender relations during the time period of the composition of the two Sanskrit epics.

Music was known to the Gandharvas, who were projected with 'masculine qualities' through their warfare tactics. People who pertained their affiliations to the Gandharvas were considered weak and not 'masculine' by nature.[73] The Gandharva is one of the prominent communities that has been shown as the guardian of the musical tradition; but this community has been often described as the one excelling in the warfare. Sometimes, the description of the warfare associated with this community seems to overweigh its artistic feature. For example, after learning both the art forms and the warfare from Gandharvas, Arjuna emphasized on what he learnt in warfare, marginally discussing the expertise in music that he achieved at Amarāvati with his brothers and Draupadi.[74] The warfare of the Gandharvas has been valorised at many places in the Mahābhārata, but apparently an attempt has been made to give the community a 'masculine' colour; probably, merely the knowledge of music and dance was a 'feminine feature' that was not taken cognizance of.

Music was something that the princes were not taught, it was not considered a sign of valour; valour was equated with 'masculinity'. For example, Gaṅgā brought up Devavrata under the supervision of Vasiṣṭha. While describing Devavrata's qualifications to Śāntanu, Gaṅgā has been depicted to have emphasized Devavrata's qualities as a warrior. An affinity towards music or related art forms did not find any passing reference.[75] Among

[73] Mbh. *Ādi-parvan*, *Caitraratha-parvan*, 109.18.

[74] Mbh. *Vana-parvan, Nivātakavacayudhha-parvan*, 168.58–59 (This *upaparvan* is not given under a separate Rubric in the critical edition given by Bhandarkar Oriental Research Institute, Pune).

[75] Mbh. *Ādi-parvan, Sambhava-parvan*, 100.35. (It must be noted here that some may argue that Gaṅgā spoke about Devavrata's expertise on the Vedas, which included the Sāmaveda as well. It implicitly implied that he must have known the musical aspects of the Vedic tradition. But this chapter attempts to focus on 'emphasis' and 'de-emphasis' on music as an art form by the early societies. In this case, warfare as 'feature of masculinity' was 'emphasized' as Śāntanu was looking for a male successor for the lineage.)

the four brothers in the Rāmāyaṇa, Rāma had the knowledge of the Gāndharva Śāstra.[76] The Pāṇḍavas gained their education under the supervision of Droṇa. However, none of them learnt music or dance specifically, except for the marginal uses, like we learnt about the usage of the conch. Though Arjuna accessed the knowledge while being in touch with the 'other' communities. However, it is interesting to know that Aśwatthāmā learnt music, and he was also interested in watching the musical and dance performances.[77] Droṇācārya imparted the knowledge of music to him; the students who belonged to the ruling families were deprived of the art as an independent discipline.

Music could be seen in transition in terms of gender roles. It is so because music was seen in binaries of masculinity and femininity; yet the powerful and pivotal characters in both the epics have been 'represented' to have transcended these boundaries of gender and learnt music and dance. This aberrant 'depiction' helped these characters to bring certain art forms out of the binaries of gender, and this romanticized the idea of music for the course of future.[78] These characters are Kṛṣṇa,[79] Arjuna and Rāma. Even in case of Aśwatthāmā, probably the imagination of a guru was such that he could transcend such constructs and Droṇa as an *ācārya* could make his son learn the art form. Also, it must be pointed out that a female deity was not yet assigned to music until this point. The vocal sound that emanates from the deep within the human body was seen as the process of 'bringing forth' of the divine figure known as Vāc[80] in the Vedas who resides at the heart

[76] Rmṇ. *Ayodhyā Kāṇḍa*, 2.35.

[77] Mbh. *Droṇa-parvan, Jayadratha-parvan*, 85.14–18.

[78] This is evident from the imagery of Kṛṣṇa which is associated with his flute in the Vaishnav tradition.

[79] Mbh. *Sabhā-parvan, Arghābhiharaṇa-parvan*, 38.

[80] Vāc, personified in the Vedas as the goddess of speech and identified at times with the Goddess Sarasvatī (the patroness of both speech and music), may refer to ordinary human speech, sound in general, animal sounds or to the divine speech principle as a curative power. Lewis Rowell, *Music and Musical Thought in Early India* (Chicago: University of Chicago Press, 1998), 42.

of our innermost being.[81] Vāc, as an antecedent to Sarasvatī, dealt with the idea of sound, not music. In the Mahābhārata, Tārkśya holds a conversation with Sarasvatī, but she talks of knowledge, not music per se; she talks of what offerings revive which features of her in a *yajña*, but she does not give any mention to her ability to play music.[82]

Also, to understand the gender construct that the Gandhavas worked in, it must be pointed out that when Arjuna reached Virāṭa's court as Bṛhannalā, he is not confused as a Gandharva at all; he was considered a eunuch, signifying a sharp difference between the Gandharva and a eunuch.[83] Also, it could be pointed out that as Bṛhannalā, Arjuna wanted to teach music to the girls and the women.[84] And again, we see that the princes were not asked to learn music. But it must be noted that the eunuchs could access the art form. So, the fluidity of music as an art form during the concerned time period was something that could control the roles of an individual. These roles could be controlled by the individuals only if they could step out of the conventional grounds of gender.

Significance of Music in Epics

The evolution of the 'idea' of music in the early Indian history has been a process. The perspectives and thoughts on music evolved through their interaction with the surroundings and, hence, emanated the similar experiences through the sounds. In order to understand the way in which people perceived music in early India, it is important for us to understand music in terms of its content. This is important, as Venkatasubramanian aptly

[81] Ibid., 6.

[82] Mbh. *Vana-parvan, Mārkaṇḍeyasamāsyā-parvan*, 186.25.

[83] Mbh. *Virāṭa-parvan, Pāṇḍavapraveśa-parvan*, 11.12. (This *upa-parvan* is not given under a separate rubric in the critical edition given by Bhandarkar Oriental Research Institute, Pune.)

[84] Ibid., 2.29.

states Marx who implied that 'music is a part of ideology, and therefore does not have a history of its own, only society as a whole has history'.[85] We dealt with this aspect in the beginning as well while discussing the transfer of the composition of the epics from the Sūtas to a Brahmanical framework.

Sengupta, while discussing the perspectives in the philosophy of art, tries to keep music and art in the religious domain to understand the way in which an art form works in a society. He points out that it is impossible to define religion in its totality, but in order to understand its components, the interaction of religion and society must be understood.[86] On similar lines, one could also point out that music could be seen as human attitude in a given time and space. And the time period of the epics is significant because it was in transition between the Vedic tradition and the Purāṇic tradition. Therefore, the attitude of humans, especially towards the texts in this age, has to be focused upon how the understanding of music was derived from its past and shaped its course in future. Scholars like Paranjape consider the Vedic tradition as the foundation of music in early India.[87]

In the year 1975, Frits Staal studied a 3,000-years-old Vedic ritual called Agnicayana, which has been conserved by the Nambudiri Brāhmaṇas in the southwest India. He observed that a ritual is primarily an activity governed by explicit rules and the way the prescribed acts are performed in it. For Staal, it did not really involve any thought process.[88] Rather, he gave stress on the rhythmic patterns which govern a Vedic ritual leading to its 'meaninglessness'.[89] Staal argued that the Vedic mantras have

[85] Venkatasubramanian, *Music as History in Tamil Nadu*, 58.

[86] Pradeep Kumar Sengupta, *Foundations of Indian Musicology: Perspectives in the Philosophy of Art and Culture* (New Delhi: Abhinav Publications, 1991), 1–2.

[87] Sharaccandra Shridhara Paranjape, *Bhārtīya Saṁgīta kā Itihāsa* (Varanasi: Chowkhamba Vidyabhawan, 2010), 17.

[88] Frits Staal, 'The Meaninglessness of Ritual', *Numen* 26, no. 1 (June 1979), 4.

[89] Ibid.

not changed in the last 3,000 years because they are meaningless sounds, and such sounds do not change.[90] But Brian K. Smith accused Staal of being selective in his approach where Staal picked up all the arguments to define the meaning of 'meaninglessness' of a ritual.[91] Smith counter argued that Staal did not see the idea which allows even the 'obsolete' activities to acquire new meanings over a period of time through the same rituals throughout.[92] However, when the Western scholars like Staal looked at the Vedic rituals as void transcendental concerns formulated by the rules with no meaning, Sengupta argued that the transcendental aspects become an extension to the human lives everywhere which are sought to harness their potential to the best. In India, the humankind has tried to focus on this particular extension of its being, considering the idea of an ultimate reality and the manifested form of the unreal.[93] Now one may wonder if we are shifting our focus to study about the idea of music emerging from the Vedic rituals while looking at music in the epics. It must be made clear that it is after the emergence of musical thought and ideas pertaining to sound that the issues related to vocal utterances began to emerge: ordinary speech, elevated speech, recitation, chant or singing. And in case of Indian music, the ancient theory of speech became a fertile breeding ground for the theory of vocal music. A word does not only carry a meaning but it also has its own distinct sound as well. It is the sound and word together that take us to its lasting meaning. The prose is created when the meaning of the word becomes more dominant. Music is born when sound gains dominance over the meaning. For example, in many of the *śikṣās*, Rowell pointed out that the emphasis has been given upon meaning. Without a perfect accent, or great quality of sound, the meaning is not conveyed in its full glory. This might signify that the music in the Vedic tradition was just beginning to prosper as an independent discipline because of its

[90] Ibid., 12.

[91] Brian. K. Smith, *Reflections on Resemblance, Ritual and Religion* (New York: Oxford University Press, 1989), 38.

[92] Ibid.

[93] Sengupta, *Foundations of Indian Musicology*, 29.

focus on the articulation; however, we have Sāmveda as text that focuses the aspects of chanting.

As far as the presence of music is concerned in the Vedic ritual, Staal had devised music to complement his framework. He drew parallels between an Indian ritual of the second millennium BCE and Western music of the second millennium CE by looking at the ritualistic elements such as the *iṣṭis* and the *soma* sequences through the elements such as refrain, cycle, palindrome, overlapping and threesomes from the Western music.[94] Also, he argued that music had been the essential part of the ritual, though it was not highly evolved at that point of time. Similarly, the evolving nature of music derived its structure from the thought that existed around.[95] He tried to focus on the amalgamation of the rituals and music and used the syntactic approach rather than to focus on the semantics because, according to him, both ritual and music were made of abstract elements.[96] In the second volume of Staal's prominent work *Agni*, Howard had contributed to make the understanding of the idea of music even more clear in the *Sāma* Vedic chants called the *sāmans*.[97] The portion of the *sāman* that is affected by the displacement is referred to as *aniruktagāna*, that is, unexpressed or unenunciated chant. Howard argued that 'the syllable substitution which takes several forms, has musical as well as verbal ramifications'. He gave an example of how when the Gāyatri mantra was adapted by the Nambudiri Brāhmaṇas, it changed its form to satisfy the equations of breaths and the tones while singing a chant.[98]

If Staal's focus on syntax semantics and Smith's arguments on the philosophy exuded by the Vedic tradition can be seen as

[94] Frits Staal, *Rituals and Mantras: Rules without Meaning* (New Delhi: Motilal Banarsidass, 1996), 178–182.

[95] Ibid., 185.

[96] Ibid., 186.

[97] Wayne Howard, 'The Music of Nambudiri Unexpressed Chant (Aniruktagāna)', in *Agni*, Vol. II, ed. Frits Staal (New Delhi: Motilal Banarsidass, 2010), 311.

[98] Ibid., 316.

complementary to each other, then it can be argued that since the time of the Vedic tradition, there has been a constant romance between sound and its meaning. Depending upon the required essence to be yielded, one dominated the other. It is very difficult to say that the Vedic tradition focused merely on sound in the form of enunciation or the prose literature tended to focus on the meaning. There had been a confluence of the two elements providing ample space to the evolution of music in early India.

And What Follows?

The two Sanskrit epics project a society that had evolved its outlook towards music further since the Vedic tradition. These are just certain aspects of the ideas relating to music which came into existence to show the conscience that the society had developed for an art form. The musicological aspects have not been covered in this study. In this regard, there are certain issues which need greater attention. For example, as far as the kinds of musical traditions which existed during the period of the composition of the epics are concerned, in the Rāmāyaṇa, Mārga[99] and Gāndharva[100] styles of music are mentioned. The first denotes the classical style, while the other is ritual centric.[101] But these two styles need further investigation in terms of their content and the ways in which communities practiced them. For example, if the two epics are examined in this direction, the community of Gandharvas require a more pragmatic approach to be studied. For the musicological aspects, the idea of *mūrchana* finds its reference in the Rāmāyaṇa[102]; and not to forget, the *Riṣabha swara* and the *śamyā tāla* which we talked about before. These ideas are important because they provided the space for the musical treatises such as the *Natyashastra* and *Brihaddeśī Saṁhitā* in the parallel or subsequent periods respectively. The two epics provide

[99] Rmṇ. *Bālakāṇḍa*, 4.36.
[100] Rmṇ. *Ayodhyākāṇḍa*, 2.35.
[101] Rowell, *Music and Musical Thought*, 10.
[102] Rmṇ. *Bālakāṇḍa*, 4.10.

an aesthete an amalgamation of visual, acoustic and textual rasa, and this aspect also needs to be looked at in its historical context to see how the theory of rasa was devised in early India.

Bibliography

Desai, Devangana. 'Social Dimensions of Art in Early India'. *Social Scientist* 18, no. 3 (March 1990): 3–32.

Pandey, Ramayandutt Shastri, trans. *Mahābhārata*. Gorakhpur: Geeta Press.

The Mahābhārata, Critical Edition. Pune: The Bhandarkar Oriental Research Institute. Entered on the website of BORI by Professor Tokunaga and then maintained/updated by Professor John Smith. http://sanskritdocuments.org/mirrors/mahabharata/mahabharata-bori.html

Vālmīki, Śrī. *Rāmāyaṇa*. Gorakhpur: Geeta Press.

4

Knowledge Traditions in Ancient India

Shri Prakash Singh

Introduction

The immensely rich cultural treasure of India not only continues to shape the wide spectrum of India's lives but also influences a major portion of Asia and other continents in one way or the other. Undoubtedly, India, known for its achievements in the field of culture, spirituality, art and architecture, has valued its intellectual tradition in distinct fields of knowledge spread over more than thousands of years, which is widely acknowledged by the scholars all across the world. Indian civilization, which has been persisting for nearly four millennia in the fields of 'eternal' knowledge, has left an impression over others and enlightened the curiosity to understand the in-depth *jnāna* (i.e., knowledge). Unfortunately, the knowledge system which we treasure to have for centuries has been on the ebb. It has been losing its prominence primarily because of intermittent political upheavals leading to systematic destruction of the coveted indigenous traditions and the institutions that supported them. The most exquisite vehicle of the knowledge tradition was language. Sanskrit was indisputably the most prominent representative language whose origin in written form is traced back to the 'Rigveda more than thousands years back' and continued for centuries through oral tradition and preservation of verbal knowledge. But Sanskrit gradually reduced to an oppressed language. The death of Sanskrit literary culture as a historical process was caused essentially, what Sheldon Pollock writes, due to four major developments:

> The disappearance of Sanskrit literature in Kashmir, a premier centre of literary creativity, after the thirteenth century; its diminished power in sixteenth century Vijayanagara, the last great imperial formation of southern India; its short-lived moment of modernity at the Mughal court in mid-seventeenth century Delhi; and its ghostly existence in Bengal on the eve of colonialism.[1]

Given this context, the chapter attempts to stress upon methodological ambiguity in understanding proper context and meaning of the specific words and notions used in the texts of Indian knowledge tradition and seeks to invoke interpretation which carry sense in the right perspective. To this end, the chapter, first, maps the history of the knowledge tradition and subsequently investigates the deep root of distortion, which progressively diluted the real meaning and understanding, and thereby causing irreparable damage to rich Indian knowledge tradition.

Knowledge Tradition

India's rich and vivid ancient tradition of elucidating and interpreting the texts is well acknowledged. Indian civilization has always accorded great value to knowledge, which may be experienced in the incredible bodies of texts embracing specific context. It has collection of huge manuscripts wedded to particular tradition. The thinkers embody domains of the knowledge. For instance, in Shrimad Bhagavad Gita, Lord Kṛṣṇa told Arjuna that knowledge is the greatest purifier and liberator of the self.

[1] Sheldon Pollock, 'The Death of Sanskrit', *Comparative Studies in Societies and History* 43, no. 2 (2001): 394–395.

India's knowledge tradition is ancient, and the unrestrained flow continues to be maintained whose roots lie in the Vedas itself. Vedas are the extensive source of India's knowledge traditions where *jnāna* has been at the focal point of all the rational and investigative issues in India.[2] The knowledge tradition of Ancient India was collected and preserved in the oral form, in which language played the pivotal role in shaping the Indian knowledge (intellectual) tradition extensively. Besides, interpretation (how the knowledge precisely got across) has always played a major intellectual role in shaping and preserving the tradition right from the Rigvedas itself.[3] For instance, Bhartrhari held knowledge as awakening of our inner self. He called it '*antarjṇata*, which is constituted of *indriya*, administered by the mind (i.e., *mana*) and the intel (i.e., *buddhi*). Finally the knowledge comes into existence with our transformed intellects and revivify the self.[4] Bhartrhari's special remark finds resonance in Rigveda in one of its verses (X. 71.1.): 'The real significance

[2] To get the theoretical underpinnings of the statement about ancient Indian knowledge tradition, the words of Sri Aurobindo had a remarkable impact. Sri Aurobindo states that in one of his letters, 'India's Rebirth': 'We Indians, born and bred in a country where *jnāna* has been stored and accumulated since the race began, bear about in us the inherited gains of many thousands of years' (Sri Aurobindo, 'India's Rebirth', 14). Further, in 1932, he enhanced his own statement as follows: '[the mother and myself] do not found ourselves on faith alone, but on a great ground of knowledge which we have been developing and testing all our lives' (Sri Aurobindo, 'India's Rebirth', 191). *Out of the Ruins of the West India's Rebirth: A Selection from Sri Aurobindo's Writings, Talks and Speeches*, Mira Aditi, Mysore, 1993.

[3] The sense of words altogether with their interpretation begins in the Rigveda itself, for instance, 1,240 instances of *nirvacana* (selection) which help in establishing the meaning through the derivation from a given verbal root. For more details, see B. N. Tewary, *Bhartiya Bhasha: Vigyan ki Bhoomika* [Introduction to Indian Linguistics] (Delhi: Sahitya Sahkar, 1972), 24–118.

[4] For more details, see Bhartrhari, *Vakyapadiya*. K. A. Subramania Iyer, trans., *Bhartrhari: A Study of the Vakyapadiya in the Light of Ancient Commentaries* (Poona: Deccan College, 1969), 123.

is that the principle of vāk (speech) creates or fashion out the manifold forms out of the waters of the Infinite ocean of the ultimate reality.'[5]

Aitareyopanishad (III 1.6) sheds light as follows: the knowledge and inner relationship is possible only by speech (vāk).

> The teacher Pāṇcālacanda considered speech itself as the Saṁhitā ... by speech the Vedas are strung, by speech the metres are made, by speech friends are united, by speech all beings (establish their intra-subjective knowledge and relation) and hence all this is speech.

Further, the Chāndogya Upanishad (VII. 2) spells explicitly that language situates at the very foundation of ethics (*niti*): 'Without speech who could explain right and wrong, good, evil, pleasant, unpleasant? (Only) Speech explains all.'

In the Kathopanishad (III. 13), as well, the identical notion finds expression with a significant appeal that 'the real self of a man' can be found through language:

'The wise should merge the speech (language) in the mind, and that (mind) in the intellect, and that (intellect) in the Great-self

[5] Bhartrhari's viewpoint is that knowledge came into existence in the form of words (*Vakyapadiya*, I.108), which signifies that all the interpretation and differences are the outcome of language itself. Hence, the wise man had said, according to Bhartrhari, 'all the world (samsara) is the result of language'. The reason is obvious that

> it is not possible to draw lines in water or to divide water; we cannot segment it—everything is merged with everything else, every particle is like every other and indistinguishable. The discrete forms and shapes are cognized through language which gives them 'names' for language is 'naming' is knowledge.

For more detail, see Kapil Kapoor, *Text and Interpretation: The Indian Tradition* (New Delhi: D. K. Printworld, 2005), 4; V. S. Agarwal, *The Thousand-Syllabled Speech (Being a Study in Cosmic Symbolism in Its Vedic Version)* (Delhi: Motilal Banarsidass), 45.

and that (great-self again) in the Self of peace (Sānta-Ātman, the real self of man).'[6]

As noted by Kapil Kapoor, it was somewhere between the 7th century BC, mostly the pre-Buddha time of Pānini, that language became the sole object of analysis, where language acts as ontology and as epistemology, altogether with the interpretation of metaphysics. The whole knowledge tradition was divided into four phases: (a) from the beginning to Pānini: pre-7th century BC; (b) from Pānini to Ānandavardhana: from 7th century BC to 9th century AD; (c) from Rāmacandra to Nageśa Bhatta: 11th century to 18th century; and (d) 19th century to now.[7]

Coming to the core issue undertaken here, the interpretation of term or word (i.e., sābda) is key to understanding the essence of knowledge as each sābda encompasses specific meaning. It is believed that few of the mantra (hyme) or sābda requires sound or vibrations which help in unfolding them. There are at least six interrelated meaning which have been identified: (a) bhavartha; (b) sampradayartha; (c) garbhartha; (d) kaulartha; (e) sarvarahasyartha; and (f) mahatattvartha.[8] A word or sābda is nothing but an image of an idea. It is immortal living entity. Word is mainstay to import the idea. Word articulates the interpretation of the ideas.[9] In the Rigveda (X. 71. 1-3), this is stated as follows:

> When, lord of our prayer! The first of speech, and the foremost, the sages uttered, giving the unnamed a name, which was their best, and their most stainless, when they with love revealed the divine secret in their souls. Where the sages formed the speech

[6] Swami Sharvananda, *Kathopanishad* (Text with English Translation), 11th ed. (Madras: Sri Rama Krishna Math, 1973), 25.

[7] Kapoor, *Text and Interpretation*, 5.

[8] K. V. Dev, ed., and M. N. Namoodiri, trans., *The Thousand Names of the Divine Mother: Sri Lalita Sahasranama*. With Commentary by T. V. Naryana Menon (Amirtapuri: Mata Amritanandamayi Math, 2000 [1996]).

[9] Avadhesh Kumar Singh, 'Word and Beyond: Questions of Meaning and Interpretation', in *Sābda: Text and Interpretation in Indian Thought*, eds. Santosh K. Sareen and Makarand Paranjape (New Delhi: Mantra Books, 2004), 107.

> (vāk) with their mind, straining it as they strain flour with the sieve, therein have friends discovered bonds of friendship, whose holy beauty lies hidden in that speech.
>
> With worship they followed the steps of the Speech and found it installed in the hearts of sages. They acquired it and gave it at many places, and seven singers intone it together.[10]

The oral texts, in the ancient Indian knowledge tradition, are highly structured and properly ordered. Oral texts, where the Indian minds are taxonomic, are based on overt organizers such as *adhikarana* and *prakarana*. These two overt organizers are based on the structural relationship and order treatment of subjects, which further enhanced 'the interpretation of statements through a four-point references to their location in the over-all text down to the particular *sutra* (formula) and *kārika* as is the case with the Rig Veda, Mahabharata, and Arthasāstra'.[11] The texts, that is, oral conceptualization, in ancient Indian knowledge traditions have gone through rigour maintenance of texts of knowledge. Earlier, the tradition of maintaining the texts of knowledge was not bibliolatrous, rather it had been through capacity of mental storage.[12] Max Muller also observed that texts in the oral traditions, which he called as 'living libraries',[13] are maintained in memory. His following remark is germane: 'This

[10] John Brough, 'Some Indian Theories of Meaning', in *A Reader on the Sanskrit Grammarians*, ed. J. F. Staal (Delhi: Motilal Banarsidass, 1972).

[11] Kapil Kapoor, 'Indian Knowledge System: Nature, Philosophy and Character', in *Indian Knowledge System*, Vol. 1, eds. Kapil Kapoor and Avadhesh Kumar Singh (Shimla: Indian Institute of Advanced Study and New Delhi: D. K. Printworld, 2005), 13.

[12] Kapil Kapoor, 'Some Reflections on the Interpretation of Texts in the Indian Tradition', in *Structures of Signification*, Vol. 1, ed. H. S. Gill (Delhi: Wiley Eastern Limited, 1990).

[13] Max Muller states that orality, as a mode in the maintenance of knowledge, constitutes knowledge in the mind, as against the literae traditions in which knowledge is kept externally. He calls them who have kept the knowledge through the act of memorization 'living libraries'. For more detail see, Max Muller, *India: What Can It Teach Us*, Indian ed. (Delhi: Munshiram Manoharlal, 1991), 132.

may sound startling, but what will sound more startling, and yet is a fact that can be easily ascertained ... here then we are not dealing with theories, but with facts, which- anybody may verify. The whole of the Rgveda, and a great deal exists now in the oral tradition.'[14]

Indian knowledge tradition within different domains has been institutionalized by numerous disciplines, *vidya* or knowledge (theoretical principles) and crafts, that is, *kāla* (applied principles). Knowledge traditions comprises of diverse fields such as philosophy, architecture, mathematics, grammar, astronomy, metrics, sociology, science, economy, polity, ethics, geography, logic, military, weaponry, agriculture, mining, trade and commerce, metallurgy, shipbuilding, medicine, poetics, biology and veterinary science.[15] The Indian knowledge tradition has dealt with 18 sort of major *vidyas* and 64 *kālas*. The 18 *vidyas* are as follows: 4 Vedas; 4 subsidiary Vedas (i.e., Ayurveda, Dhanurveda, Gandharvaveda, Śilpa); Purāna; Nyāya; Mīmāmsā; Dharamasāstra; and the 6 auxiliary sciences: phonetics, grammar, metre, astronomy, ritual and philology. Further, these constituted 18 sciences in ancient Indian knowledge tradition.[16] Knowledge traditions of ancient India are uninterrupted ones which were based on philosophy, nature and character of ancient Indian intellectual traditions. The intellectual tradition of ancient Indian knowledge system is differentiated by *jnāna* (knowledge) and *vijṇāṇa* (perceptible reality). Threefold distinctions are further classified: (a) sāttvika jnāna; (b) rājasīka jnāna; and (c) tāmasika jnāna. Adi Sānkara, who was also one of the leading minds, talks about the *visudha jnāna* (purified knowledge), which is isolated from (other) senses and established in the (inner) self. He also distinguishes between *jnāna* (knowledge) and *karma* (action) which leads to *sattva-śuddhī* (purification

[14] Ibid., 131.

[15] Kapoor, *Text and Interpretations*, 18.

[16] For more details, Sribasavarājendra in *Sivatattvaratnākara*, Vātsyāyana in *Kamasutra*, Sridharasvāmi in his commentary on Shrimad Bhagavad Gita. 10.45.64. and Sukrācāryā in *Śukranīti*.

of instrumentalities).[17] Therefore, the Nyāya contribution is to assume the validity as a parameter of different sorts of knowledge. It distinguished between the knowledge based on memory (smrti) and knowledge based on experience (ānubhava) which is further subclassified as *yathārtha* (valid) and *a-yathārtha* (non-valid).[18] Moreover, the knowledge was known as *adhyatma-jnāna*, *visudha-jnāna* and *nirguna-jnāna*, which arises in the individual self. In fact, Rajiv Malhotra has noted that Sanskrit mantras are taxingly as corresponding to the sense of vibrations which serves as the keys to apex rank of consciousness.

Malhotra argues,

> Writing is intrinsically less subtle than the inner vibrational form of the language. As a result, traditionalists consider the use of language (here, Sanskrit) prior to the written form as important. They want the revival of the language (i.e., Sanskrit) to include the oral tradition.[19]

Methodology

The biggest crippling effect in understanding the ancient knowledge tradition has been the dearth of appropriate methodologies of interpreting the terms, words, hymns and poetic expressions. Therefore, to interpret the knowledge tradition, understanding the language has been the primary concern. Drawing right sense for each word used in the knowledge tradition can only lead to right interpretation. Noticeable was the *sāstra-paddhiti* (methodology of the knowledge tradition of ancient India) which depended on the structure of the knowledge and nature of the

[17] For more detail, see The Bhagavad Gita (4.33) where it states that all action ends in knowledge, that is, all *karma* finally meets with *jnāna*.

[18] This question of 'validity' in knowledge was elaborately enhanced by almost all the different schools of thought/philosophy.

[19] Rajiv Malhotra, *The Battle for Sanskrit: Is Sanskrit Political or Sacred? Oppressive or Liberating? Dead or Alive* (New Delhi: HarperCollins Publishers, 2016), 36.

language and their relationship with the thought and the reality. Thus, the dimension of the intellectual tradition through the interpretation of language are as follows: (a) structure of the language (its phonetics and phonology); (b) its morphology and syntax; (c) nature of sound change and change in the interpretation of the words; (d) synchronic variation in the linguistic usage; and (e) philosophy of the language, its thoughts and reality.[20]

Jamini, in his *Mimamsa Sutras*, discussed all the significant issues of relating the interpretation of word and their interrelationship between the linguistic meaning and its existence, that is, the reality of the objects. Jamini further raised few objections and answered in his own style, which has had great sense for the modern minds: (a) Is not linguistic proposition? If not multivalent, essentially ambiguous? (b) Does the text not have intrinsic potential to produce its interpretation through which the readers may develop its understanding on their own? (c) How do the readers, after confronting over the distinguish meaning of the word, select the meaning of the term? and (d) What are the structure of interpretation and what are the preconditions to their denotation and connotation?[21] In that order, Jaimini's *Mimamsa Sutra*, through its philosophy of performance, is a philosophy which helps in interpreting the injunctive sentences, that is, *vidhi-vākya*. He discussed about five significant elements: (a) *vishay* (subject of investigation); (b) *samasya* (the doubts); (c) *pūrva-paksa* (prima-facie view); (d) *uttar-paksa* (the reply); and (e) *siddant-nirnaya* (principle decision).[22]

In the intellectual tradition, the significance of *sāmvad* (conversation) or dialogue has had its own relevance while explaining the knowledge through its *paddhiti*, that is, methodology. Primarily, the use of *sāmvad* or dialogue was used differently in the Upanishads. But the pertinent question which

[20] Kapoor, *Text and Interpretations,* 6.

[21] M. L. Sandal, trans., *Mīmāmsā Sūtras of Jaimini*, Vol. I (Delhi: Motilal Banarsidass, 1980).

[22] Ibid. and for more detail, see also Kapoor, *Text and Interpretation.*

needs to be addressed is whether the ancient intellectual tradition makes use of *sāmvad*. *Sāmvad* is a dynamic process of conversation, argumentation and mutual discussion of ideas between individuals, whereas dialogue involves the method in which encounter with other thinkers are essential. It is opposed to a monologue, which can formulate nothing but a dogma.[23] The knowledge tradition had come across numerous *sāmvad* which clearly reflects the variation in the knowledge tradition. The Chandogya Upanishad—where dialogues such as between *Satyakama* and his beloved mother *Jabala*, between *Yāma* and *Nāchiketa*, between *Ghora Agṇirasa* and Kṛṣṇa, between Rishi *Nārada* and *Sānat kumar*, between *Prājapati*, Indra and *Virochana*—and the Brihadaranyaka Upanishad—where dialouges such as between Prajapati and his sons and between *Yajnavalkya, Maitreyi and Katyayani*—were suffice to depict the essentiality of the discussions, that is, the process of *sāmvad*. *Sāmvad* is the process which cannot be possible without speakers having fundamental consensus, that is, both the speakers '(a) speak, (b) listen, (c) aim at truth, (d) understand each other's language, (e) understand each other's way of thinking, (f) and, do not live in two worlds contents totally differ'.[24] The method of *sāmvad* was at the heart of the Upanishads and Upanishadic ethics. Therefore, the operative terms of this methodology are as follows: (a) dialectic; (b) plurality; (c) questioning as an 'enquiring' act; (d) deferring; (e) analogy; (f) synthesis; and (g) aphorisms. Shankara said the following:

> Every word employed to denote a thing can do so only in so far as it is associated with certain *genus,* or a certain act, or a certain quality, or a certain mode of relation. The cow and horse imply

[23] Raghwendra Pratap Singh, 'Methodological Issues Concerning Hermeneutics in the Upanishads', in *Sābda: Text and Interpretation in Indian Thought*, eds. Sanotsh K. Sareen and Makarand Paranjape (New Delhi: Mantra Books, 2004), 82.

[24] A. T. Paperzak, *System and History in Philosophy* (New York: SUNY Press, 1986), 84.

genera, teacher and cook imply acts, white and black imply qualities, wealthy and cattle-owner imply possession.[25]

Panini's *Ashtadhyayi* reflects the interest to linguistics of the generative persuasion as well as linguistic theoreticians. He had a different sense of ordering the structure. The *Ashtadhyayi*, as a part of method, holds a central position in the grammatical literature, and subsequently, it assists in the interpretation and reinterpretation. In the intellectual tradition of ancient knowledge, *Dhvāni* (sound) also acts as the method of interpreting texts. The discourse of *Dhvāni*, therefore, states that these sorts of discourses/theories cannot be used only for interpreting, but these can be applied in other arts or *kāla* as well because of their aesthetic grandeur in all art forms.

In *Arthashastra*, Kautilya had elaborated variation in methodology which enumerated 32 methods of science followed in the ancient Indian society. These methods were also derived from ancient Indian philosophical systems such as *Lokayata*, *Sāmkhya* and *Nyaya*. The methods of *Anvikshiki* or *Anvikshikee* (deals with the knowledge of the self) and *Yukti* (reason) were appropriately used by Kautilya to write the science of politics. Undoubtedly, Kautilya's approach was synthetic. Kautilya was not only the politico-economic theorist but also one of the individuals who raised their voice for the cultural sophistication.

While exploring the epic literary magnificence, Annie Besant declared Mahābhārata, like *Arthashastra*, as 'the great poem in the world'. 'There is no other poem as splendid as this, so full of what we want to know, and of what is good for us to study'.[26] Not only this but she also suggests a few methods or *paddhiti* to understand this sacred text of Indian knowledge tradition such as the following: (a) the mind should be in the right frame; (b) not to

[25] Shankara, Commentary on the Gita, XIII. 12, Bhasya with Nine Commentaries, ed. M. M. A. K. Shastri (Delhi: Gita Press, 2002), 155.

[26] Annie Besant, *Mahabharata: The Epic Story of Great War* (Chennai: The Theosophical Publishing House, reprint 1978).

read it with an ignorant conception; (c) read it by *pārva*, chronologically; (d) interpret the words between the lines; and (e) what it is, actually, telling us.

Expounding Indian Knowledge Tradition

Indian traditions rely not just on the consistency of truths but also on the synthesis of truths. The Indian thinkers followed distinct paths to truth, however. Indic tradition which believes and welcomes vibrant thoughts and ideas, *ekam sat viprabahudhavadanti* (truth is one, learned refer to it with distinct names), does not prefer a singular path to truth. The ancient Indic tradition was not just for the promotion of the man's material comfort but was also for the enhancement of one's mental and physical well-being, which Lord Buddha seeks as nirvana or in the Vedic terms is called as moksha or liberation of the self. That is why knowledge has never been diverted from the socio-ethical imperatives.

Notably, it has been experienced that the Western tradition of knowledge has been held to oppose the innocence, indulged in attaining the unrestrained 'power', which is the sole reason for the fall of an individual. Knowledge is, merely, an instrument in the Western conflict model to handle the adversary. The Old Testament refers that 'man is given dominion over the fish of the sea and over the fowl of the air, and over the cattle, and over all the earth....'[27] Thus, the Western man has been granted all the superior rights over all the living entity including the Mother Earth. Therefore, at the age of Renaissance, all the significant efforts were laid to put the foundation for the material comforts of the individuals, which was promised as his sole inheritance. The history of the Western conception of knowledge has proved 'organized' knowledge as destructive.

Contrary to this, in the Indian thought system or intellectual tradition, the central objective of knowledge is not to exercise

[27] Genesis, 1.26.

the power over others rather to exercise it over self, to attain the inner self, moksha (the liberation of the self from other restrictions). In the Indian knowledge system, *jnāna* acts as an instrument of liberation of the individual from the superficial, external restraints and existential constraints to attain one's own mind and self. This is the true power, a true freedom, *āatma-bodha*, that is, self-realization. Freedom of an individual in the Indian tradition, specifically in the *Sāmkhya* thought, is defined as moksha (the liberation from *duhkha*, that is, suffering).[28] Yet this makes the Indian knowledge system more inclusive as opposed to the Western knowledge system. From the theory of *pūrva-paksa* (which has been always presented before the discussion) to *sāmvad parampara* (an act of contestation to get the path for truth), the Indian knowledge system had shown a great tolerance to others and for dissension. Indeed, the Indian intellectual tradition, through knowledge, aimed at happiness, if not comfort, and tried to enhance the harmony and peace between the nature and individuals.

Knowledge Tradition of Middle Indo-Aryan Languages: *Prākrt* and *Pāli*

The knowledge tradition of middle Indo-Aryan languages was comprised, mainly, by *Pāli* and *Prākrt*. The term *Pāli* has been derived in distinct ways. As the Buddhist scriptures, gradually written in *panktis* or lines. This led to the argument where it was assumed that *Pāli* has come from *pankti* through a process of evolution. Other narratives have considered that Palli (village) had led to the evolution of the word *Pāli*. Henceforth, *Pāli* also represents the language of rural people. As noted in the Buddhist scriptures, Buddha way before his demise, methodical his disciples to use and propagate his teachings in people's own language, that

[28] For more detail, Mahābhārata defines moksha as the knowledge which promotes the general welfare of mankind, while the Bhagavad Gita defines it as an individual attaining the knowledge which promotes the *loka-samgrahā* (the collective well-being).

is, *svakāya niruttiya.*[29] Much ink has been flown out over the epistemology of Buddhist literary knowledge. A little but significant consideration came from D. T. Suzuki who juxtaposes the discursive and intuitive levels of understanding, that is, *Viṇṇāṇā* and *Prājna*, within the *Pāli* knowledge of Buddhist tradition. *Viṇṇāṇā*, as observed by Suzuki, is the 'mode of knowledge appropriate to the world of the sense and the intellect characterized by the duality between the seer and the seen', whereas on the other hand, *Prājna* is the 'fundamental noetic principle whereby the synthetic apprehension of the whole becomes possible'.[30] *Prākrt*, undoubtedly, was derived from *Prakriti* that clearly reflects a relation with the nature. However, in this regard, *Prākrt* is the language that is related with the natural sense of the people. Many would have considered *Prākrt* as the origin or the source. Meanwhile, Andrew Ollett aptly points out that it is imperative to note that *Prākrt* is not merely an antique that should be kept in the historical annals of India's languages/knowledge tradition. Rather it significantly helps to understand how literary knowledge function in the pre-modern India. Notwithstanding, *Prākrt* provides an alternative way of pondering over knowledge tradition and language, specifically about its origin, existence, its unity and other related variations, sociality and its (literary) imaginative possibilities.[31] An interesting description of *Prākrt*, primordially as the linguistic tradition, comes from Mirza Khan in his *Gift from India*, where he states the following:

> Prākrt—the language is mostly employed in the praise of kings, ministers, and chiefs, and belongs to the world, that is to say, the world that is below the ground; they call it *Pātāl-bānī*, and also *Nāg-bānī*, that is, the language of the lowest of the low, and of reptiles of

[29] Suresh Chandra Banerji, *Historical Survey of Ancient Indian Grammars: Sanskrit, Pali and Prakrit* (Delhi: Sharda Publishing House, 1996), 40.

[30] D. T. Suzuki, 'Reason and Intuition in Buddhist Philosophy', in *Essays in East-West Philosophy*, ed. C. A. Moore (Honolulu: University of Hawaii Press, 1951), 17.

[31] Andrew Ollett, *Prakrit in the Language Order of India, in Language of the Snakes: Prakrit, Sanskrit, and the Language order of Premodern India* (Berkeley: University of California Press, 2017), 2.

mean origin, who live underground. This language is a mixture of *Sahãskirt,* mentioned above, and *Bhākhā,* to be mentioned next.[32]

Mirza Khan's narrative on *Prākrt* is sufficient to prove the distinct but diverse knowledge tradition of ancient India, which also proves the existence of other knowledge tradition which is, intentionally, neglected by many decades. It is very hard to trace the genesis of the Indian knowledge tradition. Andrew Ollett, therefore, argued that *Prākrt* because of its ancient linguistic tradition is, nonetheless, 'languages of the snakes'[33] for its tail-end long historical existence. *Prākrt,* in the linguistic tradition, was used as the primary language in literary works, such as single-verse lyrics, narratives, historical excursion and romantic prose. Undoubtedly, *Prākrt* was not just restrained to the classical Indian literary knowledge, rather *Prākrt* texts were great classics in themselves. As the knowledge of a certain language and literature was the chief element of cultural reflection, *Prākrt* was, therefore, cultivated across parts of southern Asia (from Kashmir to the region of Tamil Nadu, from the valley of Sindh to Bengal) and also, if not popular, in Cambodia and Java.[34]

Similar to Sanskrit, *Prākrt* was a language of Indian literary intellectual tradition, and it reflects the regions and other religious traditions also. *Prākrt,* even after having an enriched literary background, also became even more vulnerable comparatively to other classical languages of the Indian linguistic tradition. Reasons are many! Primarily, one of the reasons for its vulnerability is that it does not stand for any regional, national, ethnic

[32] *Duyum parākirt o madḥ-I mulūk o wuzarā' o akābir beshtar badīn zabān goyand. o ān zabān-i 'ālam ast, ya'ni 'ālam-i ki zīr zamīn ast. o ān-rā pātāl-bānī goyand … o nāg-bānī nīz nāmand … ya'nī zabān-i ahl-i asfal us-sāfilīn o mārān ki zamīnīyān o suflīyānand. o ān murakkab ast az sahāskirt, ki sābiq mazkūr shud, o bhākhā, ki ba'd az īn mazkūr shawad.* For more detail, see Mirzā Khan, *Gift from India (Tuḥfat al-Hind) of Mīrzā Khān: A Grammar of the Braj Bhākhā by Mīrzā Khān (1676 A.D.),* ed. and trans. M. Ziauddin (Calcutta [Kolkata]: Visva Bharati Bookshop, 1936), 53–54.

[33] Ollett, *Prakrit in the Language Order,* 2.

[34] M. A. Barth, *Inscriptions sanscrites du Cambodge* (Paris: Imprimerie Nationale, 1885), 234.

or religious existence. Later, scholars have cited that the *Prākrt* texts are 'homeless texts'", as there were no authentic claims by anyone for owning them and *Prākrt* itself is not part of any cultural existence. Another reason for its vulnerability is that it is deeply embedded in Sanskrit culture. Richard Pischel in his *Grammar of the Prākrit Languages* observed the following:

> The Prakrit languages are thus 'artificial languages' (*Kunstsprachen*) insofar as they have been significantly modified by poets for literary purposes. But they are not 'artificial languages' if it is thereby meant that they are whole-cloth fabrications of the poets. Entirely the same account applies to them as to Sanskrit, which was neither itself the general language of everyday life (*allgemeine Umgangssprache*) of educated Indians, nor is based on such a language, but certainly harkens back to a dialect spoken by people that was, for reasons of politics or religious history, elevated to the status of a general literary language (*Litteratursprache*).[35]

Gradually, *Prākrt* was widely seen as a dialect of Sanskrit; Sanskrit which has always cast its enriched shadow, that is, *chāya*, over *Prākrt*. As Andrew Ollett remarked that 'amongst of all the literary languages of South Asia, *Prākrt* alone was close enough to Sanskrit, both linguistically, in terms of their forms, and discursively, in terms of their co-occurrence in texts, to be read as Sanskrit'.[36] *Prākrt*, however, the language of middle Indo-Aryan tradition, was promoted as 'poetry of polity' and later on was known as the medium of 'courtly literature'.[37]

Terminologies of the Knowledge System

In order to obtain the adequate and apposite knowledge of the ancient Indian intellectual tradition, it is essential to have the precise and contextual knowledge of the terms and their appropriate

[35] Richard Pischel, *A Grammar of Prakrit Language (1900)*, trans. S. Jha, 2nd ed. (Delhi: Motilal Banarsidass, 1986), 6.

[36] Ollett, *Prakrit in the Language Order*, 10.

[37] Ibid., 23.

interpretation. The existing contradictions in interpreting the terminologies of the Indian knowledge tradition require a great deal of precautions. The terminologies are not what we read at first glance, rather it has an in-depth interpretation between the lines. As Manford H. Kuhn remarked from an ancient dictum that 'we (humans) see things not as they are but as we are' and 'we do not first see and then define: we define first and then see'.[38] Because of this ignorant sense, many thinkers categorized the Indian philosophers exclusionary, and the language they used, Sanskrit, oppressive.

This can be understood as follows: In the Vedas, we find the reference to *rashtra* or *rashtram*[39] as a personified king holding the sway over its subjects with all benign and benevolent instinct. *Rashtram* is etymologically explained as a firm and enlightened path for the welfare of the community. In the *pratham mandala* of the Rigveda, the conception of *rashtra* was discussed as, *aham rashtri sangamani vasunam Prathama yagyiyanam* (I am the beholder of this *Rashtra*; benefactor of the gods; and first among the worshipped). In the words from *Aitareya Brahmana*, *rashtram* is identified with the dominion or rule (*Ksatra*).[40] Unlike the theory of a state in the West, a mention in the Atharva Veda about the term *rashtram* is illustrative here.

Bhadram icchhantah rishiyah
swar vidayah, tapo dikshaamupanshed agre.
tato raashtram, bala, ojasya jaatam
tadasmai devaupasannmantu.

It reflects that wish from a benign which originated in the minds of seers during penance. And this wish is for the welfare for all. However, this wish is not self-centric, rather, it covers the welfare for every bit of humanity. This sense of collectivity brings the

[38] Manford H. Kuhn, 'Major Trends in Symbolic Interaction Theory in Past Twenty Five Years', *The Sociological Quarterly* 5, no. 1 (1964): 70. http://www.jstor.org/stable/4105182

[39] Rigveda, vii, 34, ii.

[40] Aitareya Brahmana, vii, 22, 31.

common welfare of all which creates the *rashtra*. If looked at the Indian equivalent of the term sovereignty, there have been varied connotations. For instance, the Indian term for sovereignty was *Ksatra*[41] or *Ksatrasi* in the Vedic literature and *Swamitva* in the *Arthashastra*,[42] whereas, on the other hand, Ghoshal, etymologically, ponders over the word *Rajyam* which means royalty or sovereignty, and derivately, it means kingdom.[43] Benoy Sarkar translates it as a form of *aiswarya*.[44] Take example of another term *Dandaniti*, which had its own specific place in the scheme of knowledge. However, *Dandaniti* does not limit only to the act of punishment, according to the Hindu political philosophy. The Sanskrit word for knowledge is *vidya*, and there are many interpretations regarding this. Kautilya, himself, accepted four branches of knowledge: (a) *Anvikshiki*; (b) constituted from three Vedas, that is, Sam, Yajur and Atharva; (c) *Varta*; and (d) *Dandaniti*.[45] Brihaspati, quoted by Kautilya, conceptualized only two *vidya*'s, that is, *Dandaniti* and *Varta*, at the same time as Sukra, in his *Sukraniti*, accepts only one kind of *vidya*, that

[41] *Ksatra*, in the general sense of dominion, rule, power as exercised by gods and men, occurs frequently from the Rigveda onwards. The word is also found in the concrete sense of rulers in the Rig Veda and later .... 'A *Ksatra-pati* is several times mentioned as an equivalent to King' in Arthur Anthony Macdonell and Arthur B. Keith, *Vedic Index of Name and Subjects*, Vol. 1 (Delhi: Motilal Banarsidass, Reprint Edition 1967), 202.

[42] H. N. Sinha, *Sovereignty in Ancient Indian Polity* (London: Luzac & Co., 1938), 18–19.

[43] U. N. Ghoshal, *A History of Hindu Political Theories* (Oxford: Oxford University Press, 1923), 84.

[44] Benoy Sarkar, *The Political Institutions and Theories of the Hindus* (Leipzig: Markert & Petters, 1922), 214. Where he talks about the term as

> the conception of external aiswarya (i.e., sovereignty) was well established in the Hindu philosophy of the state. The Hindu thinkers not only realized the sovereignty about the constituent elements in a single state. They realized also that sovereignty is not complete unless it is external as well as internal, unless the state can exercise its internal authority unobstructed by, and independently of, other states.

[45] *Arthashastra*, I, 2, 6–12.

is, *Dandaniti*.[46] According to Kautilya, *Dandaniti* deals with the means of preservation and acquisition of dialectics, Vedas and *Varta*.[47] *Dandaniti*, for him, aids *Varta* and Vedas because both the treasury and punishment are necessary for the control, both of one's own kingdom and of enemies. It is therefore, as, Kautilya said: 'It is on this art of the government that the course of the progress of the world depends.'[48] And further it remarks that 'the first three branches of knowledge are (highly) dependent for their well-being (or rooted in) on the art of punishment'.[49] The Mahābhārata, in *Shantiparva*, also illustrates the nature of *Dandaniti*.[50] It ascribes *Dandaniti* to the great God Brahma.[51] According to Bhisma (one of the classic teachers and warrior-heroes of ancient India), in *Shantiparva*, *Dandaniti* is a wide-ranging branch of knowledge, and it elaborates the fourfold ends of the man popularly culminated in the forms of *purushartha*: dharma, *artha*, *kama and* moksha.[52] The great epic Mahābhārata interchangeably used the word *Dandaniti* with *Rājadharma* (the dharma of the king). For instance, Mahābhārata reads as follows: 'when the *dandaniti* becomes lifeless, the triple *Veda* sinks, all the dharma's howsoever developed, completely perished. When traditional rajadharma is departed, all the bases of the divisions of ashramas shattered'.[53]

[46] Ibid.

[47] According to Kautilya, *Dandaniti* has four special functions to do: (a) acquisition of that which is not under control and possession; (b) preservation of that which has been acquired; (c) accentuation of that which has been preserved; and (d) righteous and due apportionment of that which has been accentuated. For more detail, *Arthashastra*, I, 4.

[48] Ibid.

[49] Ibid., I. 5. Kautilya cited it as 'तस्मादंडमुलास्तिस्त्रो विद्या:' where the first three branches of knowledge are highly relied over the concept of *Dandaniti*, an act of punishment.

[50] Pratap Chandra Ray, *The Mahabharata of Krishna-Dwaipayana Vyasa: Udyoga Parva* (Calcutta: Bharata Press, 1890).

[51] Ibid., in Shantiparva, ix, 28–79.

[52] Ibid., 22.

[53] Ibid., xii, 28–29.

The term Varna, besides its real interpretation, is considered as the caste and is blamed for the discrimination among the individuals in the society. None of the present thinkers and scholars have made a real interpretation of the term Varnas. Erroneously, the misleading myth is that the prevalent caste system, hierarchically dividing the society with intrinsic unequal structure, stemmed from the Varna system. Such disingenuous impression represents the false tendency of looking at the ancient Indian sociocultural organizations. Discussing the early Vedic period, V. M. Apte says that the Rigveda refers to the Varnas in such a manner that it cannot be considered as discriminatory or hierarchical. He elucidates that the Brahmanas do not constitute a high caste or race, officiating at the services of the deities, and they do not limit to the men of priestly families at the age of Rigveda. For him, there is no such ample evidence of prohibitions of inter-dining or intercaste marriage among the Varnas which are mostly considered as abhorrent acts in the contemporary time.[54] P. V. Kane's, a notable Indologist, interpretation of the Dharmashastra is relatable in this context in which he emphasizes that 'the discriminating provisions based on caste and the ascription of minor or grave sins had become a dead letter and were not being enforced by the Kings of India by the twelfth century CE at least'.[55] In contrast to the contemporary viewpoints over the distorted interpretation of Varnas, the egalitarianian view in texts, which was reflected through the *sāmvad* of Yudhiṣṭhira in the Mahābhārata, shows something that was really practised in the ancient India. According to the Mahābhārata,

> the marks of the shudra are found in a brahmin; but a shudra is not necessarily a shudra nor a brahmin a brahmin. In whomever a brahmin's marks are found, he is known as a brahmin and in whomever they are not found, him we designate as a shudra.[56]

[54] Arvind Sharma, *Hindu Egalitarianism* (New Delhi: Rupa Publishers, 2006), 61.

[55] Ibid., 60.

[56] Ibid., 43.

Bhupendranath Datta, throwing light on this issue, writes as follows: 'Varna was not a caste and, caste originally had an economic basis. It was the occupation of a group of men that determined their status in the society ... the *varna* was a fiction in historical period but the occupational grouping became the reality'.[57] Further, he added that 'the original Hindu society did not know the caste system. In the primeval days of the Vedas, the Varnas were the representation of the social grades and as such they were clauses and not stereotyped hereditary castes'.[58]

Coming to the term 'dharma',[59] derived from the root *dhri* meaning to hold and sustain, which is right from the beginning has been subjected to distorted meaning equating it with the Western notion religion. The two terms in two different traditions carry different meanings; nonetheless, misleading sense prevails and incessant effort gets piled up upon wrong sense, subsequently generating whole lot of ambiguous interpretation. For instance, dharma is not based on theology and institutions, rather it is merely a path of life. Dharma is, perhaps, the most comprehensive notion in the Hindu political thought.[60] It has been used and is still in existence since the days of Rigveda.[61] As advanced by many thinkers and scholars, dharma was sovereign in ancient India which acts as the natural law.[62] During the Vedic period, the term dharma signifies

[57] Bhupendranath Datta, *Studies in Indian Social Polity* (Calcutta: Purabi Publishers, 1944), 450–451.

[58] Ibid., 444.

[59] Dharma is the principle which can sustain any object. Gradually, it has its root from the term *dhri*. ध्रुवां भूमिं पृथ्वी धर्मणा घृताम, Atharva Veda, xii, p. 17.

[60] G. H. Mees has listed numerous meaning and implications of dharma. Dharma, sometimes, was the following: (a) ethical duty and virtue; (b) good works; (c) religious duty and virtue; (d) ideal society; (e) identical with God and absolute truth; (f) divine justice; (g) convention: code of customs and traditions; (h) common law; and (i) international or intertribal law. For more detail, G. H. Mees, *Dharma and Society* (London: N. V. Servire, The Hague and Luzac & Co., 1986), 8–9.

[61] *Rigveda*, I, 22, 18; I 164, 43, 50; iii, 3, I; iii, 60, 6.

[62] Benoy Sarkar, *The Political Institutions and Theories of the Hindus*, 207–210.

only ordinance and law; but when it is fused with the term *rita*,[63] it emanates the combined sense of the virtue and morality. The word 'dharma' also has been mentioned in the Upanishads.[64] In the Upanishads, the notion of dharma is rather broadly conceived. According to the Upanishad, there are, particularly, three branches of dharma: (a) sacrifice; (b) austerities; and (c) brahmacharin.[65] Moreover, the Vedic notion of law the concept of dharma assumed two meanings: (a) it became identified with a moral or an ethical view of life; and (b) it became identified with the social duties and orders.[66] According to Kautilya, dharma carries at least three meanings: (a) in the sense of social duty; (b) moral law based on truth; and (c) as civil law.[67] Even the concept of *Rajadharma* is comprised of *Dharmasutras*[68] from the Mahābhārata and Manusmriti. The concept of *Rajadharma* in *Kamandakiya Nitisara* is to act as *Parthiva*, the ruler of earth coming closer to modern conception of sovereign. *Rajadharma* in *the Rajdharmānusasana parva* of the Mahābhārata entails as follows: 'he is the best of kings

[63] *Rita* firmly stands for the order. It meant by the fixed and fundamental course of the natural objects. Beside the natural entity, it also stands for the physical order of the universe and ritualistic nature in the Vedic and post-Vedic period. According to Rudolf Otto, the term comes from the root *ar* (to arrange, to order and to regulate). Cited in Mees, *Dharma and Society*, 10.

[64] In Upanishad, the term 'dharma' meant as follows:

> dharma is the force of force or power of power. There is nothing higher than dharma. Henceforth, even a weak man rules a stronger person with the help of dharma, as with (the help of) a king. It is equivalent to truth. Hence, if a man speaks the truth, they say he speaks the dharma and if he speaks dharma, they say he speaks the truth.

For more detail, see Brihadaranyaka Upanishad, I, 4, 14.

[65] For more detail, see Chandogya Upanishad, ii, 23.

[66] For more detail, see Tattiriya Upanishad, I, 11.

[67] *Arthashastra*, vi, I.

[68] According to P. V. Kane (*The History of Dharmashashtra*, Vol. II, 965), the notable Indologist, the king is not only the head of the civil administration and the fountain of the justice but he is also the final controlling authority in preserving religious and spiritual institutions. The king is to punish the people for the branches of the religious and spiritual codes.

in whose dominions men live fearlessly like sons in the house of their sire'.[69] It was only the theory of *Rajadharma* which allows a king to use dharma or *adharma* simultaneously at the time of 'dharma at crisis'. Quoting a notable sage Bharadwaj's statements, Bhisma told Yudhiṣṭhira to use *Rajadharma* even in the most adverse and critical conditions and that the king is not supposed to divorce from ethical and moral path.[70]

In Shrimad Bhagavad Gita, Sri Kṛṣṇa also dealt with the theory of *Rajadharma* while talking to Arjuna:

> Besides, even if you consider your own duty, you ought not to falter, because there is nothing more meritorious to a *Kshatriya* than a warfare enjoined by duty. And O Partha! This war, which is indeed a door of heaven, found open without effort, falls to the lot of only those kshatriya's who are fortunate. But, if you will not carry on this righteous warfare, then you will have abandoned your duty and lost your honour and incurred sin.[71]

Dharma in later *Pāli* Buddhism found five categories in the following order: (a) *karmaniyama* or order of facts and result; (b) physical inorganic order; (c) order of plants: organic orders; (d) order of conscious life; and (e) order of dharma.[72] R. K. Mookerjee, throwing light on the dharma, holds that 'Hindu thought counts dharma as the true sovereign of the state, as the rule of law. The King is the executive called the *danda* to uphold and enforce the decree the dharma as the spiritual sovereign'.[73]

[69] Kamandakiya Nitisara, section iv, 33.

[70] 'A person or king should never act in accordance with these rules. These measures laid down by me (Bhisma) should be taken recourse to only in times of extreme distress. Inspired by the motive of doing good to you, I have said this for instructing you in counteracting the use of these measures by the enemy'. For more detail, see Shantiparva, xl, 70.

[71] Bhagavad Gita, ii, 31–33.

[72] Sarvapelli Radhakrishnan, *Indian Philosophy*, Vol. 1 (Oxford: Oxford University Press, 2009 [1923]), 374.

[73] R. K. Mookerjee, *Chandragupta Maurya and His Times*, (New Delhi: Rajkamal Publications, 1943), 79; idem, The Fundamental Unity of India, *Hindu Civilization*, (Bhartiya Vidya Bhawan, 1954), 100.

Conclusion

The Indian knowledge tradition predominantly has been served by Sanskrit as a potent traditional means of communication that descended from the Vedic period to the early modern period in the Indian history, encompassing religious and philosophical texts, poetry, prose, art, medicine, science, etc. Unfortunately, the interpretation of words or notions in the texts of Indian knowledge tradition, ascribed in the specific context drawing out specific meaning, has often been subjected to immense distortion. The in-depth understanding of the *sāstra-paddhiti* is a crucial factor. The transition of ancient Indian knowledge system from the concrete to abstract, materialism to idealism, *Cārvaka* to *Vedanta* and *Dhvāni* to *sābda-brahman* has moved in the opposite direction to the Western pattern of knowledge. Therefore, any attempt of overlapping the sense of a particular notion with other traditions is bound to damage the real meaning that our knowledge tradition tends to convey. This can be put in a re-paraphrased elucidation of Bhartrhari. He writes as follows: 'Mind acquires critical acumen by interacting with the other tradition; even though one knows nothing if he doesn't know about his own tradition'.[74] But unfortunately, how Kapil Kapoor reviews and comes up is as follows: 'now what does one know, knows almost nothing about his own tradition?'[75] In the present-day context, this can further be suitably re-paraphrased: if one does not know about his own tradition, then it is deliberately designed so as to not know.

[74] Bhartrhari, *Vakyapadiya*.

[75] Kapil Kapoor, *Knowledge, Individual and Society in Indian Tradition* (Chandigarh: Saini Memorial Foundation Lecture, Panjab University).

5

Violence and Non-violence in Indian Religious Traditions

Dinesh Kumar Singh

The study of the concept of violence/non-violence in the religious and philosophical traditions is a complex and sensitive subject. It has great relevance to understand and comprehend social and political processes in contemporary times.

The adherents of various religions characterize their traditions as a gospel of non-violence, peace and tolerance. Conversely, many people argue that the religion has been used for persecution, oppression, murder and torture of people who disclaim adherence. They substantiate their argument by citing examples of forced conversion in Christian and Islamic religions. Some argue that religion uses violence when it deviates from its ideal principle.

The idea of non-violence has featured in the discourse of Hindu, Buddhist, Jain and Sufi religious traditions. It was believed that social harmony, non-violence and tolerance of others' beliefs were central and guiding principles of ancient traditions. These unique features have been contrasted with those traditions which emphasize notions of crusade and Jihad. Despite the projected image of Indian religious traditions as a gospel of non-violence, violence has been observed in India's religious and philosophical traditions.

The civilization and intellectual roots of ancient India shaped the political thought of Gandhi and Nehru. Gandhi engaged with the idea of *yajñas* (sacrifice), ahimsa (non-violence) and renunciation which appeared in Indian religious traditions. Bhimrao Ambedkar engaged with the Indian philosophical traditions for the emancipation of Dalits from the iniquitous Hindu social order. The ideas of violence and non-violence were reflected in the writings of Ambedkar. The chapter attempts to look at the issue of violence and non-violence in Hindu religious text, Buddhist text, and other literature and practices of ancient India. It seeks to explore new perspectives on this issue.

Gandhi engaged himself with the Hindu, Jain, Buddhist religious traditions and their world view of non-violence, sacrifice and renunciation. The Bhagavad Gita was seen by him as a treatise which espoused the theory of non-violence. He believed that the idea of non-violence is deeply rooted in Indian religious traditions. He used the concept of truth and non-violence as a powerful strategy to launch an anti-colonial movement.[1]

Bhimrao Ambedkar seriously engaged himself with Indian religious traditions. He reflected on the Hindu social and religious issues from rationalist perspectives. The main purpose of his engagement with the philosophy of Hinduism was to provide a creative critique of Hinduism and to establish casteless society which would be based on the principle of justice. His two important books, *Philosophy of Hinduism* and *The Hindu Social Order: Its Essential Principles*, critiqued the existing Hindu

[1] Bhikhu Parekh, *Colonialism, Tradition and Reform: An Analysis of Gandhi's Political Discourse* (New Delhi: SAGE Publications, 1989); Shruti Kapila and Faisal Devji, eds., *Political Thought in Action: The Bhagavad Gita and Modern India* (Delhi: Cambridge University Press, 2013).

social order based on the philosophy of Hinduism.[2] He was of opinion that the principle of equality, liberty and fraternity had no place in Hinduism. He considered Buddhism as the 'gospel of non-violence'. Like Buddha, he supported justified violence. He suggested the untouchables for embracing Buddhism which stood for equality and fraternity. He considered Buddha as a rationalist and progressive religious thinker.[3]

Vinayak Damodar Savarkar understood the Hindu religious text and ancient history differently. He was the most important Indian thinker who wanted to Hinduize politics and militarize Hindu. He considered non-violence in negative connotations. He emphasized the necessity of violence for the Hindus to fight foreign aggressors. He considered Gita's battle literally. He developed the argument about an 'ethical premise of violence against non-Hindus in India'.[4]

Vedic Period and Non-violence

The idea of non-violence and non-violence in the Vedic rituals has appeared in the writings of the authors of numerous philosophical, legal, epical, poetical and other works in the Sanskritic-Prākrtic tradition up to the modern day. The important studies by P. V. Kane, Ludwig Alsdorf, Hanns-Peter Schmidt,

[2] B. R. Ambedkar, *Philosophy of Hinduism*, in Dr Babasaheb Ambedkar: Writings and Speeches, Vol. 3, Compiled by Vasant Moon (Bombay: Education Department, Government of Maharashtra, 1987); Idem, *The Hindu Social Order: Its Essential Principles*, in Dr Babasaheb Ambedkar: Writings and Speeches, Vol. 3, Compiled by Vasant Moon (Bombay: Education Department, Government of Maharashtra, 1987).

[3] B. R. Ambedkar, *Buddha or Karl Marx*, Critical Quest, taken from BAWS, Vol. III (New Delhi: Education Department, Government of Maharashtra, 1987).

[4] Vinayak Chaturvedi, 'Rethinking Knowledge with Action: V. D. Savarkar, the Bhagavad Gita and Histories of Warfare', in *Political Thought in Action: The Bhagavad Gita and Modern India*, eds. Shruti Kapila and Faisal Devji (Delhi: Cambridge University Press, 2013), 158.

Jan C. Heesterman, Boris Oguibenine, Herman W. Tull, Henk Bodewitz and Upinder Singh are concerned with the Vedic and Dharmashastric literature.[5]

Conflict, war and violence were prevalent in the Vedic period. After intoxicating Soma's drinks, God Indra smites his enemies with his thunderbolt. The Rigveda, which is the oldest Vedas, narrates the story of Indra who represents masculine ethos. It tells the story of not only a fierce battle between different groups of Aryans but also between Aryans and Dasa or Dasyus. In the Vedic times, the tribal chief or clan chief ruled over the state. The post-Vedic period witnessed the emergence of the hereditary king. Kurus was the first state in India which appeared in the narrative of the Vedic texts. The emergence of the monarchical states was intimately connected with the Varna hierarchy which was emerging. The Abhishek ceremony was in practice for the sprinkling of water at the time of anointing the king. The practice of sacrifice such as the Rajasuya, Vajapeya and Asvamedha prevailed where the king used to stand in the centre. The king was symbolically elevated to a position of a paramount power through these sacrifices. The Vedic text presents narratives in which kings and clan chieftains appear as warriors, as a protector of the Brahmanas and as performers of sacrifice.[6]

It is very difficult to construct a narrative of ahimsa in the early Vedic text. The story tells the tale of sacrifice and violence which was in the form of victim immolation. It was full of tales of sacrifice in which the sacrificers vied with each other for wealth such as cattle. The deadly contest, sacrifice and counter sacrifices have been narrated in the text. Brahmodayas practice (question and answer) in the form of verbal contest was prevalent in which

[5] Jan E. M. Houben, 'To Kill or Not to Kill the Sacrificial Animal (Yajnapasu)? Arguments and Perspectives in Brahminical Ethical Philosophy', in *Violence Denied, Violence, Non-violence and the Rationalization of Violence in South Asian Cultural History*, eds. Jan E. M. Houben and Karel R. Van Kooij (Leiden & Boston: Brill, 1999), 107.

[6] Upinder Singh, *Political Violence in Ancient India* (London: Harvard University Press, 2017), 22–24.

vituperation is heightened, and this process reaches a point where the loser remains silent or accepts death. Laurie Patton observes the following:

> One passage in a Vedic ritual text mentions the passing of a car, or chariot, through someone else's sacrificial fires and ritual enclosure, thus signifying a kind of battle. And even in the most innocuous of Vedic rituals, the agnihotr, sacrificer still retains a vajra, a sword.[7]

Heesterman discusses that the idea of violence is inherent in sacrifice. In the most well-known story of Sunahsepa, Varun was persuaded by king Hariscandra's rigid *tapas* to give him a son. A son was given to him on the divine condition that the king sacrifice him back to the god. Brahmana Sunahsepa is persuaded by the king to substitute for sacrifice. When Sunahsepa is about to be killed, he recites the correct mantra. He finally succeeds in releasing himself, the king and his son. Sage Vishvamitra adopts Sunahsepa. The adoption witnessed rivalry and violence amongst his brothers.[8]

Sacrifice involves death and death involves sacrifice. There is discussion of human sacrifice in the *Satapatha Brahmana*. A hymn refers to a primeval sacrifice in which a giant named Purusha was the victim. Houben observes that when the description of the sacrifice reaches the position when the victim is likely to be sacrificed, the language of the text changes to a narrative mode and past tense: 'Victims had the fire carried around them, but were not yet slaughtered. Then a voice says to the sacrificer and priests, addressing them as Purusa: Do not establish (samtisthipa) them (as victims), because if you did establish them, purusa would eat purusa'.[9] There is strong evidence that Vedic text represents a

[7] Laurie L. Patton, 'Telling Stories about Harm: An Overview of Early Indian Narratives', in *Religion and Violence in South Asia: Theory and Practice*, eds. John R. Hinnells and Richard King (London: Routledge, 2007), 13–14.

[8] Ibid., 16.

[9] Quoted in Ibid., 14.

masculine martial ideology that justified promoted and directed violence against the people outside of a tribe.[10]

The Upanishadic philosophy emphasized esoteric knowledge which talks about liberation from the cycle of birth, death and rebirth. It used sacrifice as a reference point. It focused upon the ideas of eternal self (Atman) and world soul (Brahmana). The Upanishad and Aranyakas do not reject the sacrifice in the favour of philosophy. They debate, redefine and interiorize sacrifice.

Dharmashastra was a new discipline which was devoted to explication and discussion of dharma. P. V. Kane was of opinion that early Dharmashastra was documented in the 6th century BCE.[11] Early Dharmashastra came to be known as Dharmasutras. Except for two references of ahimsa in the Chandogya Upanishad, non-violence, as a principle, appears for the first time in the Dharmashastra.[12] The Dharmasutras codify violence as a function of caste ideology and connects violence and dharma with the duties of the four Varnas and life stage of Ashrama system. The punishment for killing was decided on the basis of Varna and caste system. *Apastambha Dharmasutra*, *Vashistha Dharmasutra* and *Gautama Dharmasutra* codify violence to standing of the individual in the social structure.[13]

Renunciation, Asceticism and Non-violence

The origin of Jainism is older than Buddhism. The emergence of Jainism and Upanishadic thoughts are reported at the same time. Both Jainism and Buddhism heralded the break with the Vedic religious thought. Jain philosophy approached the

[10] Singh, *Political Violence in Ancient India*, 24.

[11] P. V. Kane, *History of Dharmasastra*, Vols. 2 & 3 (Pune: Bhandarkar Oriental Research Institute, 1941–1946).

[12] Henk W. Bodewitz, 'Hindu Ahimsa and Its Roots', in *Violence Denied, Violence, Non-violence and the Rationalization of Violence in South Asian Cultural History*, eds. Jan E. M. Houben and Karel R. Van Kooij (Leiden & Boston: Brill, 1999), 23.

[13] Patton, 'Telling Stories about Harm', 30–31.

relationship between power and knowledge with new perspectives. Renunciation and non-violence became the most debated ideas in Indian culture with the emergence of Buddhist and Jain religious traditions.[14]

This period witnessed the emergence of the beginning of critique of violence and propagation of ideas of non-violence. Three types of answers are advanced for locating the idea of non-violence in Indian religious traditions. The relationship between Brahmanical, Jain and Buddhist asceticism remains a matter of dispute among the scholars for more than a century. Jacoby Herman was of opinion that Brahmanas did not borrow asceticism from the Jain and Buddhist. The *Baudhayana Dharmasutra* rules for ascetics predate a developed Buddhism and Jainism. [15]

One school of thought opined that the idea of non-violence originated within Brahmanical Vedic tradition. H. P. Schmidt is exponent of this thought. He observes the following[16]:

> From a casual survey of the material collected in the preceding paragraphs it might appear that the idea of ahmisa originated among the world-renouncers, was gradually adopted by the Brahmanas and was finally considered to be rule for the whole society whose values were determined by the precedent of the Brahmins.

He connects the ahimsa doctrine with the Atman doctrine, which opines that there is an Atman in all living beings. Killing a living being would mean killing the Atman. Another school of thought saw it as originating from non-Vedic tradition, which was exemplified as Buddhism and Jainism. According to a third school, the idea of non-violence emerged simultaneously in the Brahmanical, Buddhist and Jain religious traditions. Heesterman and Alsdorf were of opinion that ahimsa was not a monopoly of Jains and

[14] Ibid. Also see Patrick Olivelle, *Ascetics and Brahmins: Studies in Ideologies and Institutions* (London: Anthem Press, 2011).

[15] Houben, 'To Kill or Not to Kill the Sacrificial Animal', 132.

[16] Henk W. Bodewitz, 'Hindu Ahimsa and Its Roots', in *Violence Denied, Violence, Non-violence and the Rationalization of Violence in South Asian Cultural History*, eds. Jan E. M. Houben and Karel R. Van Kooij (Leiden & Boston: Brill, 1999), 23.

Buddhists but, on the contrary, was a common Indian movement in which Brahmanism, Buddhism and Jainism shared equality.[17] Asceticism and renunciation prevailed within the Brahmanic Vedic and Upanishadic traditions. But these ideas and practices became more pronounced during the emergence of Buddhism and Jainism. Both traditions rejected the Vedic religious thought and its notion of sacrifice. It vigorously emphasized that salvation consisted in lifelong celibate renunciation. They created monastic order for monks and nuns and provided institutional space for renunciants for building strong sense of community identity. Non-violence was the central focus of both Jainism and Buddhism.

Jain Religion and Issue of Non-violence and Violence

The abstinence from violence is more pronounced in Jainism than in all religions of the world. The members of the Jain monastery and the laity were required to vow non-violence. Among the world's religions, the Jain followed the principle of non-violence more vigorously. They present themselves as the adherents of the 'religion of non-violence'. Ahimsa as the ethical concept was considered as the central principle of the Jain religious thought. The Jain authors maintained that it lies at the base of the distinctive Jain ontology. *Ahimsa paramo dharmah*, that is, 'non-violence is the highest religion' is an important slogan of Jainism. The idea of ahimsa as the central principle gets reflected in both older Jain literary writings and contemporary writings. The principle of ahimsa influenced the Jain in performing Jain worship, and consequently, they adopted the non-Aryan puja. The principle of non-violence has been an important guiding principle of moral and spiritual virtues of Jain religious traditions. The following has been commented about the Jain traditions and Parshva, the 23rd Tirthankara:

> Various ethical themes in Jain teaching come together in the figure of this fordmaker: compassion, non-violence, fellowship with all

[17] Ibid., 29.

> living creatures.... Jainism can today be said to be an actively proselytizing religion only in that it advocates the universal practice of vegetarianism and non-violence.[18]

The Jain tradition sees the universe as inhabited by sentient beings ranging from humans with five senses to tiny organism called *Nigodas* with single senses. They believed that the plants, earth, water, fire and air are inhabited with sentient beings. They graded the level of value of harming. Harming a *Nigoda* is not so serious when it is compared to harming an animal. It is suggested that harming living beings involves suffering to both the victim and persons who carry the act. They prescribed the laity and Jain monks to desist from injuring living beings. Jain monks are expected to follow strict rules and take care of not harming or injuring any kind of living beings. Vegetarianism was strictly observed by the laity, Jain monks and nuns. This practice was not strictly followed in the Buddhist religious traditions.[19] The Jain tradition's excessive concern for ahimsa and protection of the smallest life forms has been ridiculed and criticized. It was seen as a tradition which stands for vegetarianism. Sinclair Stevenson in her book *The Heart of Jainism* ridiculed the claims of Jain tradition. She portrayed the hollowness of the 'heart of Jainism'.[20]

Question was raised regarding the impossibility of practising the principle of non-violence in the absolute terms. The Jain tradition tried to resolve this problem by classifying violence into different categories. They differentiated violence which emerged due to unintentional injury from violence which originated from intentional harm. Violence may emerge from self-defence for the protection of the life of monks and the laity. This kind of violence

[18] Robert J. Zydenbos, 'Jainism as the Religion of Non-violence', in *Violence Denied, Violence, Non-violence and the Rationalization of Violence in South Asian Cultural History*, eds. Jan E. M. Houben and Karel R. Van Kooij (Leiden & Boston: Brill, 1999), 185–186.

[19] Singh, *Political Violence in Ancient India*, 27. Also see, Padmanabh S. Jaini, *The Jaina Path of Purification* (Delhi: Motilal Banarsidass, 1979), 167–172.

[20] Zydenbos, 'Jainism as the Religion of Non-violence', 186.

was justified in certain circumstances. The justification of violence in the defence of a monk can be found in *Uttaradhyayana Sutra* of the 3rd century. The descriptions are that Hariskesa, an untouchable who has become Jain monk, is attacked by Brahmanas when he was seeking for alms. A deity intervened the attack and beat up the Brahmanas. The narrative described here attempts to establish the moral superiority of Jain ethical values over Brahmanical moral values. This kind of violence was portrayed as a form of necessary violence, and it was justified. It clearly shows that violence can be justified when there is a threat to the monks.[21] From 6th to 7th centuries CE, the *Brhatkalpa Bhasya* of Sanghadasa was considered as the most authoritative text on the monastic rules of the Jain tradition. It justified violence on the part of Jain monks to protect their fellow renunciants. It defended the killing of five-sensed living beings while defending the monastic group. It describes the narrative of the monk who killed three lions while his companions slept in the monastery.[22]

Violence as an idea has figured in the Jain doctrinal text. Sutra VII:13 of the *Tattvartha Sutra*, an important text of the Jain tradition, defines violence as 'the harming of life under the influence of the passions'. Pujyapada, Bhaskaranandi and many other commentators have unanimously agreed about the interrelationship between Kasaya and violence. In Jain text, Kasaya is defined as passion. Commenting on it, *Purusarthasiddhyupaya* of Amratacandra Suri, a text of the 10th or 11th century, argues the following:

> All this is himsa, because it is the cause of harm in the form of affecting the soul. Falsehood etc. are mentioned merely for the sake of instructing the pupil. Whatever is a cause of injury to life forces (pranas) in their objective or subjective form, due to association

[21] Paul Dundas, 'The Non-Violence of Violence: Jain Perspectives on Warfare, Asceticism and Worship', in *Religion and Violence in South Asia: Theory and Practice*, eds. John R. Hinnells and Richard King (London: Routledge, 2007), 44.

[22] S. B. Deo, *History of Jain Monachism* (Poona: Deccan College, 1956), 388.

> with Kasaya, is surely himsa. The non-appearance of attachment etc. is ahimsa; the summary of Jain scripture is that their appearance alone is himsa. There is no himsa in the case of one who is firm in his conduct and who is not affected by attachment etc., because it is only due to injury of life-forces (that there is himsa).[23]

The renunciants are expected to strictly follow the avoidance of himsa, but there was relaxation for the laity. It prescribed *mahavratas* or great vows for the renunciants and *anuvratas* or lesser vows for the lay people. The vow of ahimsa prevailed in both the vows. The laity who are burdened with the task of everyday mundane activities 'can not avoid a certain degree of himsa in daily life'.[24]

The practice of warfare and military violence figured in the scriptural text of Jainism. The *Bhagavati Sutra*, the largest text of the Jain tradition written in the early centuries of the Common Era, portrayed the Jain perception of war and military violence. It described two battles which took place during Mahavira's lifetime in which large-scale violence took place. In the 'Battle of the Thorns like Great Stones', king Kuniya defeated a tribal confederacy, which involved the death of 8,400,000 combatants. A similar massacre took place in another battle where he was engaged. The text recounts how Gautama, Mahavira's disciple, held the view that a combatant killed in a war is reborn in heaven. But Mahavira comments upon this event and rejects the idea that dead soldiers in a battle will go to heaven and declares that they will be reborn in the lower realms of the existence as animals. He gives an example of advanced Jain Varuna to clarify further that his decision to fight in self-defence and the piety of his death led to his rebirth in heaven. The narrative of Varuna, a highly religious person of Vaishali, tells us that he was compelled by king Kuniya to fight in the battle. He vowed not to attack anybody until he himself was attacked. In the war, a deeply wounded Varuna killed his foe. He left the battlefield, paid homage to Mahavira

[23] Zydenbos, 'Jainism as the Religion of Non-Violence', 195–196.
[24] Ibid., 197.

and died a religious death. It was narrated in the text that all the warriors who fight in self-defence and then die in battle are reborn in heaven. The text was influenced by a Hindu epic, and it discussed the martial world that is portrayed in it where a glorious death in a battle is reckoned to lead to death. It does not condemn the outbreak of war. The perusal of the Jain versions of the Hindu epics and Puranas of the medieval times shows the necessity of violence to maintain social morality. There are several Jain versions of Rāmāyaṇa where the story of Rama and Sita are depicted in accordance with the Jain tradition.[25]

The Jain tradition's attitude towards war varies. The story of the principle of non-violence as adopted by the Jain warriors was narrated in the famous story of 'Bahubali'. In the 8th century, Jinasena, in his work *Adipurana*, describes the narrative of Bahubali trying to prevent a full-fledge battle with his half-brother Bharata for inheriting their father's kingdom. He defeats his enemy and refrains from killing him and leaves the battlefield for the forest in search for liberation. Unlike the Bhagavad Gita where Arjuna is urged by Kṛṣṇa to fight the Kauravas at the battle of Kurukshetra, this Jain text does not subscribe to the creative role of battle. It suggests that the requirements of warfare can be balanced by non-violence.[26] In his famous work entitled *Samayasara*, the Digambara Jain monk alludes to the philosophy of Bhagavad Gita. Kṛṣṇa's famous sermon in the Bhagavad Gita narrated the ultimate impossibility of killing or being killed due to the immortality of the soul. Kundakunda states the following: 'He who thinks I kill or am being killed by other beings is foolish and ignorant. The man of knowledge is at variance with this'. He located this philosophy in the Jain karmic theory. Differing with the Bhagavad Gita's philosophy, he emphasized that death and killing are the outcomes of the actions in the previous existence which are responsible for a particular intensity of life-karma.[27]

[25] Dundas, 'The Non-violence of Violence', 45–46.
[26] Ibid., 46.
[27] Ibid., 46–47.

The *Sthananga Sutra*, a Jain canonical text of probably the early Common Era, discusses the case of asceticism. The *Parisaha* constitutes an internal part of the ascetic life of the Jain monk and nun. It consists of a regularly performed religious exercises and self-mortification in the form of fasting to destroy karma. This practice of asceticism was considered as a form of violence on the ground that he inflicts violence upon his body. It is considered as a form of self-sacrifice. It is basically a reconfiguration of the ancient Vedic ritual offering. In a reaction to these Jain religious practices, early Buddhism de-emphasized the role of asceticism. Jain religious tradition's response to various kinds of violence is that an attempt should be made to minimize rather than eliminate violence. It distinguishes between different levels of violence and different levels of truth, a mundane and soteriological.[28] In the Jain tradition, respect for life, charity towards suffering living beings and principle of non-violence have got important positions. But it has an ascetic tendency. Compared to the world's most organized religion, it is the most ascetic. The monks, nuns and renunciants are expected to strictly follow austerity and engage in fasts. It is believed in the Jain tradition that these practices motivate individuals to detach from the external world. Sallekhana or Samadhimarana is a practice which advocates the separation of the soul from its physical body. The Jain religious death of Sallekhana is considered with very high reverence. The persons who have died in these practices have been commemorated in literature, monuments and inscriptions. These practices may seem violent to the people of other religion. It is antithetical to the principle of non-violence which has been the cardinal ethical value of the Jain tradition.[29]

The Jain doctrine believes in the principle of non-violence. The kings and ministers of the Gangas, the Rashtrakutas and the Hoysalas, well-known dynasties of South India, were supporters of the Jain religion. They planned and engaged in the wars to expand the dominion of the state. General Chamundaraya of

[28] Ibid., 48–50.
[29] Zydenbos, 'Jainism as the Religion of Non-violence', 187–188.

the Ganga dynasty in the 10th century was a renowned ferocious person in the battlefield; he had Jain leanings, and he patronized the statue of the Jain saint Bahubali known as Gommateshwara at Shravanabelagola in Karnataka.[30] Paul Dundas maintains that Indian historians faced the dilemma of describing the activities of Jain kings. The kingship even involved violent activities.[31]

Buddhism and Non-violence

Buddhism is associated with the principle of non-violence. It advocates precepts of non-violence. The Buddhist monk, the laity and the king are advised to follow it. B. R. Ambedkar has summarized the basic tenets of Buddhism which has been derived from the Tripitaka. To view God as the centre of religion is discarded in the Buddhist religious traditions. It does not consider salvation as the centre of religion; it discards the practice of animal sacrifice as the centre of religion; it treats all human beings as equal. It denounces war unless it is for truth and justice.[32]

The physical, verbal and mental aspects come under the idea of violence. The physical conduct that causes unwholesome states to increase and wholesome states to diminish includes murderous activity and activity inflicting injury and harm. Harsh, hurtful and offensive speech are verbal conduct that cause unwholesome states to increase. Unwholesome mental conduct includes ill-will, hatred and the idea of injuring or killing. The dharma prescribes righteous conduct which causes the unwholesome state to diminish and wholesome state to increase. One scholar comments as follows: 'Here someone, abandoning the killing of living beings, abstains from killing living beings; with rod and weapon laid aside, gently and kindly, he abides compassionate to all living beings'.[33]

[30] Ibid., 188.
[31] Ibid., 191–192.
[32] B. R. Ambedkar, *Buddha or Karl Marx*, 3–4.
[33] Singh, *Political Violence in Ancient India*, 39.

Buddhism prescribes benevolence to living beings. It is an important principle which the monks, the laity and the king must follow. The Buddhist text vehemently criticizes animal sacrifice. The Kutadanda Sutta describes the narrative that 700 bulls and rams were tied to sacrificial posts and were ready for slaughter. The Buddha in the meantime arrives and tells the story of the King Mahavijita who was ready for animal sacrifice. He was dissuaded by his chaplain not to perform the sacrifice. The king agreed and performed a bloodless sacrifice. The Buddha disclosed that he was the same chaplain in the earlier birth. He preached his followers the futility of bloody animal sacrifice. He prescribed his followers to give gifts to ascetics, provide shelter for the monastic order and to follow dharma. These activities are more effective than the *yajñas*. He argued that the attainment of enlightenment is the highest sacrifice.[34]

In one of the early Buddhist texts, the *arhat* (perfected Buddhist saint) is advised to restrain themself from knowingly depriving a living being of life. Another Buddhist text depicted the following:

> that: 'a man or woman who kills living beings, who is murderous, who has blood on his or her hands, who is given to blows and violence, who is without pity for living beings' will as a result be reborn 'in a state of misfortune, an unhappy place, a state of affliction, hell.[35]

A group of three Buddhist text narrates the response of Buddha when he was approached by professional soldiers asking the questions which they had heard about a soldier who was killed when he was engaged in battle and will reborn among the gods. The Buddha discards this mistaken belief and opines that they will be born in hell. Other texts narrate the attitude of Buddha towards non-violence. It describes how the Buddha himself

[34] Ibid., 40.

[35] Rupert Gethin, 'Buddhist Monks, Buddhist Kins, Buddhist Violence: On the Early Buddhist Attitude to Violence', in *Religion and Violence in South Asia: Theory and Practice*, eds. John R. Hinnells and Richard King (London: Routledge, 2007), 59.

'refrains from killing living creatures, discards sticks and swords, and is considerate and full of concern, remaining sympathetic and well disposed towards all creatures and beings'.[36] The Buddha's teachings prescribe benevolence to living beings and advises the followers to turn away from violence towards all living beings. Theravada Buddhist ritual has chanted the message which has been depicted in the Buddhist text *Metta Sutta* or *Discourse on Friendliness*. It aspires to ensure protection and safety to humanity. It quotes as follows:

> one should not wish another pain out of anger or thoughts of enmity. Just as a mother would protect with her life her own son, her only son, so one should cultivate the immeasurable mind towards all living being and friendliness towards the whole world.[37]

The earliest Buddhist text such as Pali Nikayas and Chinese Agamas have condemned violence in all its forms. It prescribed monks and the laity to cultivate the virtues of friendliness and compassion towards the whole world. All forms of violence were renounced by the Buddhist tradition.[38]

Buddhism: Kingship, War, Punishment and Peace

The issue of political violence was raised in the Samyutta Nikaya. It tells the story of a period when Buddha was living among the Kosalans in a small hut. Buddha reflects in the following words: 'Is it possible to exercise rulership righteously; without killing and without instigating others to kill, without confiscating and without instigating others to confiscate, without sorrowing and without causing sorrow?'[39]

The Buddhist ethical principle emphasized non-violence, but it was difficult for the king to rule without engaging in violence. He

[36] Ibid.
[37] Ibid.
[38] Ibid., 62.
[39] Singh, *Political Violence in Ancient India*, 40.

permitted the use of force. The Buddha responded to a question asked by a senapati or the commander–in–chief of Vaishali. He asked Buddha: 'The Bhagvan preaches ahimsa. Does the Bhagvan preach an offender to be given freedom from punishment? ... Does the Tathagata prohibit all war even it is in the interest of Truth and Justice?'[40]

Buddha replied as follows:

> You have wrongly understood what I have been preaching. An offender must be punished and innocent man must be freed.... A man who fights for justice and safety cannot be accused of himsa. If all the means of maintaining peace have failed, then the responsibility for himsa falls on him who starts the war.[41]

The strict application of the Buddhist ethical principle of benevolence to all living beings symbolizes the rejection of all kinds of war. The stories depicted in the Jataka and its commentary narrate the story of Prince Temiya who abhors the horrible kind of violence associated with the kingship and decides to become an ascetic. There is a story of King Mahasilavant who does not defend himself by military forces when attacked by enemy forces. Quoting a warning directed at a Turkish chieftain, P. Demieville observes that 'Buddhism makes people good and weak and is, in its principle, opposed to war and violent conflicts'.[42]

Ashoka considered himself as a Buddhist *upasaka* (follower) and had been associated with the Buddhist sangh. There are two distinct sets of sources of evidence to find out Ashoka's attitude towards violence and non-violence. A set of contemporary edicts and inscriptions is the first source and a set of legends depicted in the Buddhist texts such as *Ashokavadana* and *Mahavamsa* is the other source. Ashoka came to rule the Mauryan throne in

[40] Ambedkar, *Buddha or Karl Marx*, 12.

[41] Ibid.

[42] Quoted in Lambert Schmithausen, 'Buddhist Attitude towards War', in *Violence Denied, Violence, Non-violence and the Rationalization of Violence in South Asian Cultural History*, eds. Jan E. M. Houben and Karel R. Van Kooij (Leiden & Boston: Brill, 1999), 51–52.

269 BCE and expanded the territory of his kingdom. He engaged himself in the Kalinga War. The 13th major rock edict talks about his remorse at the death of over 100,000 Kalingans. He bemoans suffering which was caused by the war and military campaign. Other inscriptions speak of his leaning towards Buddhism. He even supported to Ajivikas. His policy strives for tolerance and mutual understanding among different religious groups. He motivates the people to respect the ascetic and Brahmanas. The central aspects of Ashoka's dharma were benevolence and non-violence towards all living beings. As opposed to violence, he talks about conquest by means of dharma. He appeals to the people of his kingdom to refrain from anger and injuring and killing all living beings. He himself refrains from harming and killing living beings. It also indicates that he may have abolished capital punishment.[43]

Buddhacharita, *Ashokavadana*, *Mahavamsa* and Jataka were the most important Buddhist texts which discussed the relationship between the king and Buddhahood in contrasting perspectives. In Buddhism, different models of kingship emerged. In the Buddhacharita, renunciation and enlightenment were considered as superior to kingship. The kingship was rejected, and renunciation and enlightenment got prominence. In the *Ashokavadana*, the king was seen as a religious patron. He was seen as a proselytizer as opposed to the principle of non-violence. The Jatakas portray a king who possesses the virtue of compassion and self-sacrifice. The representation of a king based on the Buddhist sites does not portray the king in a military role. The king has been shown as a religious person and a donor. But Ashoka's visit to Ramagrama on a military mission is an exception.[44] Buddhist texts *Ashokavadana* and *Mahavamsa* portray Ashoka as an uncompromising and exclusive supporter of Buddhism. In *Ashokavadana*, 18,000 Jains/Ajivikas were killed because of one Jain follower's portrayal of a picture depicting the Buddha bowing down at the feet of their master. Such violent acts against

[43] Gethin, 'Buddhist Monks, Buddhist Kins, Buddhist Violence', 70.
[44] Singh, *Political Violence in Ancient India*, 175.

the followers of other religious schools were not condoned by Ashoka. Buddhist text *Mahavamsa* emphasizes the king Dutthagamani in a violent role.[45]

One cannot deny the inevitability of war and conflict within the system of kinship. The kingship cannot function without war and conflict. But there has been a contradiction between the Buddhist teaching and prevailing historical reality. Theravada Buddhist monk composed an important text known as *Mahavamsa* on the island of Lanka a little before 500 CE. The text narrates that Dutthagamani, fearless wicked leader, wanted to become the ruler of the whole of the island of Lanka. In his military campaign, he wreaked havoc and slaughtered millions of people. The king was distraught at these events. A group of eight *arhats* declares that the king's deed is not a hindrance in any way to heaven. They ignored the slaughter of millions and justified violence.[46]

Early Buddhist thought condemns the acts of violence. The systematic literature of both the Theravada and Sarvastivada Abhidharma similarly condemns violent acts. One can notice the variety of attitude towards violence in Theravada Buddhist text. For understanding the ambivalence of attitude towards violence, Steven Collins divides 'the protean category of dharma' into two modes. In the first mode, dharma functions as the practical moral framework and depends on circumstances. Here violence is allowed. In its second mode, dharma considers all forms of violence as wrong.[47] Schmithausen observes the following:

> one of reasons for the frequency of war even in Theravada Buddhist countries seems to have been that in these countries governments and politics continued to be guided to a large extent by their own system of values, which, being derived from, or at least strongly influenced by, ancient Indian of law, politics and administration, focused on maintaining and extending

[45] Gethin, 'Buddhist Monks, Buddhist Kins, Buddhist Violence', 70–73.
[46] Ibid., 59–60.
[47] Steven Collins, *Nirvana and Other Buddhist Felicities: Utopias of the Pali Imaginaire* (Cambridge: Cambridge University Press, 1998), 451–466.

> power and were thus quite different from the Buddhist system of values.[48]

In the later period, Buddhism justified the violence of a king. It even justified the violence of rebels. Buddhist traditions advocated the separation of a king from renunciants and gave primacy to the latter's supremacy.

The discourse on non-violence did not have major impact in the field of political sphere because of the ambivalent attitude of the dominant intellectual and religious traditions.

The king's use of force and war was not rejected by Buddhist and Jain texts. It was recognized that it was impossible for the king to practice absolute non-violence. The religious texts and political narratives of ancient histories of North India showed a fierce competition between Brahmanism, Buddhism and Jainism. Ashoka's edict conveyed the dissension and discord within the Buddhist sanghs. The 12th major rock edict indicates religious discord.

The complex relationship between a king and a Brahmana could not be resolved in Hinduism. It could not establish the superiority of dharma over the King. It remained ambiguous. But both Jainism and Buddhism established the superiority of Jina or Budha over the king.

The Mahābhārata and Rāmāyaṇa: Non-violence and Violence

The Mahābhārata is an important Hindu religious epic which is full of ambiguities and contradictions. Dharma, kingship, violence, non-violence and war have been discussed from multiple perspectives in the epic. When the characters of the epic are faced with dilemma and perplexed questions, the answers offered by

[48] Schmithausen, 'Buddhist Attitude towards War', 52.

them indicates several alternatives. The characters take their decisions after engaging in deliberations with others. It does not provide quick and readymade solutions to the most fundamental problems of human existence. It discusses serious moral questions in narrative forms. A vibrant discourse on moral philosophy is found in the Mahābhārata.[49]

The Mahābhārata contains many stances which tell the story of violence. It is pervaded by violence. Kṛṣṇa, while driving the chariot in the battlefield of Kurukshetra, urges Arjuna to take up arms and fight the battle. It advocates to Arjuna to follow Kshatriya Dharama in accordance with Hindu Philosophy of life. But it also contains different alternative positions. It is claimed by our sages that ancient Hindu traditions condemned himsa and advocated the principle of ahimsa. Bhisma, the paragon of knowledge and grand uncle of Pandavas, hands over dictum to Yudhiṣṭhira in *Anusasanaparvan*. The dictum *ahimsa paramo dharmah* or 'non-violence is the highest religion' should be observed by the Brahmanas and renouncers. While responding to a question by Yudhiṣṭhira regarding dharma, Bhisma tells the story of an encounter between a Brahmana ascetic named Jajali and Jain monk Tuladhara. At the end of the story, Tuladhara's teaching of non-violence prevails as the true path of liberation. The philosophy of harmlessness finds expression in the Mahābhārata. In the *Anusasanaparavan*, Yudhiṣṭhira asks the questions to God Brhaspati, who happens to pass by Bhisma's bed of arrows. Brhaspati teaches the lesson of non-violence and advocates abstention from hunting animals. After listening to Brhaspati's teachings on non-violence which are familiar within the Upanishadic and Brahmanical traditions, Bhisma advocates the practice of vegetarianism. He argues that it should be practiced by both renouncers and the laity. Dumont opined that the

[49] Singh, *Political Violence in Ancient India*, 60. See Bimal Matilal, 'Moral Dilemmas: Insights from the Epics', in *The Collected Works of Bimal Krishna Matilal*, ed. Jonardon Ganeri (New Delhi: Oxford University Press), 2015, 22–23.

practice of non-violence and vegetarianism was introduced to the Hindu society from Buddhist and Jain renouncers.[50] Non-violence is the greatest dharma for all Varnas. The Mahābhārata combines notions of self-control, non-violence, austerity, oneness and yogic samadhi into a unified practice and ideology.

Alf Hiltebeitel observes that *paramo dharmah* occurs 54 times in the Mahābhārata, and it is conjoined with the word ahimsa only four times. Non-violence was ideal for the renunciants, and it was very difficult to practice it in absolute terms. Anrsamsya (compassion) also occurs in the Mahābhārata. It is understood as goodwill and empathy. Anrsamsya was the practice followed by the people in a worldly life. *Anrsamsyam paro dharmah* or 'non-cruelty is the supreme dharma' features eight times in the Mahābhārata. It has more positive connotations than ahimsa.[51] The 'Aranyaka Parvan' narrates the dialogue between Yudhiṣṭhira and Dharma, appearing as Yaksha. Dharmaraj responds to Yaksha's question, 'what is the greatest virtue?' and opined that *anrsamsyam paro dharmah*, that is, 'non-cruelty is the supreme dharma'.

Mukund Lath argues that Anrsamsya rather than ahimsa has supreme significance in the epic.[52] Some scholars held contrary opinions. The central message of the Mahābhārata is neither Anrsamsya nor ahimsa. It is very difficult to locate the central message in the epic because of its inherent multivocal nature. It alternates between different alternatives and formulations.[53] There are many narratives which tell the story of violence in the

[50] Christopher Key Chapple, 'Ahimsa in the Mahabharata: A Story, a Philosophical Perspective, and an Admonishment'.

www.sutrajournal.com/ahimsa-in-the-mahabharata-by-christopher-key-chapple

[51] Alf Hiltebeitel, *Rethinking the Mahabharata: A Reader's Guide to the Education of the Dharma King* (New Delhi: Oxford University Press, 2001).

[52] Mukund Lath, 'The Concept of Anrsamsya in the Mahabharata', in *The Mahabharata Revisited*, ed. R. N. Dandekar (New Delhi: Sahitya Akademy, 1990), 113.

[53] Singh, *Political Violence in Ancient India*, 74.

Mahābhārata. J. L. Mehta held the opinion that non-violence and compassion are the highest duties of an individual.[54]

The two most prominent Sramans, that is, the Buddhist and the Jain, denounced animal sacrifice for the appeasement of gods. It was practiced in the Vedic rituals. Sramans' advocacy of non-violence criticized the himsa-oriented Brahmanical practices, and it provided the condition for Mahābhārata's Anrsamsya.[55]

But the Mahābhārata warns that the excess of non-violence is disastrous for a state and a king. Bhisma advises the vacillating Yudhiṣṭhira as follows: 'Nothing great can be achieved through pure compassion (Anrasamsya). Further, people do not hold you in much respect for being gentle, self-controlled and excessively noble and righteous.... The behavior you want to follow is not the behavior of Kings'.[56]

The Mahābhārata narrates the dialogue between Bhisma and Yudhiṣṭhira in which the former suggests the latter that it is impossible to practice absolute non-violence. Nobody in the world has a livelihood that does not involve doing some amount of violence. The dialogue between Brahmana Kaushika and a hunter teaches the lesson that philosophical life inevitably involves killing. Even walking by a person involves killing. The hunter works in a slaughterhouse. The hunter is doing his duty because of his deeds performed in the previous life. One does not incur sin by violence that is connected to one's hereditary calling. The main teaching of the Mahābhārata is that non-violence cannot be practiced by a king. Violence is necessary for the welfare of the world. Kings cannot maintain its territorial integrity without killing enemies. It is impossible for a king to practice non-violence.

[54] J. L. Mehta, 'The Discourse of Violence in the Mahabharata', in *Philosophy and Religion: Essays in Interpretation* (New Delhi: Indian Council of Philosophical Research, 1990), 250.

[55] Sibaji Bandyopadhyay, 'A Critique of Non-violence' [Seminar]. https://www.india-seminar.com/2010/608/608_sibaji_bandyopadhyay.htm

[56] Quoted in Singh, *Political Violence in Ancient India*, 74.

In the epic, Bhisma suggests Dharmaraj that a kingdom is a place where violence took place. A king engages in a war, and it involves killing and violence. It is the dharma of a Kshatriya to protect the people. It is the most sinful of all dharmas. Violence is inherent in Kshatriya dharma and kingship. It can only be atoned.[57]

In Rāmāyaṇa, the hero Ram does not claim his right to the throne and obeys the command of his father for *Vanvas* (exile in forest). Unlike the Pandavas, he does not resort to violence. He moves to the forest along with his brother and wife. Valmiki, the composer of the Rāmāyaṇa, outpours grief and compassion in sloka meter when the male of a pair of sweet-voiced Krauncha birds are killed by a Nishada hunter. Valmiki was instructed to document the story of Ram in the same sloka meter. The epic talks about the important values like compassion. It depicts many events where violence is decried. It also tells us that Ram resorts to violence when necessary. The story of King Sagar's sons relates to kingship, sacrifice and violence. In order to locate and search for the king's sacrificial horse which was stolen by the God Indra, the princes engage themselves in violent activities by digging up the earth and killing its creatures. On the intervention of Brahma, the carnage is stopped. There is another story of King Dasaratha who kills an ascetic when he goes on a hunting expedition on the banks of the Sarayu river. It was a violent act by King Dasaratha. He was cursed by the ascetic's father that he will meet the same fate and die grieving for his own son. This curse led the royal kingdom of Kosala into the succession crisis of the throne.[58]

Brother Lakshmana requested Ram to use force for his elevation. Ram's mother Kausalya also favours this idea. But Ram refuses the idea of Lakshmana and obeys his father's command. He addresses to Lakshmana: 'So abandon this way of thinking based on the noble Kshatra dharma. Think like me and follow dharma, not violence'.[59] Unlike the Pandavas of the Mahābhārata,

[57] Ibid., 75–77.
[58] Ibid., 88.
[59] Ibid., 89.

Ram does not resort to violence against his brother to seize the kingdom. Bharata visits the forest to meet his elder brother Ram. Lakshmana advises Ram to kill him. Ram motivates Lakshmana to refrain from violence. However, Ram resorts to violence in order to rescue his wife from demon Ravana, the king of Lanka.

Arthashastra

Kautilya composed the *Arthashastra*, the manual of statecraft, around the 4th century BCE. Like *Dharmasutras*, similar attitude towards violence is found in this text. But unlike those texts, the affairs of the state and caste equally figures in Kautilya' political thinking. *Arthashastra* (1.3.13) prescribes ahimsa for all people and all classes together with Satyam and Saucam. Bodewitz observes that Brahmacarya and Aparigraha are the missing elements. It suggests that unlike celibate practitioners and vows of poverty, ahimsa had reached a larger audience.[60]

The detailed discussion and classification of force, injury and violence in the political and social sphere has been documented in his book. The injury is often used for violence. He differentiates verbal injury (*vak-parusya*) from physical injury (*danda parusya*). Physical injury is seen as 'touching' (*sparsanam*), 'menacing' (*avagurnam*) and 'striking' (*prahatam*). Theft, injury to property as well as injury to animals, plants and trees come under the category of physical injury. He talks about the punishment for those persons who are causing injury in Chapter 3.19 of the book. He provisions for the hierarchy of expiation depending upon the nature of the injury.[61]

Kautilya discusses the term ahimsa as the general code of ethics applicable to all categories of people belonging to all Varnas and Ashramas as well as to the king. He suggests the following duties to all people: nonviolence, truthfulness, freedom from

[60] Bodewitz, 'Hindu Ahimsa and Its Roots', 37.
[61] Patton, 'Telling Stories about Harm', 22.

malice (*anasuya*), compassion, purity (*sauca*) and forbearance (*ksama*). He also suggests to the sage-like king (*rajarsi*) to refrain from violence and to avoid yearning for other person's wife and property.[62]

Kautilya describes the course of action to be decided by the king while pursuing foreign policy. The criteria for deciding the course of action depend on his assessment of his own and his enemies' strength. He supports the king to initiate all measures that are essential to maintain and enhance the prestige of his kingdom. He has pragmatic thinking about state-initiated violence. Unlike Upanishads' vision of the metaphoric attitude towards violence, *Arthashastra* has a worldly and pragmatic attitude towards violence.[63]

The Brahmanism, Buddhist and Jain religious traditions do not preach war. They recognized the necessity of justified violence by the state. There is no single theory of kingship and violence. Both the Buddhist and Jain traditions held the view that it was impossible to practice non-violence in absolute terms.

Bibliography

Jatavallabhula, Danielle Feller. 'Ranayajna: The Mahabharata War as a Sacrifice'. In *Violence Denied, Violence, Non-Violence and the Rationalization of Violence in South Asian Cultural History*, edited by Jan E. M. Houben and Karel R. Van Kooij. Leiden & Boston: Brill, 1999.

Kangle, R. P. *The Kautilya of Arthasastra* (Part 1 & 2). Delhi: Motilal Banarsidass, 1972.

Verhagen, Pieter C. 'Expressions of Violence in Buddhist Tantric Mantras'. In *Violence Denied, Violence, Non-Violence and the Rationalization of Violence in South Asian Cultural History*, edited by Jan E. M. Houben and Karel R. Van Kooij. Leiden & Boston: Brill, 1999.

[62] Singh, *Political Violence in Ancient India*, 120–121.

[63] Patton, 'Telling Stories about Harm', 22–23.

6

Medicinal Concepts and Institutions in Precolonial India

Shankar Kumar

Early Indian medical treatises that stand largely encapsulated in the corpus of Ayurveda,[1] besides detailing health and healing practices, constitute a rich repository of cultural data. So overwhelming is the immersion of these treatises in culture of the subcontinent that G. Jan Meulenbeld, credited with having produced a multivolume history of Indian medical literature with stunning comprehensiveness that takes into its fold works from the 'classical age' of Indian medicine down to the ones written in the 20th century, commands that Indian medicine 'cannot adequately be studied and understood without acquaintance with its history and ways of thought'.[2] Fortuitously then, a reading of early Indian medical treatises can heuristically offer us critical

[1] Charaka, Sushruta and Vagbhata are regarded as the great trio or big three (*Brhat-Trai* or *Vrddha-Trai*) of Ayurvedic literature. See Priya Vrat Sharma, ed., *History of Medicine in India* (New Delhi: Indian National Science Academy, 1992), 175.

[2] G. Jan Meulenbeld, *A History of Indian Medical Literature*, Vol. I A (Groningen: Egbert Forsten, 1999), 2.

insights and understanding of the ways and means by which pre-modern Indians made use of and viewed the things around themselves: in other words, a subject matter that is loosely sought to be apprehended by the term 'Indic'. While it would almost be anachronistic to use the present Western medicinal principles and practices as the point of departure to understand and analyse early Indian medicine, the taxonomical categories and imageries that they used to visualize and understand human physiology and health go a great length in capturing the essence of what constitutes Indic.

Ayurveda: A Living Craft

All through its history, Ayurvedic practices and pharmacopoeia kept registering change, and it would be erroneous to visualize it as being frozen in time. Also noteworthy is the fact that unlike the Greek medicine that long lost its dominant position in the West and is only residually present within Islamic medicine, Ayurveda is 'a living and still developing practice, and an ongoing literary activity'.[3] The decisive empirical falsification of a plethora of ancient assertions, be it the geocentric model of Aristotle or the traditional Greek theory of the four elements,[4] which characterized the rise of modern science around the 6th and 7th centuries in Europe, is something that conspicuously eluded Indic intellectual cosmos.

Indic medical tradition, despite several insertions, accommodations and even reinvention in the last century as *Navya Ayurveda* (New Age Ayurveda), never severed its umbilical cord with the ancient. Despite having lost the privileged and mainstream status to its Western counterpart since the colonial times, Ayurveda, as an alternate system of medicine, has leveraged its holistic and ecologically consistent therapeutic conceptualizations

[3] Ibid., 1.

[4] Jonathan Daly, *How Europe Made the Modern World* (London: Bloomsbury Academic, 2020), 97.

to emerge as an adjunct, even supplement, to the localized and ecologically insulated approach that has become proverbial of the mainstream Western medical treatments. Under the aegis of the Government of India, Ayurveda comes under the Ministry of AYUSH (Ayurveda, Yoga, Naturopathy, Unani, Siddha, Sowa-Rigpa and Homeopathy). It is entrusted with the responsibility of being a facilitator for upgrading the AYUSH educational standards, quality control and standardization of drugs; improving the availability of medicinal plant material, research and development; and generating awareness about the efficacy of the systems in India as well as abroad. As in 2010, there existed 9 national institutes and 3,277 AYUSH hospitals of which 2,458 were exclusively for Ayurvedic system. It also had 24,289 dispensaries of which 15,353 were Ayurvedic. In the same year, there were 478,750 registered Ayurvedic practitioners[5] and 7,494 Ayurvedic manufacturing units. The latest *Annual Report of the Ministry of AYUSH (2018–2019)* lists 401 Ayurveda, 11 Siddha and 53 Unani colleges affiliated with 59 universities across the country. With the continued survival of Ayurvedic practices not being the focus here, this essay seeks to illustrate some of the critical conceptualizations underpinning ancient Indian medicine and demonstrate their similarities and departures with respect to its Greek counterpart, thereby attempting to arrive at what could be understood as Indic in substantial terms, beyond merely the facile and superficial. A very early description of hospitals in *Charakasamhita*,[6] subsequently ratified by an eyewitness account of Fa Hsien in the early decades of 5th century CE, is also discussed to lend institutional credibility to the medical conceptualizations discussed in the chapter. Problems appended to such an exercise of culling out something specifically Indic

[5] In spite of nationwide data on Traditional Community Health Care Providers (TCHPs) not being available, it is estimated that their numbers are nearly the same as those of AYUSH practitioners for Ayurveda, Unani, Siddha and *Sowa-Rigpa*, around 7.5 lakh, or of biomedical physicians. See 'Medical Manpower AYUSH 2015'. Accessed 10 June 2017 at http://ayush.gov.in/sites/default/files/Medical Manpower Table 2015.pdf

[6] *CaSu* 15.1–15.7.

from the myriad formulations and conceptualizations in ancient Indian medicine from the issue of its desirability/futility and attempts to move towards non-ethnocentric universalism also comes in for a condensed treatment in this chapter. Historian Sanjay Subrahmanyam's assertion that 'early modern world must be understood as a porous network of regions and local communities rather than as a patchwork of well-defined states'[7] is pertinent here, particularly because our exercise will deal with ideas, ideals and its circulation across the territorial connotation of the term Indic and Greek. Seductive academic charm of using terms and notions such as 'connection', 'circulation' and 'global history', which provide enough historiographical traction today,[8] will, however, be rigorously tested by historicizing the concepts chosen to be compared across cultures and also highlighting the departures in their treatment to arrive at what could truly stand as Indic. For instance, some of the concepts, categories and processes central to Ayurveda will be compared with respect to their presence/absence in the then-existent Greek medical practices and formulations. While the discovered similarities would hint at the 'connected' and in-circulation aspects of the exercise, the departures and uniqueness would be a pointer towards their Indic quotient.

Being an all-embracing system with several layers, it is very difficult to identify the foundation of Ayurveda. Yet a cluster of ideas can be identified that characterizes Ayurveda in many important

[7] See Sanjay Subrahmanyam, *Explorations in Connected History: From the Tagus to the Ganges* (Oxford: Oxford University Press, 2004).

[8] 'We should also be wary of the legitimizing effect that can result from the simple import of things from other academic or scientific contexts that are rarely explained or translated: being responsive to novelty does not necessarily mean that we have to abandon a critical view point'. For an interesting discussion on the hazards of making across-the-domain comparisons and, therefore, the need for historicizing the categories in question before making such comparisons see, Caroline Douki and Philippe Minard, 'Global History, Connected Histories: A Shift of Historiographical Scale?' *Revue d'histoire moderne et contemporaine* (translated from the French by Cadenza Academic Translations) 2007/5, no. 54-4 (2007), 7–21.

ways. The relation between humours (*dosha*), body tissues (*dhatu*) and waste products (*mala*); doctrine of three humours (*tridosh vidya*), namely wind (*vaata*), choler (*pitta*) and phlegm (*kapha/ shleshman*); emphasis on moderation, balance or equilibrium; invoking cosmic physiology to understand critical processes of human physiology, such as circulation of fluids and digestion involving fire (*agni*) and water (*soma*); osmosis between living creatures and environment; resemblance through contagion of physical proximity; manipulations and synthesis of food ingredients, involving mixing (*samyoga*) and perfecting (*samskara*), that are hinged on gestures from daily life; the vast combinative system, involving manipulation of the chemical and organic materials, being hinged on the imagery of the layout of a meal are some of the conceptualizations that can characterize Ayurvedic system. While discussing the 'scientific' premise of these Ayurvedic presumptions would be carried out at one level, the chapter will, at another level, explore the congruence of these conceptualizations underpinning Ayurvedic practices and formulations with its Greek counterpart to understand its Indic dimension.

The issue of 'scientific' premise and prescriptions of Ayurveda and other traditional medical practices, like Unani, has been particularly looked at, quite critically, ever since the introduction of the Western biomedicine or 'Allopathy' or '*Angrezi dvai*'[9] (English medicine) in India. At one level, the competition posed by the Western medicine pushed the traditional practitioners of these crafts into diligently re-interpreting their untenable concepts and categories all through the 19th and the following centuries. Resultantly, the incoherent aspects of Ayurveda were plumbed into giving a coherent and sanitized look to it, and ancient terms for various physiological and patho-physiological processes were tailored to suit the requirements and parameters of the Western medicine. It was claimed that the Ayurvedic compilation into eight parts by Charaka, Sushruta and Vagbhata included sections

[9] Helen Lambert, 'Popular Therapeutics and Medical Preferences in Rural North India', *Lancet* 348 (1996), 1706–1709.

on anatomy, physiology, therapeutics, surgery, midwifery, etc., and that they were a 'theoretically complete and rationally evolved medical system'.[10] In order to buttress their image as scientific practitioners, they consciously distanced themselves from quacks and family-based hereditary practitioners of traditional medicine. At another level, however, operating as the things were under structural constraints of colonial circumstances, this led to the new legitimacy accruing not to the heterogeneous, no-formal erstwhile practitioners of traditional medicine but to the homogenized, formal, linguistically and religiously identifiable practitioners of the new avatar of traditional medicine. The Orientalists' urge to include indigenous medicine as a significant part of the new college curriculum and the hardened colonial bureaucratic attitude, following 1857, resulted in the development of a curriculum that displayed little resemblance or relation to the linguistic plurality as well as medical practices that characterized traditional Indian medicine. Hindi, tinctured with Sanskrit, became the language for Ayurveda, and Urdu, with little bit of Persian and Arabic, became the language of Unani. The homogenization of traditional medicine under new languages, Hindi and Urdu, went on to envelop other diversities and soon dovetailed into the Hindu–Muslim polarization.[11]

Yet another work by Guy Attewell[12] also asserts that Unani Tibb and Ayurveda were a cosmopolitan profession, with the practitioners and the patients not segregated on religious lines.

[10] Kavita Sivaramakrishnan, *Old Potions, New Bottles: Recasting Indigenous Medicine in Colonial Punjab 1850–1945* (New Delhi: Orient Longman, 2006), 133.

[11] The homogenization of these traditional medical practices into neat categories with language and religion as its identifiers is a phenomenon that has carried over to the contemporary times. The Government of India organizes the two, Ayurveda and Unani, into separate administrative branches under AYUSH. This clean distinction is not attested in older sources. For more, see, Guy Attewell, 'Beyond the Label: An Essay on Unani Tibb's Entangled History', *Biblio* 12, nos. 9 &10 (September–October, 2007), 27–28.

[12] Guy Attewell, *Refiguring Unani Tibb: Plural Healing in Late Colonial India* (Hyderabad: Orient Longman, 2007).

However, with the Ayurvedic revival becoming increasingly associated with communal identity and distinct vernacular traditions in the colonial period, it became difficult to accord cosmopolitan character to it anymore. The colonial context also meant that Ayurveda was shorn of orthogenetic growth, and it were the non-medical concerns such as the politics of nationalistic pride and issues of patronage that peddled the image-makeover of Ayurveda and its practitioners. Medical issues such as efficacy of Ayurvedic drugs, people's access to its treatment, its role in public health, etc., were not reckoned with in the process of resurrection of Ayurveda as a unified, sanitized and scientific body of knowledge. Instead, the Ayurvedic practitioners sought to engage themselves in the emerging network of exchange of news through publications in journals and equally eagerly sought to combine Western medical therapies in diagnosing and treating diseases. Despite the inadequacy of human anatomical details[13] being very much a matter of fact in traditional Ayurveda, it is no wonder that, displaying the same colonial hangover, many of the modern practitioners of Ayurveda, most notably Swami Ramdev, are also seen trying to establish the credibility of their Ayurvedic prescriptions and drugs by alluding to them being tested by modern scientific laboratories in terms of their biochemical constitution!

Inconsistencies in anatomical detailing and anthropocentric taxonomical principles of classifying materia medica, among many other inaccuracies in terms of biochemical composition

[13] But the heart was not a pump in the ayurvedic view of the body, nor did the blood circulate in the post-Harveian sense. There was certainly no concept of a contrast between venous and arterial circulation, and several of these vessels are most commonly seen as being rooted in the naval, not the heart.

See Dominik Wujastyk, *The Roots of Ayurveda* (New Delhi: Penguin Books, 1998), 37. 'The heart is thought to be the seat of consciousness, as well as being the receptacle for energy. The ducts and pipes are based in the naval'. For an interesting discussion on Sharangadhara's compendium (probably composed around 1300 CE) detailing Ayurvedic understanding of human anatomy, see idem, 302–327.

of tissues, or otherwise, prompt Zimmermann to disparagingly remark that in the absence of physiology and anatomy, the doctors in Ayurveda could, at best, offer only prognosis (the course taken by illness and the signs that heralded crises, accidents, solutions) and not a logical diagnosis.[14] What, therefore, emerges from our discussion of the pre-modern medical practices across its negotiation during the colonial period, particularly of the Ayurveda, is that their resilience is increasingly predicated on their ability to appear as scientific as possible, rather than anything intrinsic. The terror, or compulsion, of maintaining scientific pretence has also resulted in halting the orthogenetic way of the growth of Ayurveda. It is this brash putting-aside of the Ayurveda as not-scientific over the past couple of centuries that needs to be relooked.

The Issue of Scientificity and Comparison with Its Greek Counterpart

The existing image of science, with which we almost seem to be possessed, has been substantially altered by several brilliant works including the one by Thomas Kuhn.[15] Talking of the increasing difficulties in distinguishing the 'scientific' component of past observation from what their predecessors had declared unscientific, Kuhn goes on to infuse a new meaning and substance to the term scientific. This is pertinent to our discussion here because the imageries drawn from cosmological functioning, cooking and cuisine have been verily used in Ayurveda to understand human physiology and even prescribe drugs. On the face of it, from the perspective of conventional understanding of science which was the frame of reference during the 19th century, such postulations will look unscientific. And it is this labelling that Ayurveda and

[14] Francis Zimmermann, *The Jungle and the Aroma of Meats* (Delhi: Motilal Banarsidass, 1998), 20.

[15] Thomas S. Kuhn, *The Structure of Scientific Revolutions* (Chicago: The University of Chicago, 1962), viii.

its practitioners were trying to avoid. However, Kuhn's work has offered a new perspective to look at the history of scientific thoughts and practices by placing them against the prevailing 'paradigm'.[16] He, for instance, writes the following:

> The more carefully they study, say, Aristotelian dynamics, phlogistic chemistry, or caloric thermodynamics, the more certain they feel that those once current views of nature were, as a whole, neither less scientific nor more the product of human idiosyncrasy than those current today. If these out-of-date beliefs are to be called myths, then myths can be produced by the same sorts of methods and held for the same sorts of reasons that now lead to scientific knowledge. If, on the other hand, they are to be called science, then science has included bodies of beliefs quite incompatible with the ones we hold today. Given these alternatives, the historians must choose the latter.[17]

Elaborating further about the new image of science, Kuhn writes as follows:

> Rather than seeking the permanent contributions of an older science to our present vantage, they attempt to display the historical integrity of that science in its own time. They ask, for example, not about the relation of Galileo's views to that of modern science, but rather about the relationship between his views and those of his group, i.e., his teachers, contemporaries, and immediate successors in the sciences. Furthermore, they insist upon studying the opinions of that group and other similar ones from the viewpoint—usually very different from that of modern science—that gives those opinions the maximum internal coherence and the closest possible fit to nature.[18]

The categories and conceptualizations, at times predicated on the imageries and processes drawn from everyday phenomena like

[16] Kuhn defines it as universally recognized scientific achievements that for a time provide model problems and solutions to a community of practitioners.

[17] Kuhn, *The Structure of Scientific Revolutions*, 2.

[18] Ibid., 3.

cooking, or intricate network of tubes and capillaries carrying water into the soil—a clear reminder of irrigation of agricultural fields, used verily in the Ayurveda to understand human physiology, therefore, cannot simply be brushed aside as fanciful imagination and unscientific. It rather needs to be seen if the contemporaries, in our instance, the Greeks, given their time period being roughly the same, that is, around the beginning of the Common Era, were also using similar concepts and categories in medical practices. An answer in affirmative would hint at internal coherence with which these healing practices were being pursued. For example, *tridosha-vidya*, or the doctrine of the three humours, namely wind (*vaata*), choler (*pitta*) and phlegm (*kapha*) which is credited in the Ayurveda with regulation of the overall health in human beings, finds its echo in the contemporary Greek humoral system of Hippocrates and Galen.[19] Ayurvedic emphasis on moderation, balance and equilibrium in almost all activities, say food, sleep, sex or even dose of medicine, finds reverberation in the contemporary Greek medical tradition as well. Extending the principle of moderation and equilibrium to the domain of cultural behaviour, Charaka, for instance, instructs that an intelligent person should not overindulge in a habit even in acceptable things such as 'exercise, laughter, talking, travelling, village behaviour, or staying up all night'. He further writes that '[a] person who indulges to excess in these and similar activities will perish violently, like a lion tugging at an elephant'.[20] A parallel to the Ayurvedic concept of *samayog* (equal mixture, congruent junction) could be found in the Greek idea of *Krasis* (temperament to achieve the 'correct mean').[21] In fact, *Krasis* constitutes the central idea of Hippocrates in his work *On Ancient Medicine*. Quite like the Ayurveda, the Greek term uses the imagery of 'temperament' of the juices in foods to visualize and achieve the 'correct mean' of bodily humours by harmoniously mixing the substances with antagonistic attributes

[19] Wujastyk, *The Roots of Ayurveda*, 4.

[20] Ibid., 55.

[21] Zimmermann, *The Jungle and the Aroma of Meats*, 129.

to compensate for and moderate one another. The convergence between the two contemporary medical ideas and prescriptions cannot be more striking. Both borrow from two gestures of daily life, that is, mixing and cooking, to arrive at and leverage the same principle of compensating through contraries to attain the desired meaning or equilibrium. One of the key formulae in the Ayurvedic pharmacopoeia is the art of mixing (*samyoga*) and perfecting (*samskara*). Incidentally, this is elaborated in a hemistich that is common to both *Charakasamhita* and *Sushrutasamhita*.[22]

While it is well known that the curative principle of using things which constitute corresponding contraries to the detected causes of the humoral symptoms happens to be the centrepiece of Ayurvedic treatment, the Greek parallel, even here, is too striking to be missed. Alcmaeon, in Greek medical tradition, is acknowledged as the one to whom they owe the idea that 'health results from the *isonomia* of contraries'.[23] Zimmermann suggests that this therapeutic action in the Greek tradition involves two simultaneous aspects: compensation of contraries and moderation of extremes. We have already alluded to the familiar Ayurvedic processes by which the two, compensation of contraries and moderation of extremes, are achieved by mixing (*samayog*) and cooking (*samskara*). Incidentally, cooking and mixing forms almost an indissoluble pair in Greek medical tradition. In India, even today, it is a common practice to have the kitchen and cooking managed only by the Brahmanas,[24] since cooking (*samskara*) requires operations beyond eclectically mixing (*samayog*) the ingredients. It rather is a knowledgeable intervention that requires studied and careful manipulation of the ingredients (*samskara*), keeping in mind the compatibility of the constituents. In the Ayurvedic terminology, this is referred to as *satmya* (a thing which agrees with one).

[22] *CaSu* XXVII, 276a; *SuSu* XLVI, 391a.

[23] Zimmermann, *The Jungle and the Aroma of Meats*, 128–129.

[24] For an interesting discussion around this theme and its ritual pertinence, see Charles Malamoud, *Cooking the World Ritual & Thought in Ancient India* (Delhi: Oxford University Press, 1996), 7–22.

Our attempt to understand the real import of the term *satmya* as a key concept, probably Indic, in Indian medical tradition leads us to unravel yet another imagery, hence cultural, that underpins the Ayurveda. This is the idea of inherent affinities. We have earlier alluded to Thomas Kuhn's invocation of 'paradigm' in understanding pre-modern scientific conceptualizations. So, the physicality of sensory perception getting used as an imagery to understand the working of other domains is not rare to find in pre-modern societies. Therefore, the logic of physical injury on touching an inappropriate object probably gets transposed in matters of food, ailments and cure as well. Charaka, while tackling the question of possible sources of ailments, uses the expression 'an unwholesome association of sense and object' (*asatmyendriyarthasamyoga*). He goes on to say that a wholesome sense object is one, which is beneficial.[25] What, therefore, underpins this notion of a thing being 'wholesome', 'compatible', or 'a thing which agrees with one' (*satmya*) is the principle of inherent affinities.[26] This principle is also invoked in understanding the relationship of health and season cycle.

Having broached the issue of 'connected history' in the sense of these ideas and premises having characterized medical traditions of other cultures as well during the period, we need to check if this was so elsewhere too. While the evidence to this effect may not be directly available, Charaka[27] himself (or maybe one of the redactors of the text, given the layered nature of the matter contained!) enumerates various regions, most outside the subcontinent, and mentions the kinds of food that the people of these regions are habituated to consuming. Meat, wheat and mead for the *Bahlikas, Pahlavas, Chinas*, *Shulikas, Yavanas* and *Shakas*; fish for the Easterners, while milk for the people of Sind; oil and sour tastes, referred to be particularly to the likings of the *Ashmakas* and *Avantikas*; tubers, roots and fruits for the people of *Malaya*, while milk for the Southerners,

[25] Wujastyk, *The Roots of Ayurveda*, 45–46, 68.
[26] Ibid., 46.
[27] *CaCi* 30. 316.

and drinks for the Northeasterners; barley, wheat and cow's milk are mentioned to be particularly liked by people in the central region. Most importantly, Charaka instructs that 'one should prescribe medicines that are in harmony with the affinities of these people, since such affinities give rapid strength and do little harm even in excess'.[28] Given that Persians, Chinese, Scythians and, probably, the Greeks (if one were to understand *Yavanas* as Greeks) are mentioned with their food habits, one can presume that the writer was aware of the appropriateness or compatibility (*satmya*) of medicines to be provided to them. While the available sources do not allow us to ascertain whether these foreigners, including the Greeks, also deployed the principle of compatibility or wholesomeness in their medical traditions, a more intensive research or fortuitous chancing of sources can help in joining the missing dots in our effort to use 'connected history' perspective to probe the issue. It is suffice to say, however, that in the absence of any such parallel concept elsewhere, compatibility and wholesomeness of food or medicine may be regarded as exclusively Indic. It is noteworthy that the idea of compatibility/appropriateness of food/medicine finds its logical extension in another elaboration in *Charakasamhita*. Talking about the therapeutic principles Charaka alludes to natural bodily constitutions (*deha-prakriti*).[29] This is interesting because the Ayurveda in current Indian parlance is counterpoised to the principles of allopathy, the latter being premised on incompatible intervention through drugs or surgery on the disease being treated. This, of late, is getting a lot of traction in *navya* Ayurveda. *Deha-prakriti* for Charaka, however, is essentially about humoral predisposition of bodies. So, humans born with balanced choler (*pitta*), wind (*vayu/vaata*) and phlegm (*kapha*) need to take food that are appropriate/compatible (*satmya*) to their bodily constitution; only those born with bilious, windy or phlegmatic humoral constitution need to be treated by substances of antithetical attributes.

[28] Cf. Wujastyk, *The Roots of Ayurveda*, 42.
[29] Ibid., 43–44, 55–56.

Another key conceptualization permeating the Ayurvedic corpus is the one by which circulation of fluids in human body is sought to be understood and apprehended. Humours, understood in the Ayurveda as one of the three permanent bases of human body apart from body tissues and waste products, are conceived of as physical substances, semifluid in nature, that regulate the state of body. While the congruence of the Ayurvedic doctrine of the three humours and ancient Greek humoral system, as outlined by Hippocrates and Galen, has already been alluded to, what is of interest here is that even the principle or cosmic physiology underpinning the circulation of fluids and stages leading to digestion in human body appears to be similar. A dialectical relation mediating between the Sun (associated with heat and fire/*Agni*) and the Moon (*Soma* and its association with cold rays nourishing the saps) is a recurrent theme in Sanskrit literature, with some having been composed even prior to *Charakasamhita*. This imagery of cosmic physiology, around which the Ayurvedic understanding of flow of humours is weaved, suggests that the Moon (*Soma*) nourishes the saps that run beneath the soil in a network of capillaries through its coldness, while the Sun through its heat/fire (*Agni*) captures all the unctuosity of beings. The Greek medical tradition, as articulated by Hippocrates in his treatise *On Regimen*, too borrows the paradoxical idea of 'a wet fire and a dry water from Anaxagora's cosmology'.[30] Ayurveda's visualization of digestion furthers this fire–water dialectic polarity. Noteworthy, here, is the fact that the root word for cooking and fire in Sanskrit happens to be the same, that is, *pach*. Further, the digestive force is also identified with the root *agni*, that is, *jatharagni*.[31] The understanding of human physiology, particularly flow of fluids, in this pre-Harvey[32] period could not quite have chosen a better cosmic imagery and, simultaneously, could not quite have shown a more remarkable

[30] Cf. Zimmermann, *The Jungle and the Aroma of Meats*, 131.

[31] Wujastyk, *The Roots of Ayurveda*, 5.

[32] See Daly, *How Europe Made the Modern World*, 93.

congruence of its application across cultures. The scientificity of such assertions has already been discussed earlier in the chapter with respect to Kuhn's 'paradigm'.

Medical Practices and Institutions That Grew in Orthogenetic Fashion

The consensus across the cultures having been established in this case, it is pertinent to mention Zysk's scholarly work[33] that has convincingly established that congruence of ideas and concepts in Indian and Greek medical tradition notwithstanding, a great deal of concepts and even materia medica of the Ayurveda actually evolved orthogenetic ally through the continuous accretion at the hands of ascetics from around the middle of the first millennium BCE in India. Be it the iconic *tridosha* etiology or several other taxonomic principles (such as external–internal, substantial–non substantial foods) that went on to characterize the Ayurveda centuries later, Zysk furnishes a range of evidence, mostly drawn from the ascetic traditions of Buddhism, to demonstrate and identify the substrata of healing practices and codification principles on which the theoretical sophistication of the Ayurveda rests. It is suggested that the streak of empiricism present in ancient wandering physicians (*vaidya/bhisaj*) coalesced with the remarkable emphasis on direct observation[34] betrayed by the Buddhist ascetic physicians; and with the wandering ascetics taking to a more stationary existence in the early Buddhist monasteries, the medical lore even got codified and documented to which the early Ayurvedic practices owe significantly.

[33] Kenneth G. Zysk, *Asceticism and Healing in Ancient India: Medicine in the Buddhist Monastery* (Delhi: Motilal Banarsidass, 1998).

[34] 'Such information pertaining to the acquisition of anatomical knowledge by the early Buddhists contributes much to our understanding of the evolution Indian anatomy and to the connections between sramana, Buddhists, and ayurvedic medicine'. See Zysk, *Asceticism and Healing in Ancient India*, 36–37.

Orthogenetic growth of a range of Ayurvedic principles and practices in an anterior historical context than that of the Greek is a pointer to its Indic substratum, contemporaneous similarities or acquaintance of the subsequently codified Ayurveda with its Greek counterpart notwithstanding. We have already alluded to the Buddhist monasteries as the nascent institutions where early formalization of healing practices, that were hitherto eclectic and esoteric, could have taken place. While it has been argued that etiology, materia medica and taxonomical principles of the ascetic heterodox and Buddhist monastic periods of around the middle of the first millennium BCE bear a remarkable formative resemblance to the early classical treatises of Charaka and Sushruta, something on similar lines can be proposed to have happened in the instituted-ness of hospitals.

Hospital, civil in nature, as a functional institution at Pataliputra (modern Patna) has been famously commented about by the 5th century Buddhist traveller from China, Fa Hsien. Important as the description is, what it ratifies as a functional institution, in terms of what Charaka had to say about hospitals in idealized terms centuries earlier than Fa Hsien's visit, is more important. Wujastyk regards the description by Fa Hsien as

> one of the earliest accounts of a civic hospital system anywhere in the world and, coupled with Caraka's description of how a clinic should be equipped, suggests that India should may have been the first part of the world to have evolved as organized cosmopolitan system of institutionally-based medical provision.[35]

Described as charity hospitals established by the heads of the *Vaishya* families, Fa Hsien lists a cross section of poor and maimed people who were examined and given medicines for cure at these hospitals. The stay of the patients and provisioning for medicine was available in-house. In effect, the description seems to physically testify the existing form of the ideal type

[35] Wujastyk, *The Roots of Ayurveda*, 2.

of an Ayurvedic hospital that Charaka[36] has mentioned in his treatise. Seen in conjunction with Emperor Ashoka's edicts informing us about planting of medicinal herbs which are suitable for men and animals and a number of passages from the Sanskrit and *Pāli* literature talking about the merits of establishing *arogyashala* (halls for health) and medical institutions, Charaka's description of hospital does not seem to be historically untenable. They in fact lend a lot of historical credence to the Indic claim of being the place where institutional health care in South Asia evolved first.

Concludingly, it emerges from our discussion that the range of conceptualizations underpinning early Indian medicine, despite showing apparent similarities with its Greek counterpart, appears to be nothing more than stylized congruence in visualizing human physiology in the pre-modern times. Given the compulsion of comprehending and operating with limited anatomical and biochemical compositional awareness, early Indian as well as Greek medicine made use of the limited number of cosmic physiology and other imageries to systematically present the details. With respect to our allusion to Kuhn's 'paradigm', there seems nothing unscientific about them. The discussed similarities and congruence should rather be understood in terms of 'consensus' among the pre-modern communities than any organic linkage across the two civilizations. Evolutionary and orthogenetic growth of medical and healing techniques including its materia medica in the ascetic traditions of Buddhism and otherwise in Indian history, as shown for the Ayurveda in Zysk's works, further cuts into this apparent congruence. Historical anteriority of healing and medicine in early India, having been convincingly proved to be prior to their systematization as a coherent medical epistemology in the classical treatises of Charaka and Sushruta, further opens the possibility of their presentation using the current cosmological imageries and idioms, such as fire–water

[36] *Ca Su*, 15.1–15.7. Also see Ibid., 75–78.

polarity, osmosis between living creatures and environment, resemblance through contagion of physical proximity, to name a few. The 'connected' aspects of medical traditions of the Indic and the Greek might more be a consequence of this systematization using current imageries, idioms and metaphors rather than anything substantial or organic. Indic component, likewise, lay in the material, institutional and processual substrata of asceticism that accounted for the orthogenetic growth of Indian medicine, subsequently systematized as a coherent epistemological account, the Ayurveda.

7

Concept of Shaktitva and Women Saints in Medieval Maharashtra

Sonali Chitalkar

Introduction

The concept of feminist episteme has become so large and hegemonic that it has obscured indigenous understandings of the concept of *prakriti* or what Western feminist thought as gender. Indian history offers us ample examples of empowered women. These have, however, been so far analysed within a colonial framework of thought, once again imposing Western ideas of gender, patriarchy and empowerment on women in Indian history who had different existential conditions. The gender-based explanation for the freedom experienced by Lalleshwari, Mirabai and various other women saints in India are interpreted as having stood out against 'patriarchy'. Such interpretations are restrictive and fall strictly within the colonial frameworks of understanding. The Indic understanding of gender is best exemplified in the indigenous philosophical tradition of Sanatan Dharma and is marked by some essential characteristics which, interestingly, enhance the diversity of perception within the tradition and establish it as a separate field of academic and religious interest, while, at the same time, it endows it with the spirit of individuality and liberality, thereby rightfully earning it a place on the timeless Sanatan philosophical continuum.

This study tries to build an alternative framework of analysis for understanding women empowerment as Shakti.

Understanding Indian Women

The Sanatan understanding of gender is not based on a dichotomy between the masculine and feminine identities and roles. It is not about compartmentalization, or about creation of the public and private contingent spheres, rather it is about working of social cooperation and a principle of spiritual unity. The analogy given to the idea of gender relationships as the linkage between the *prakriti* and *purush* is also applied to a conceptualization of the cosmos in the form of Maya and Brahmana. *Prakriti*, Maya and Shakti are depicted as the context and situation as well as the source of power for the sustenance of all life. *Purush* is widely interpreted in Vedic Sanskrit as *atman* (*Pure-sheteiti-purushah*) or a manifestation of the Brahman, while the Vedanta and Upanishads see it as the Brahmana itself (*Tat-tvam-asi*). However, Shakti or Maya are neither a contradictory or antagonistic force to the Brahmana or *purush* and nor is it merely an instrument for creation, subjugated to its creator who is seen as a Superior Truth or as a priori reality. The self or the soul is a manifestation of the Para Brahmana who is considered to be both the 'creator' of whatever exists and is also the element of which everything is 'created'. It is to feel what lies within. This experiencing is *Antardrishti*. It is not merely a practice, or a ritual, rather it is the state of being and facing one's own undiscovered potential and limitlessness. The *sadhak*s divert their mind from their worldly surroundings towards their own soul and search the innermost sanctum sanctorums of their hearts in search of the truth. And ultimately, this search leads them to the entirety of their worldly existence when they reach a state where they realize that the *tatva* (element) within them and around them is the Brahmana itself.

The flexibility of *Antardrishti* gives her powers of liberation, self-realization and self-acknowledgement which could never have been gained by something like Rawlsian 'veil of ignorance' or reductionist feminist reasoning. It allows the *sadhak*s to start from the point of their own choice, be it gender, and then discover their own position within that particular sphere which, instead of turning into a compartment for parochial ideology, becomes the stepping stone to greater discoveries and newer dimensions for the individual self, as well as for the entirety of existence, the Brahmana, it is believed to contain.[1]

The essential philosophical bearings of Shakti, and of the rich didactical and narrative tradition associated with it, occur in the form of the ideas of *Bhavnatmak*, as opposed to the rationality of both erstwhile Indian and prominent Western philosophical traditions of feminism and of liberalism and others. Shakti is *Bhavnatmak* rather than rational. One of the main thrusts of Western feminism was the acceptance and extension of the Enlightenment of individualism and rationality to women. Shakti is not bound by rationality.

Contexualization

Women not only read the Vedas, they also write them. It is true that Vedic scriptures do not force anyone to engage above and beyond their capacities and wishes; therefore, in Vedic civilization, a woman had the choice to simply dedicate herself to family, children, husband and home, but such occupations do not constitute a limitation, an obligation or a priori duty.[2] The *grihasthashrama* (or the household) and the idea of *matritv* or motherhood were not conceptualized as a public–private divide, as opposed to contemporary portrayal, rather they were perceived

[1] See Chandrakala Padia, ed., *Feminism: Tradition and Modernity* (Simla: IIAS, 2002), 210.

[2] For a detailed explanation, see A. S. Altekar, '*Position of Women in Hindu Civilization: From Prehistoric Times to the Present Day*', https://archive.org/details/in.ernet.dli.2015.100033/page/n29/mode/2up10

as the sphere of cooperation between the two major forces of gender in society, the *prakriti* and the *purush*. *Purush* itself was interpreted in the Vedic literature as the *atman* or the 'Brahmana', which was genderless, and the *prakriti* was its context as well as the source of Shakti or power, which was necessary for the sustenance of life and order.

The Harita Dharmasutra tradition of Maitrayanayi school of Yajurveda described two categories of women, namely: (*dvi vidha striyah, brahmavadinyah sadyovadhvas ca, tatra brahmavadini namupanayana magnindhanam svaghre bhikshacharyeti*).[3]

The first type of women described by the Dharmasutra included the revered *Brahmavadinis* (those who were not married and were Vedic scholars), who chose to dedicate their lives to the study, practice and teaching of Vedic knowledge and endeavoured towards self-enlightenment and self-realization of the Brahmana. They were perceived as knowledgeable, enlightened and independent women and were not expected to engage compulsorily with household duties or marry, and marriage was a matter of their own consent, rather than a compulsion. They were not ritually or socially prohibited from marrying either. Some prominent examples from this tradition include the names of women saints such as Sikata, Nivavari, Apala and Visvavara from the family of Atri, Angirasi Sarasvati from the family of Angirasa, Yami Vaivasvati, Sraddha, Ghosha, Surya, Indrani, Urvasi, Sarama, Juhu and Paulomi Saci, who are associated to the mantras of Rigveda. A particularly famed *Brahmavadini* by the name of Lopamudra had great knowledge of Sanskrit and Tamil. Her name, mystical in its own right, means 'completely absorbed in the self'; though she has been categorized with *Brahmavadini Rishi-patnis*, as she later married Agastya Rishi. Two mantras of the Rigveda are attributed to her.

[3] For more details, see Parama Karuna Devi, *Introduction to Vedic Knowledge* (Puri: Pavan House, 2011), 71, http://jagannathavallabha.com/pdf_engl/Introduction%20-%20complete%20-%20amazon%20template%208.5%20x%2011.pdf

It is said that some Vedic scholars named their literary works after their wives or daughters, as in the case of the Vedanta commentary called Bhamati and the mathematic treatise called Lilavati. However, we cannot dismiss the possibility that such texts have in fact been written or composed by women whose names they bear, because there is no specific documentation for the authorship of these works.

Rigveda *Suktas*[4] have explicit and evident attributions to female authorship. Book 14 of Atharvaveda and various sections in several more books also have feminine origins traced to various female rishis. The Vac *Sukta* (Rigveda 10.125), which concerns the revelation of the Vedas, is attributed to the Rishika Vagambhrina. A particular section of the Atharvaveda which is focused on the subjects of domestic rituals, marriage, etc., is attributed to a Rishika. Several parts of the other 19 books of the Atharvaveda are attributed to women. There is also a mention of a specific category of women's rituals which were meant to be celebrated exclusively by women referred to as *strikarmani.*

Women scholars also held positions of reverence and honour like their male counterparts. A list of highly esteemed Rishikas is provided by the ritual texts of the Vedas, and the students were expected to offer their homage to them during their learning of the divine texts. Major instances include the *Ashvalayana Grhyasutra* and *Shankhayana Grhyasutra*, which list female Vedic gurus such as Sulabha Maitreyi and Vadava Prathiteyi. Certain Vedic texts also present women as authorities on the details of the Vedic rituals, like the Aitareya Brahmana 2.9 which cites the opinion of the Female Vedic Authority Kumari Gandharva-grihita regarding the ritual of *Agnihotra* (the daily celebration of the fire sacrifice).

Some texts are specifically destined to be recited by women, such as the mantras of the Madhyandina Yajurveda, the *Apastambha*

[4] At least the following Rigvedic *Suktas* are ascribed to women, 10-134, 10-39, 10-40, 10-91, 10-95, 10-107, 10-109, 10-154, 10-159 and 10-189.

Dharmasutras and the *Srautasutras* on the Vedic ceremonies. Also, many mantras from the Yajurveda are specifically meant to be recited by women. Even when men recited the other slokas, the presence of women was implicit: the recitation of the Samaveda is intended to be accompanied by the music of the instruments played by women. In Kena Upanishad, Uma Brahmavidya appears to dissipate Indra's ignorance with her teachings: apparently Adi Shankara saw this discourse as very important because he wrote no less than two different and subsequent commentaries on this one text.

The esteemed *Brahmavadini*s who swore to the vows of Brahmacarya were also subjected to the upanayan sanskara just like the boys, making them *dwija* (twice born) too. They also had the right to engage in the performance of the Agnihotra and the Veda-adhyayana sanskara (daily study of Vedic scriptures), and these were started at a very young age with the only difference existing that owing to their physical disposition, girls were not required to mandatorily adhere to the stringent obligations concerning austerities prescribed for males. Consequently, they had the liberty to decide to spend their Brahmacarya period in their natal homes while receiving private tuition. They were excused to obtain their *bhiksha* (ritual alms) from family members rather than from strangers. These alternative rules have also been cited in the lost text, frequently cited by commentators, known as *Yama-Dharmashastra*.

Nevertheless, it would be a grave error to interpret this liberty of choice as a mandatory norm of confining women's education to the household. Instead, even in the post-Vedic period, as described by the renowned sage Panini, girls attended Vedic schools known as Charanas. At times, they were also free to reside in hostels or *chhatri-sala* for pursuing their studies, unperturbed. In the words of another famed grammarian Katyayana, whose working period is dated sometime after Panini, one of these schools was specifically famous owing to its special grammar course delivered by Apisali, a prolific grammarian who lived before Panini. In the *Mahabhasya*, his famed work, Patanjali describes a school for female students where knowledge associated with Mimamsa philosophy was the focal point of education. He also distinguishes between beginner and advanced students who were defined by the terms *adhyetri* and *manavika*, respectively.

When they chose to marry, the *Brahmavadinis* looked for men who were equally dedicated to the cultivation of spiritual knowledge and practice. Some famous *rishi-patnis*, respected and famous at least as much as their husbands, were Romasa the wife of Svanya, Anasuya the wife of Atri, Maitreyi the wife of Yajnavalkya, Arundhati the wife of Vasistha, Vasukrapatni, Ghosha, etc. *Brahmavadinis*, as contrary to popular Western assumptions, were not confined to their austere life and had the liberty to experience all four ashramas of organized life, from *grihasth* to sannyas, like their male counterparts. It is said that Gargi attained perfect realization in the stage of Brahmacarya, Chudala in the *grihasthashrama*, Maitreyi in the stage of vanaprastha and Sulabha yogini as a sannyasini. This Sulabha bhikshuni ('sacred mendicant') was famous for her vast and deep knowledge of the Mahābhārata.

Vedas were revealed to the same number of women as men; those who were married to and were themselves Veda scholars were known as *saadhya vadhus*.

Those who were not married and were Vedic scholars, nevertheless, were referred to as *Brahmavadinis*. Atlekar further observes that *Purva Mimamsa Sutra* is more abstruse than algebra, and apart from men, a number of women were adept in its operations. This information is given in Kaasakritsanaas (Maha Bhashya). Until 788–820 AD, Hindu women scholars were studying Vedas, adjudicating religious discussions, even when male scholars such as Acharyas Sankara and Mandana Mishra were debating—both accepted Ubhaya Bharati as judge (adjudicator).

Bhakti Movement

Bhakti movement is an important milestone in cultural and religious history of medieval India. It marked an important departure from the focus on complex ritualistic traditions prescribed by the Vedas and other texts as a medium of reaching to the Divine, to a philosophy of uncanny love and devotion to a God who came to be seen as a caring and loving entity, rather than as a guardian, with whom intimate personal relationships of the devotees could be formed and sustained. Absolute devotion to God was seen as the only prerequisite for bhakti and, consequently, for attaining moksha or oneness with the Divine, and this essential message was dispensed both through deep philosophical knowledge and through complex rituals.

Bhakti saints believed in religious egalitarianism. All Bhakti saints claimed that salvation can be achieved by all. They did not make distinction of caste. Most of the saints of Bhakti movement belonged to diverse social backgrounds. All of them used regional languages for propagating the Bhakti tradition. Despite the diversity of traditions and the plurality of practices, the various local manifestations of the Bhakti movement shared certain common tenets such as belief in the god, emphasis on belief in one Supreme god, devotion to God as the way to attain salvation, necessity of guru (teacher) to attain bhakti, stress on noble life and conduct, equality among all devotees and discarding of excessive rituals.

Bhakti movement in Maharashtra, North and East India also denounced the caste organization and the power of Brahmanical scriptures. Vaishnavite movement centred on Rama and Krishna's lives in North India propagated Saguna Bhakti. Chaitanya, Tulsidas and Mirabai were the main exponents of this type of bhakti.[5] The path of salvation is expressed through the medium of poetry, songs, dance and kirtans. It was also influenced by *Nathpanthis*, who were very popular among the lower classes.

[5] Steven Rosen, ed., *Vaisnavi: Women and the Worship of Krishna* (New Delhi: Motilal Banarsidass, 1996), 165.

Varkari Sampradaya

The Varkari sampradaya is a regional manifestation of the Bhakti movement which flourished in many parts of Maharashtra. Like other variations of the Bhakti cult, the Varkaris, too, have a chief deity who is the focal point of worship, and he is known as Vitthal, which is considered as an alternative name of Vishnu. The etymology of the term 'Varkari' can be directly traced to a Sanskrit terminology Varkari which can be roughly translated as 'a group of devotees', referring specifically to those who made a pilgrimage to Pandharpur. Molesworth[6] (1863) also describes the Varkaris as a pilgrim sect who went, either on a monthly or an annual basis, on a pilgrimage to their sacred place of worship located at Pandharpur. Dnyaneshwar and Namdev, two prominent figures of the Varkari tradition, use the term Varikar (or the one who engaged in the act of Vari), and probably this evolved into Varkari. Therefore, the term 'Varkari' is exclusively used for pilgrims travelling to Pandharpur.

Regarding the composition of the community, the Varkari community is formed by local independent groups despite the uniformity of traditions. However, the term 'community' or *sampradaya* should not be misinterpreted as a sectarian monastic organization in the orthodox Hindu or Buddhist sense. Rather than order, these communities were more about the similarities of religious and traditional practices.

Varkari is a part of Vaishnava sampradaya; the Varkari sect is believed to be a part of the larger Vaishnava sampradaya whose chief worshipping deity is Lord Vishnu, but, nevertheless, there remains major differences to be observed between the two. The Vaishnava sampradaya derived its philosophy and other traditions from traditional sources such as the Puranas and Bhagavad Gita and also from older Vedic literature of Upanishads.

On the other hand, the Varkari sect, owing to its origination during the Bhakti movement, evolved as an entirely devotional

[6] A Compendium of Molesworth's Marathi and English Dictionary by Baba Padmanji, downloaded from http://ia802704.us.archive.org/1/items/compendiumofmole00mole/compendiumofmole00mole.pdf

sect and traces its philosophical tradition to the Advaita philosophy (monism) of Shankaracharya (who, in turn, is believed to belong to the Shaiva tradition, an alternate tradition as compared to the Vaishnavas.)

Dnyaneshwar

Among the popular saints of Varkari tradition, Dnyaneshwar is revered as the founder of Varkari sect. He wrote a simplified version of the Bhagavad Gita, which is known as Dnyaneshwari, because of which he is often credited with the revival of Bhagavad Dharma. In an early attempt to outline the foundational philosophy of the Varkari sect, Dnyaneshwar chose a form of dialogue as his mode of explanation and raised the following three questions.

1. Regarding the nature of the Absolute Truth or *Jagadish*, The Supreme God?

To this, Dnyaneshwar responds by saying that the *atman* and the Brahmana are one and the same. His response reflects strong influence of the Advaita thought. The influence is reaffirmed when he further says that this ultimate reality is the one which gets manifested in various forms.

2. Regarding the nature of *Jeev*, Soul.

Dnyaneshwar says that people suffer because they exist in a state of ignorance of the Ultimate Truth. To make him realize the Ultimate Truth is to get him rid of the sufferings. 'Moksha' or liberation lies in the state of realization of the Ultimate Truth, which brings an end to all worldly sufferings. The Jeev or the soul becomes one with the Brahmana, or the Ultimate Reality, and this oneness can be achieved in different ways. Dnyaneshwar mentions three prominent ways of achieving self-realization and liberation: Dnyan Marga, Karma Marga and Bhakti Marga.

3. Regarding the nature of the world, *Jagat*.

The last question acts as the hinge between the first two and seeks to deepen as well as clarify their meaning. Dnyaneshwar asserts that despite the fact that there is only one Ultimate Truth, there exist multiple versions and manifestations of the same. Shankaracharya sees this as a pessimistic view and attributes this multiplicity of perspectives to *agyan* or lack of knowledge.

However, Dnyaneshwar takes a different and a more accommodating stance on this plurality of truths and attributes it to the many modes of experience which lead to discovering diverse forms of the world and refers to this diversity of experience as *dnyanacha vyavhaar* or nature of knowledge. Dnyaneshwar also asserts that despite its plurality, the visible world is temporal and transient and what can be experienced is merely a partial manifestation of the Truth, which goes on manifesting itself in new forms all along an everlasting continuum.

Summing up, like most post-Vedic philosophies, the Varkari philosophy, in essence, also reasserts the meaning of human life in its search for and experience of the Truth. However, it retains the original liberality and individualism of the tradition whereby the choice of the mode and form of experience is granted to the person seeking the Truth. All those who make efforts to seek and experience the Ultimate Reality become enlightened and are elevated to the status of being revered and looked up to. Therefore, it preaches that everyone can and should seek to become liberated. Dnyaneshwar considers bhakti as the best medium of seeking to understand the ultimate reality.

Bhakti is not based on strict observation of ritualistic traditions. It presents simplistic, inclusive and more flexible forms of approaching the Divine. Within the Varkari sampradaya, this is exemplified by the simple practices of Naamsmaran and Jap. It literally means repeating or remembering the name of the God. It is seen as the easiest and yet the most crucial medium to reach him. It is extended to more pleasurable and communal forms of bhajan and kirtan, which involve singing, dancing and other forms of artistic expression. Bhajan and kirtan are prominent forms of musical expression of devotion for the Divine within Hindu tradition. They comprise not only of singing of the God's glory but also stories and anecdotes associated with the relationships between the deities and their devotees, as well as various forms of worship and social teachings. Total surrender to the God is considered as the only way of communicating with the Divine. Enchanting a sacred chant 'mantra', performing bhajan and kirtan, reading of sacred texts of Dnyaneshwari, *Eknathi Bhagwat* and Tukaram's Gatha are considered as the ways of communicating with Vitthal. *Navvidha Bhakti* (nine forms of devotion) is considered as a way of worshipping Vitthal. The tradition of *Navvidha* or *Navdha Bhakti* can be traced back to as early as Tulsidas's 'Ramcharitmanas' wherein Rama, while visiting the Bhil saint Shabri, propounds these nine principles of showing love and devotion to God, which are simple and flexible. This philosophy focuses on two major aspects of Hindu piety: first being the establishment of a personal and intimate relationship with a human-like deity and second being the nurturing of social and moral virtues such as *dan* (giving) and compassion. It is the comprehensive exponent of a devotee's body becoming the centre of religious experience, as well as the medium of internalizing, and becoming one with the Divine.

On the one hand, the conceptualization of the worshipped deity is what gives the various traditions of the Bhakti movement their specific flavour, while, on the other hand, the portrayal of the deity as the receiver of the bhakta's devotion and love in the form of a friend, a lover or family provided a factor for the acknowledgement of the diverse Bhakti traditions as the era of Bhakti movement within Indic tradition.

The Varkari sect is no exception to this. Vitthal or Pandurang is central to Varkari sampradaya. He is considered as a form of Vishnu, and this sect is known as the Vaishnava sect. This is also known as the Bhagavad Dharma. Hindu philosophy describes *utpatti* (creation), *sthiti* (sustenance) and *laya* (destruction) in the form of Brahma, Vishnu and Mahesha (Shiva), respectively. The world is considered as the creation of God, but this creation is not a passive activity based merely on need or on the rhetoric of a whim, rather it has been made with love and is composed of the love of God Vitthal. Since bhakti, that is, devotion, is the inherent part of love element, it is the most appropriate way of attaining the God. The concept of bhakti or devotion is seen as the pinnacle of love, wherein one, through one's perseverance and efforts, becomes one with the beloved Lord himself.

Many Abhangas (poems) of the saint literature describe the greatness of Vitthal, expressing the same sentiment. For instance, Sant Eknath says as follows: 'We cannot think of anyone but Vitthal. He has been our family Deity and his worshipping is the ritual of our family'. Like many prominent figures of the Bhakti movement, the Varkari saints also rose from common social, economic and political backgrounds. They truly represented the masses. They used folk medium and local languages to enlighten the masses. While doing so, they did not disregard or look upon with contempt at what the classical languages had offered them. The dichotomy of the great and little traditions falls flat with a closer look at the Varkari tradition whereby they chose whatever they perceived as relevant and necessary from classical traditions, and also enriched them by making their own contributions. They spoke in the language of the people, established a dialogue with them, propagated their message and disseminated knowledge in local languages. Multiple ways of communicating with the deity were established along with a vibrant diversity of languages and an equally diverse tradition of different ways of looking at the deity and at the relationship between the deity and the devotees.

The Varkari saints' contribution to Marathi literature is immense. Various literary forms were created by these saints enriching Marathi literature. It includes Abhanga, Ovi, Gavalani, Bharude, etc., (different forms of compositions, Maharashtrian Saints chose to express them). All of them used these forms for enlightening the common people. The tradition was started by Dnyaneshwar followed by Namdev, Eknath, Tukaram, Savtamali, Janabai, Muktabai and many more.

Janabai and Soyrabai

Bhakti in the medieval period in Maharashtra was composed of compositions such as Ovi, Bharude and Abhanga. Abhangas of female Varkari saints discussed here are being studied for prominent themes. Overall, the Bhakti saints of India, including the Varkari saints, whether female or male, wrote around themes of daily life including work, experiences in social settings and the daily issues arising out of life. For them, the daily process of life was joyous, and their chosen deity was a part of this routine.

The literature understudy pertains to the section of Maharashtrian society that lies at the margins, and they faced extreme socio-economic conditions. However, the literature in question does not dwell on the agony but rather focuses on the joy of a life of bhakti. The primary focus of all Bhakti literature is the utter irrelevance of material life and total submission to the deity. This enables the bhakta to fill life with infinite joy and ecstasy and makes us capable to endure hatred, procure love, distribute joy and share the agony of the marginalized. Another feature of the literature under survey as well as Bhakti literature in general is the focus on the Guru who leads us to think of the truth about life in its totality. In Varkari literature as in other Bhakti forms, there is derision for fixated and formal religious practice as well as social norms and sanctions.

The relationship between the bhakta and the deity is also a unique one. The deity who is normally at a distance from the worshipper moves extremely close to the bhakta in Varkari and other Bhakti literature. For women Bhakti saints, the deity comes across as the saviour, the lover, the soulmate and the husband. His participation in the daily life of the bhakta is an essential format with Bhakti saints. The deity picks the burden of the bhakta, be it the burden of the daily routine of life or the problems of social nature. The deity was also someone who would listen to them and redress their grievances. The saints such as Tukaram and Chokhoba could endeavour to be bold enough to protest against this order and rose almost like a warrior asking people to come up with a weapon to fight against injustice if the situation demanded.

Thus, the male saints could afford to be aggressive, but the women folk could do little about it since they were fated to suffer the pangs of gender discrimination and wanted to assert it, provided they were given a chance. The situation of those women who belonged to the downtrodden community was more precarious than those who belonged to the cast Hindu community.

What were the motivations for women such as Soyrabai and Janabai to take up Bhakti? One major point of debate is whether women were drawn to Bhakti because of marginal circumstances and Bhakti provided a medium to resist the inequalities of society. A case in point would be women such as Lalleshwari and Mirabai who faced failed institutions like marriage or women such as Soyrabai, Janabai and Kanhopatra who resisted caste and associated travails. Were these women questioning societal norms through Bhakti?

What was the contemporary social reality they had to face? Women's lives were centred around family and marriage. Roles for men and women were clearly defined. Women had a focal role to play in domestic chores and looking after children. While analysing the poetry of Janabai and Soyrabai, one would like to focus on the social and spiritual dimensions of their marginalization and would take up a few of their Abhangas for a detailed analysis.

Janabai

The plight of Sant Janabai is quite unnerving as she was born in a backward family. She lost her mother and father early in her childhood. Having nobody to fall back, she went to Pandharpur and got refuge in the family of Sant Namdeo, one of the prominent Varkari poets who composed his poetry in the vernacular Marathi and propounded equality and brotherhood. Janabai remained under his patronage and composed about 340 Abhangas and devotional songs.[7]

[7] See Susie Tharu and K. Lalita, eds., *Women Writing in India. 600 B.C. to the Present. Volume 1* (New York: The Feminist Press at the City University of New York, 1991), 83. https://archive.org/details/womenwritingininin00thar

Most of her Abhangas deal with her relationship with God which was purely Plutonic and never erotic. She sees Vitthal as her mother and longs for his eternal love, not only in this life but also after her death, in every rebirth she might have to undergo. Her Abhangas are still sung all over Maharashtra and a few of them also have been translated into English. Unlike Kanhopatra, Janabai registers her anguish with a subtle sense of humour. The following Abhanga brings out her sense of deprivation and disadvantage:

Your wife and mother stay at your feet And sons are placed proudly in front. This woman is kept on the doorsteps No room for the lowly inside

O Lord how I want your embrace!

When will you call Dasi Jani yours.[8]

Janabai calls on the Lord and draws his attention to His selfishness stating that He cares for only His family and neglects His devotees like her who are striving for his love and mercy. She expresses her dissatisfaction for she is being kept out of the temple because she is of a lowly origin. Several of her Abhangas reveal as to how she was grappled by a sense of emptiness, dejection and rejection. For example, look at the following Abhanga:

If the Ganga flows to the Ocean

And the Ocean turns away

Tell me O Vitthal

Who would hear her complaint Can the river reject its fish?

Can the mother spurn her child?

Jani says O Lord

You must accept those who surrender to you.

[8] Yardi Anjali, *Five Poems*. http://www.shadowtrain.com/shadowtrain/id108.html

The metaphor of Ganga–Ocean, river–fish and mother–child relationships explicitly speaks of her striving for the kind of solace which otherwise she would not think of getting in the world where all relationships are based on selfishness. In the following poem, Janabai expresses her sense of loss and longing for the grace of filial affection she could not enjoy since she had lost her parents at a very early stage of her life. The poem brings out her emotion of loneliness and powerlessness. She writes as follows:

Mother is dead father is dead Now Vitthal take care of me O Hari my head is itching

I am your child

And have no one of my own.

Vitthal says to Rukmini

'There's no one to care for my Jani'

Taking oil and comb in his hands He combs and braids my hair:

Finishing the braid he knots it.

I say, now please rub my back.

Jani says O Gopala,

Help celebrate the festival

Of the powerless.

In another poem titled 'The Grindstone', Janabai uses the grindstone as a symbol suggestive of several meanings. The grindstone then was the only means to grind the grains for flour required to prepare the bread Bhakari. It used to be made up of two hard stones, of heavy chips adjusted on a shaft fitted in the ground with a wooden handle to pull the upper chip in a circular motion so that the grains when poured from the hole above would get crushed and make into fine flour. In the earlier times, the most tiresome job of the housewives was to grind the grains. Manual grinding required great amount of energy to pull the wooden shaft and thrust the heavy chip into circular motion. A single lady could hardly do it and hence would call some other lady either from the family or from the neighbouring house to help her. Thus, the duo would occasionally sing together songs based on popular myths and legends from ancient scriptures received from the legacy of the folk traditional narratives. Sometimes, these lyrics depicted intense emotional ruptures of familial and filial affections. Look at the following lines:

> *My lovely grindstone How sweetly it spins As I sing your praise Come to me my Lord.*[9]

She relates the grindstone as a source link to concretize her relationship with the Lord. The spinning of the wheel and singing synthesize the self with the super self. The crushing of the grains serves as the metaphor for the values of sacrifice and the cycle of birth, death and rebirth. The two wooden handles stand for the world and the spirit, and the five fingers for the five senses. As the grains are churned, the senses too are led to refinement shunning the coarse and ascending to ecstatic joy. Look at the following lines:

> *Twin poles of world and Spirit are the smooth wooden handles my five fingers grasp by turns come to me my Lord.*

The grindstone for Janabai is like life that grinds her to extract its essence known as bhakti. She compares life with a boiling vessel, which is cleared of its broth; when put to adversity emerges with victory. In many of her Abhangas, Janabai calls on the Lord and requests him to help her in the domestic chores such as sweeping, cleaning, washing and grinding. She expresses her gratitude to him for helping her and sharing not only her disillusionment but also for becoming the lowest within the

[9] See, Sarah Sellergren, 'Janabai and Kanhopatra: A Study of Two Women Saints', in *Images of Women in Maharashtrian Literature and Religion*, ed. Anne Feldhaus (Albany: SUNY Press, 1996). https://www.google.co.in/books/edition/Images_of_Women_in_Maharashtrian_Literat/ooV3Rz9zQvQC?hl=en&gbpv=1&dq=sarah+sellergren+janabai+and+kanhopatra&pg=PA214&printsec=frontcover

lowest caste and helping her out of her responsibilities. Thus, her poetry signifies social awakening. It reflects not only her disadvantageous state but also her feminine sensibility, moral compunction and self-respect.

The poets of the Bhakti movement and a majority of their followers and audiences were lower caste Hindu women. Their poems which were replete with pure devotion to the Divine, also reflected a wide variety of common sentiments associated to their personal as well as social lives which were expropriated both by the listeners and by the poets themselves. Bhakti poetry, dating back to as early as 3rd century in South India and almost 10th century in North India, attracted large audience from among the marginalized in the society, such as women and 'untouchables', and was composed in the local languages of the masses. A similar poetry from Janabai is as follows:

> Cast off all shame, and sell yourself in the marketplace; then alone can you hope to reach the Lord.
>
> Cymbals in hand, a *veena* upon my shoulder, I go about; who dares to stop me?
>
> The pallav of my sari falls away (A scandal!); yet will I enter the crowded marketplace without a thought.
>
> Jani says, My Lord I have become a slut to reach your home.

डोईचा पदर आला खांद्यावर | भरल्या बाजार जाईन म ||धृ||

हात घ ऊन टाळ खांद्यावर व णा| आता मज मना कोण कर ||1||

पंढर च्या प ठ मांडडयल पाल| मनगटावर त ल घाला तुम्ह ||2||

जन म्हण द वा म झाल व सवा| डनघाल क शवा घर तुझ ||3||

In this poem, Janabai, a 13th century poet from a low-caste Sudra family, presents herself as shrugging off social conventions, enshrining women's honour (covering her body) and taking up musical instruments (cymbals and the veena) to go sing and dance in the marketplace. Janabai, though a low-caste woman, was brought up in the household of Namdev, a popular poet-saint, and thus was treated with a certain amount of respect in light of the egalitarian ethos of Namdev's message.

Nonetheless, she is still well aware of her 'place' in society; she is a servant, one who is perhaps more aware of social conventions; because of her association with Namdev, she is here apparently flaunting these very conventions, imagining herself as a woman who is utterly outside the bounds of respectability. Shedding these bonds of respectability, she is left with nothing. In essence, there is nothing standing between herself and her Beloved Vithoba, another name for Krishna, incarnation of the god Vishnu in human form.

Soyrabai

अवघा रंग एक झाला

रंडग रंगला श्र रंग म-तं पण ग ल वाया,

पाहता पंढर च्या राया नाह भ दाच त काम पळोडन ग ल क्रोध काम द ह असोडन डवद ह सदा समाडधस्त पाह

पाहत पाहण ग ल दुर म्हण चोखखयाच महार अवघा रंग एक झाला

Soyrabai is a Vithhal bhakta and the wife of Chokhamela, also a parambhakta of Vitthal of Pandharpur. She belonged to a family of Vitthal bhaktas. The family of Soyrabai was fully immersed in the worship of Vitthal. As the wife of Chokhamela, Soyrabai became 'one with the path of her spouse'. She found the expression of her bhakti in composing a wide variety of Abhangas devoted to Vitthala.

In the above verse composed by Soyrabai, her caste is seen upfront. As per the practices of the contemporary society, Dalits were not allowed to enter the precincts of the temple. Chokha and Soyrabai belonged to the Mahar Maang caste. They were not allowed to enter temples.

In the present Abhanga, Soyrabai has drawn a picture of being so immersed in Vitthal Bhakti and Naamsmaran that her entire worldly existence is reflected in Vitthala. This is the supreme state of bhakti, a state of total immersion in the paramatma. The pinnacle of bhakti is the total merging of the colours of a bhakta's life with that of the paramatma. In reality, this is the state of Samadhi of Ashtangyog, which Soyrabai has reached, a state in which no dichotomies of 'me' and 'you' exist, a state of Advaita in which the bhakta is 'ekroop' with the paramatma and there is no consciousness of the body or of society.

This is a state of bhakti that is often discussed with reference to Mirabai and Lalleshwari. While Mirabai had accepted Krishna as her 'husband' and subsequently set out to destroy all social conventions in the pursuit of Krishna, Lalleshwari was a Shiva bhakta who gave up all social pretensions. She was the naked saint of Kashmir. For her clothes signified a barrier in the bhakti for Shiva, so she shed all barriers. Interestingly, this bhakti takes the form of 'Aham Brahmasmi'. The devotion to a 'Sagun' deity God, Vishnu, Krishna and Brahma, becomes irrelevant. In Hindu thought, these are mere ways to be one with paramatma, who is not an external force. The bhakta loses everything for her bhakthnath. For the women saints of India, this is also a state in which bindings of the feminine form are surpassed. When Soyrabai was in the state of Samadhi, all such barriers disappeared. Bodily awareness was lost to her. Enemies were ineffective, and the lures of the five senses were subsumed. At this level of Samadhi, the Seen (Vitthal), the See-er (The Bhakt) and the Darshan (the experience) are all one with each other.

She credits her Samadhi to the guidance and presence of her husband Chokhamela. She is 'चोखखयाच महार'. She identifies herself as the wife of Chokha. In every Abhanga, she uses the same name. The husband is also the soulmate who guides her to a state of Samadhi in the bhakti of Vitthal.

Another of Soyrabai's Abhanga is focused on the magic of bhakti in breaking down caste barriers. Chokha and Soyrabai were of Dalit caste. Such persons were not allowed to enter the temple or draw water from the well. Soyrabai calls this 'छळ' or 'cheating. The Brahmanas of Pandharpur were creating obstacles for Chokha and Soyrabai by not allowing them Darshan of Vithoba in the temple. Division of bhaktas by caste was never the intent of Vithoba. Soyrabai feels sorry that they have to undergo such humiliation. However, she has faith in her deity. He arranges things in a way that the bhakta is redeemed. She has full faith in her Vitthala, and he responds as is promised in the Gita Chapter 9 Verse 22:

अनन्याश्चिन्तयन्तो मां ये जना: पययुपासते | तेषां श्चनत्याश्चियुयक्तानां योगक्षेमां वहाम्यहम् || 22||

The Lord takes care of the bhakta who approaches him with full faith. Vithoba arranges things in a way that the Brahmanas of Pandharpur are unable to believe their eyes. The entire pantheon of rishis, devtas and holy beings are assembled in the house of Chokha. Soyrabai's house is decorated with flowers and Riddhi–Siddhi are standing in the doorway to welcome the guests. Rangoli floor designs have been drawn to make the house of Chokhamela beautiful and welcoming. A number of festive food items being made, and rows and rows of Brahmanas are partaking the prasad. The assembled gods and divinities shower their blessings. The caste question is resolved in the most amazing way by the synergy between the bhakta and the Isht devta. The wayward Brahmanas who were cheating Chokha and Soyrabai have been shown the right path. There is actually no caste in bhakti. These are man-made restrictions that have been imposed by man on man.

Conclusion

A close study of the Abhangas of Soyrabai and Janabai shows that they received hardly any recognition in their times. Their poems are the turbulent voices of womanhood responding to the context of the community for their welfare. One of the major impulses behind their outpour of poetic creativity was their concern for the social transformation. Their poetry is characteristic of their powerful longing for it through spirituality. Their voices remain distinct into the realm of feminine sensibility and spirituality. Women are required to rethink, redefine and reconstruct the notions of the feminine, femininity and all about their feminist voices, aspirations, practices and ideology. The poems of Kanhopatra and Janabai could be studied as cultural documents reflecting the best of the feminist aspirations and the womanhood capable of guiding the community of women, particularly in terms of the challenges they have to face while interacting with different situations in private and public domains.

8

Knowledge Traditions and Institutions in Precolonial India

Niraj Kumar Jha

India before the British rule, contrary to the dismal state of education and knowledge in the country during the colonial rule and the decades following India's Independence, was a leading country in the field of education and dissemination of knowledge. Sunderlal, an acknowledged historian, captures the education system functioning in India during the precolonial times. There were four types of educational arrangements covering well the nook and cranny of the country. First, there were innumerable Brahmana preceptors who taught students at their homes. Second, there were *tols* or *vidyapeeths* (seats of learning) located in the major cities, which imparted higher education in Sanskrit literature. Third, there were maktabs and madrasas, which imparted education in Urdu and Persian to both Muslims and Hindu students. Fourth, every village had at least a school for the education of children. The traditional panchayats, which the British destroyed as they consolidated their hold over India, maintained schools as one of their prime functions. Sunderlal refers to Max Muller and Ludlow as cited in *India*, a book written by Keir Hardie, a British Parliamentarian of repute, to show the state of education in India. Max Muller had reckoned, on the basis of official documents and a missionary report, that there were 80,000 schools in Bengal alone, one school for every 400 of the population, before the British occupied Bengal. Ludlow wrote about whole India in his book *History of British India* that in every Hindu village, which had retained their old form, the children generally were able to read, write and cipher, but where the British swept away the village system, as in Bengal, there the school system also disappeared. Sunderlal quotes from the 'Report of the Select Committee on Affairs of the East India Company' made in 1832 that '... the peasantry of few other countries would bear a comparison as to their state of education with those of many parts of British India'.[1] The superiority of the Indian education system was an observed and acknowledged fact.

Indigenous Education

Dharampal (1922–2006), a Gandhian scholar and historian, debunked many myths, manufactured and propagated by the apologists of the British Empire, showing the erstwhile indigenous education system in poor light contrary to the official reports of the colonial administration itself.[2] He quotes Mahatma Gandhi, who had the idea what the British had done to education in India. Gandhi in his address at the Royal Institute of International Affairs, London, on 20 October 1931, had stated the following:

> I say without fear of my figures being challenged successfully, that today India is more illiterate than it was fifty or a hundred years ago, and so is Burma, because the British administrators, when they came to India, instead of taking hold of things as they were, began to root them out.[3]

[1] Sunderlal, *Bharat Mein Angreji Raj* [English Rule in India], 2nd ed., Vol. III (Allahabad: Omkar Press, 1938), 1119–1121.

[2] Dharampal, *The Beautiful Tree: Indigenous Indian Education in the Eighteenth Century* (Goa: Other India Press, 2000).

[3] Ibid., 6.

Dharampal also cited the very colonial records to substantiate Gandhi's observation. In fact, William Adam (referred to as a missionary above) had estimated that about 100,000 village schools existed in Bengal and Bihar around the 1830s. The estimation was based on the impressions of various high British officials and others who knew the different areas well. Even earlier, Sir Thomas Munro, Governor of Madras (16 September 1814–10 July 1827), had testified that every village had a school in the Madras Presidency. The senior British officials had observed similar arrangement in the newly acquired territories organized as the Bombay Presidency in around 1820. G. L. Prendergast, a high-ranking official, had noted that there was hardly a village, great or small, throughout their territories in which there was not at least one school, and in larger villages there were more than one school. Dr G. W. Leitner recorded the similar state of education in Punjab in around 1850.[4]

It was not only that the Indian population was well-covered by schooling and the people were well-educated. Even the method of imparting education was such that Andrew Bell, an educationist, after returning from India in the early 19th century, applied the same method of teaching in Britain which he had experienced and experimented in India. A letter from the Court of Directors to the Governor-General in Council of Bengal, dated 3 June 1814, acknowledged the following:

> The mode of instruction that from time immemorial has been practiced under these masters has received the highest tribute of praise by its adoption in this country, under the direction of the Reverend Dr. Bell, formerly chaplain in Madras; and it is now become the mode by which education is conducted in our national establishment, from a conviction of facility it affords in the acquisition of the language by simplifying the process of instruction.... This venerable and benevolent institution of the Hindoos is represented to have withstood the shock of revolutions....[5]

[4] Ibid., 18.

[5] Sunderlal, *Bharat Mein Angreji Raj*, 1122–1123.

The method of education extensively practiced in the 19th century, in which abler students having learnt their lessons from the teacher in turn taught other students, was known as the Madras System of Education or mutual instruction or monitorial system.[6] Vincent A. Smith recounted the following:

> The monitorial system commended itself to Mr. Andrew Bell, who was in charge of an educational institution at Madras in the closing years of the eighteenth century. He brought the idea home, where it was taken up by his follower and rival, Lancaster, but soon degenerated into a 'caricature' of the Indian system. Montessori copied the Indian practice of teaching writing before or simultaneously with reading. Thus it appears that in two particulars the proud West has learned something from the humble village schools of the East.[7]

Another remarkable feature of the precolonial education was that it was highly inclusive. Hard data from the areas where these were collected unmistakably state that both teachers and the taught belonged to various castes and notably even from the scheduled castes, as they came to be categorized later on. Contrary to even the widely held perception that only the upper caste Hindus and the ruling elite of Muslims received education during pre-British times, the actual scenario is quite different, at least among the Hindus in the districts of the Madras Presidency and that more significantly in the Tamil-speaking areas and also from the two districts of Bihar. It was the group termed as 'Soodras', which is mostly spelt as Shudras, and the castes considered below the Shudras which predominated in the thousands of traditional schools surviving by that time. The reports of the collectors of the Madras Presidency (from Ganjam in the north to Tinnevelly in the south and Malabar in the west) on the indigenous education,

[6] Encyclopaedia Britannica, 'Monitorial System', https://www.britannica.com/topic/monitorial-system; Wikipedia, 'Monitorial System', https://en.wikipedia.org/wiki/Monitorial_System

[7] Vincent A. Smith, 'Review of Ancient Indian Education by F. E. Keay and A History of Education in Ancient India by Nogendra Nath Mazumder', *History* 4, no. 16 (January 1920): 217.

based on the surveys carried out during 1822–1825, clearly refutes the widely held assumption of the traditional education being a preserve of the high castes. The Madras Presidency being predominantly Hindu, that is, the Hindus constituting 95 per cent of its total population, the breakup of the students receiving education is quite revealing. In the Tamil-speaking areas, students from the twice-born castes ranged from 13 per cent in South Arcot to some 23 per cent in Madras. Muslims constituted less than 3 per cent in South Arcot and Chingleput and on the higher side 10 per cent in Salem. The Shudras and other castes below this caste together constituted about 70 per cent in Salem and Tinnevelly at the lower end, and their numbers went up to over 84 per cent in South Arcot. In Malayalam-speaking Malabar, the proportion of the twice-born castes was below 20 per cent of the total. As Malabar had a larger Muslim population, the Muslim school students made up nearly 27 per cent of the total. And in this area too, the Shudras and the other castes were in far greater numbers, as they accounted for some 54 per cent of the total schoolgoing students. It was only in the Telugu-speaking districts that among the schoolgoers, the twice-born students had greater numbers. The Brahmana students were in the range of 24 per cent in Cuddapah to 46 per cent in Vizagapatam. The Vysees, or Vaishyas, constituted 10.5 per cent of the students in Vizagapatam, and the percentage went up to 29 per cent in Cuddapah. Muslim students made for the 1 per cent of the students in Vizagapatam for the highest to 8 per cent in Nellore. The Shudras and other castes still had the substantial numbers in the range of 35 per cent in Guntoor to over 41 per cent in Cuddapah and Vizagapatam.[8] However, the number of girls in the schools was negligible. Except the district of Malabar and the Jeypoor division of Vizagapatam district, where girls joined the school in good numbers, the girls from the Brahmana, Kshatriya and Vaishya castes were practically non-existent in schools. The Hindu girls who went to schools were from the Shudras and other castes. Some Muslim girls also attended the school.[9]

[8] Dharampal, *The Beautiful Tree*, 27–30.
[9] Ibid., 42–43.

This is also remarkable that the kids were admitted to schools at an early age as found in the aforementioned Madras surveys. Generally, the students were admitted to schools at the age of 5. The years of school education varied as per the reports from district to district. The collector of Cuddapah found that to be only two years, but mostly the recorded periods of school education varied from a minimum of five to a maximum of about 15 years. The given information also indicates that the schools ran for very long hours; starting early in the morning at 6 AM, the schools continued until the sunset or even later with two breaks for meals in between. The schools taught reading, writing and arithmetic. The surveys listed the books in use in the schools as well. Bellary had a list of 23 books, whereas Rajahmundry listed 43 books. The selection has a fine mix of literary and utilitarian texts. The collectors had different views about the quality of education imparted, but some indeed considered it to be useful. The collector of Madras noted as follows: 'It is generally admitted that before they (i.e., the students) attain their 13th year of age, their acquirements in the various branches of learning are uncommonly great'.[10]

The surveys had a column for the count of colleges too. Many districts of the Madras Presidency did not find any college existing in their respective areas, but several districts recorded their existence. In total, 1,094 institutions of higher learning were recorded in existence in the Presidency. The district of Rajahmundry had the highest count of 279 with a total of 1,454 scholars, followed by Coimbatore with 173 such places hosting 724 scholars, Guntoor having 171 of them with 939 scholars, Tanjore having 109 with 769 scholars, Nellore having 107, North Arcot having 69 with 418 scholars, Salem having 53 with 324 scholars, Chingleput having 51 with 398 scholars, Masulipatam having 49 with 199 scholars, Bellary having 23, Trichnopoly having 9 with 131 scholars and Malabar having 1 old institution maintained by the Samudrin Raja with 75 scholars. In most of

[10] Ibid., 30–33.

the other districts, the collectors reported higher learning in the Vedas, law, astronomy, mathematics, ethics and other disciplines being imparted in Agraharams or homes, whereas Brahmana students formed a smaller portion of students attending schools. In the institutions of higher learning, they almost monopolized the studies of theology, metaphysics, ethics and, to a large extent, the study of law. But even in places of higher learning, scholars from various backgrounds and castes had considerable presence in the disciplines of astronomy and medical science. Data from Malabar show that out of 808 scholars studying astronomy, only 78 were Brahmanas, and of the 194 students studying medicine, only 31 were Brahmanas. Rajahmundry recorded five Shudra scholars in the institution of higher learning. In the practice of surgery, it was the barbers who excelled.[11]

In Malabar, the family of Samudrin Raja supported the institution of higher learning there. The collector of Madras reported that while scholars from the poorer Brahmana families received their education without any payment, others contributed in accordance with their means. In addition, the Brahmanas were endowed with land or revenue grant and were in turn obligated to perform their religious duties and impart education to the willing scholars. The collector of Cuddapah clarified that no school or college was supported by public contribution in his district. The students moved to the houses of the preceptors between the age of 10 and 16, often travelling 10 to 100 miles from their villages, to stay there until the completion of their education. Many of them were too poor to afford their expenses. They were supported entirely by charity, which they received from the Brahmana households as alms on daily basis and the householders obliged them cheerfully. The collector of Guntoor too noted the absence of any public institution of higher learning and informed that subjects like theology, law, astronomy, etc., were privately taught by the Brahmanas of learning without getting any fees or reward. They met their expenses by means of maunium land which had been

[11] Ibid., 33–35.

granted to their ancestors by the ancient zamindars of the district and by the former government on different accounts. The collector of Guntoor noticed the same trend: the scholars from the poorer families sustained on the alms given to them by the villagers and those from better-off families paid around ₹3 per month, but that only covered expenses on victuals.[12]

The collector of Masulipatam referred to the Vedas and the Shastras being taught in the institutions of higher learning or privately in Brahmana homes. The Shastra, he explained, was the common term for all those sciences available in Sanskrit language, namely law, astronomy, theology, etc. The district of Rajahmundry provided a list of books used at the colleges, which are as follows as spelt in the report: *Roogvadum*, *Ragoovumsam*, *Yajoorvadum*, *Coomarasumbhavem*, *Samavadum*, *Moghasundasem*, *Sroudum*, *Bharavy*, *Dravedavedum*, *Maukhum*, *Nunlauyanum*, *Nayeshadum*, *Andasastrum*, *Siddhanda Cowmoody*, *Turkum*, *Jeyoteshem*, *Durmasastrum* and *Cauveyems*. In Rajahmundry, the Persian colleges used the following books: *Caremah Aumadunnanmah*, *Harckarum* in Persian, *Inshah Culipha* and *Goolstan*, *Bahurdanish* and *Bostan*, *Abdul Phazul Inshah*, *Calipha* and *Khoran*. In the traditional Sanskrit colleges, it can be inferred that the Vedas, various Shastras, the Puranas, epics, mathematics and astronomy were taught. The Sanskrit classics were very popular. The collector of Guntoor drew attention to a very important aspect of the Indian education. He noted that scholars desirous of deeper studies in theology travelled to Benares and Navadweepum, etc., where they stayed for years to take instruction under the learned pundits of those places.[13]

Another prominent feature of the existing education system of Madras Presidency was the practice of private education at home. Many collectors mentioned that boys and, especially, girls received education at home from their parents or relatives or

[12] Ibid., 35–38.
[13] Ibid., 36, 38–39.

from privately engaged tutors. Agraharams, in particular, were places where scholars studied at the residences of the preceptors. The data suggest the practice being widespread. Malabar and Madras districts provided data about the teaching arranged by the parents for their wards on their own. In Malabar, the number of scholars receiving education in private was about 21 times the number of those attending the single college existing there. The Malabar data also records 194 persons studying medicine. The data from Madras regarding the number of boys and girls being taught at home is 4.73 times of the students attending schools. On the basis of data available, it can be assumed that the number of those studying theology, law, astronomy, metaphysics, ethics, poetry and literature, medicine, music and dance at home was many times the number of those who were receiving such education institutionally. Among the private tutors, according to the data, the Brahmanas and the Vaishyas accounted for half of the total number, but even among the private tutors, there were 28.7 per cent from the Shudra castes and 13 per cent from other castes (below the Shudras).[14]

The 'Adam's Reports' or the *Reports on the State of Education in Bengal, 1836 and 1838* was semi-official, based on a mix of observations and limited surveys and consisted of three reports produced in a staggered manner covering different areas. Its first report as mentioned earlier had estimated 100,000 schools existing in Bengal and Bihar, most of the villages having one school. In addition, he calculated the existence of institutions of higher learning to be 1,800 in Bengal and made another estimation of these institutions together hosting 10,800 scholars. He observed that the schools were run from the houses of the respectable native inhabitants or some house existing nearby their homes. The institutions of higher learning unlike schools had designated buildings made of clay consisting of 3 to 5 rooms at some places and mostly having 9 to 11 rooms, of which 1 was a dedicated study room. The same trend as observed in the Madras Presidency

[14] Ibid., 39–42.

can be seen here too. The scholars stayed in the same building, and their foods and clothes were provided by the teachers with the support of the locals.[15]

Adam's second report was based on a study of a particular thana (area coming under a police station): Nattore in the district of Rajshahy. He recorded the existence of 27 elementary schools with only 262 students within the age group of 8 to 14 years, but the children occasionally studied at home. However, the schools of learning numbered 38 and hosted 397 scholars, of which 136 were local and 261 had come from distant places, and the scholars were in the age group of 11 to 27 years.[16]

Adam's third report, based on the surveys of select districts of Bengal and Bihar, that is, major part of the district of Murshedabad (20 thanas out of 37 thanas of the district), the districts of Beerbhoom and Burdwan in Bengal, and South Behar and Tirhoot in Bihar to be precise, is the most extensive of his reports based on the ground-level surveys. He recorded 2,566 schools functioning in the surveyed areas. Very remarkably, like the Madras surveys, this report too brings out the diverse social background of both the teachers and the taught in the schools. Though the larger number of teachers came from Kayastha, Brahmana, Sadgop and Aguri castes, but a significant number of teachers belonged to 30 other caste groups which included 6 teachers from even the Chandals. Among the pupils of the elementary schools, there were even a greater variety, and no caste group, it appears, remained unrepresented. The Brahmanas and the Kayasthas nowhere numbered more than 40 per cent of the total. In the two Bihar districts, together, they formed no more than 15 to 16 per cent. More surprisingly in the district of Burdwan, students from the Dom and Chandal castes numbering 61 each together almost equalled the 126 students of the Vaidya caste. The district Burdwan even had 13 missionary schools, but, as Adam records, the total number of Dom and Chandal scholars

[15] Ibid., 46–49.
[16] Ibid., 49–52.

in them were only 4, and the scholars from 16 of the lowest castes together numbered only 86, whereas 674 scholars from these castes were in the native schools.[17]

Adam's report shows that the schooling in these districts followed a systematic pattern of teaching. The age of admission to the elementary schools varied from 5 to 8 years and of leaving from 13 to 16.5 years. Education went through four stages. At the first stage, which took about 10 days, the pupils learnt to form the letters of the alphabet on the ground with a small stick or slip of bamboọ, or on a sandboard. The second stage, extending from 2.5 to 4 years, was distinguished by the use of palm leaf (*pana*) for writing, and scholars learnt to write and read at this stage and memorized the *Cowrie* Table (a numeration table as far as 100), the *Katha* Table (a land measure table), the *Ser* Table (a weight measure table) and others. At the third stage, of 2 to 3 years, scholars wrote on the plantain-leaf and learnt addition, subtraction and other arithmetical rules. During the fourth and final stage, lasting up to 2 years, the scholars used paper for writing and were expected to read the Rāmāyaṇa, *Mansa Mangal*, etc., at home and be adept in accounts and drafting of letters and petitions, etc. One important component of the school curricula was the teaching of accounts, both commercial and agricultural.[18]

There were 353 Sanskrit schools in the areas of Adam's surveys. The teachers in the schools were predominantly from the Brahmana caste and offered specialized education in grammar, logic, law, literature, mythology, astrology, lexicology, rhetoric, medicine, Vedanta, Tantra, Mimamsa and Sankhya. The age of admission varied and did not offer a pattern, but the period of study ranged from 7 to 15 years. The number of Persian schools was 694 and of Arabic schools was 31 with the strength of 3,479 and 175 scholars, respectively. The age of admissions in the Persian schools ranged from 6.8 years to 10.3 years, and the education went on for about 11 to 15 years. Interestingly, over

[17] Ibid., 52, 54.
[18] Ibid., 52, 53, 55.

half of the scholars pursuing Persian were the Hindus, mostly from the Kayastha caste. Arabic was largely studied by Muslims scholars, but report records 14 Kayasthas, 2 Aguris, 1 Teli and 1 Brahmin studying Arabic.[19]

About 45 years after Adam's reports, Dr G. W. Leitner prepared an even more voluminous survey of indigenous education in Punjab, and his findings confirmed the similar widespread arrangement of education in Punjab, which he found had declined since the British took over. Leitner observed the following:

> Respect for learning has always been the redeeming feature of 'the East'. To this the Panjab has formed no exception. Torn by invasion and civil war, it ever preserved and added to educational endowments. The most unscrupulous chief, the avaricious money-lender, and even the freebooter, vied with the small landowner in making peace with his conscience by founding schools and rewarding the learned. There was not a mosque, a temple, a dharmasala that had not a school attached to it, to which the youth flocked chiefly for religious education.... There were also thousands of secular schools, frequented alike by Mahomedans, Hindus and Sikhs, in which Persian or Lunde was taught.... There was not a single villager who did not take a pride in devoting a portion of his produce to a respected teacher.... In short, the lowest computation gives us 3,30,000 pupils (against little more than 1,90,000 at present) in the schools of the various denominations who were acquainted with reading, writing, and some method of computation; whilst thousands of them belonged to Arabic and Sanskrit colleges, in which Oriental Literature and systems of Oriental Law, Logic, Philosophy, and Medicine were taught to the highest standards. Tens of thousands also acquired a proficiency in Persian, which is now rarely reached in Government and aided schools or colleges.[20]

The available documents do not have any reference to training in different crafts or technologies, and also there is little about music and dance. The latter two might have been taken care of by the temple organizations, but the training in crafts appears

[19] Ibid., 53, 55, 56.
[20] Ibid., 341–342.

to have escaped the attention of the observers; and they seemed to be more interested in the crafts and the technologies used and they did not bother to take note of how these valuable skills were passed from one generation to another. The probable reasons are that these skills were learnt as family tradition or group occupations at the workplace itself. However, the methods of training in technologies and crafts, and improvisation of technologies which occurred over time need to be explored.[21]

The 1822–1825 Madras Presidency data, the report of W. Adam on Bengal and Bihar 1835–1838 and the later Panjab survey by G. W. Leitner basically record the state of indigenous education suffering gross neglect and decline after the onset of the British rule. In the Bombay Presidency, just after the defeat of the Peshwas in 1818 by which most of the territories of the Presidency were acquired, the 'Report of the Bombay Education Society' for 1819 had this observation: 'There is probably as great a proportion of persons in India who can read, write, and keep simple accounts, as are to be found in European countries'.[22] Sir Thomas Munro wrote in his minute of 10 March 1826: 'The state of education here exhibited, low as it is compared with that of our own country, is higher than it was in most European countries at no very distant period'. Obliviously, Munro was talking about a system in decay, and yet he found the system superior to the one prevailing in Europe not much before. Even the comparison is silent about the state of education in Britain itself. Dharampal clarifies that in the data pertaining to Britain, the term 'at no very distant period' really meant the beginning of the 19th century, which had been the real start of the Day schools for most children in the British Isles.[23] And he makes a studied comparison which deserves serious attention:

> According to this hard data, in terms of the content, the and proportion of those attending institutional school education, the

[21] Ibid., 58.
[22] Ibid., 375.
[23] Ibid., 42.

> situation in India in 1800 is certainly not inferior to what obtained in England then; and in many respects Indian schooling seems to have been much more extensive (and, it should be remembered, that it is a greatly damaged and disorganized India that one is referring to). The content of studies was better than what was then studied in England. The duration of study was more prolonged. The method of school teaching was superior and it is this very method which is said to have greatly helped the introduction of popular education in England but which had prevailed in India for centuries. School attendance, especially in the districts of the Madras Presidency, even in the decayed state of the period 1822–25, was proportionately far higher than the numbers in all variety of schools in England in 1800.

Dharampal also points to the girls missing from the Indian schools then as per the data and India lagging behind only in that in comparison to England, but Dharampal conjectures that girls at that time mostly studied at home and here the available data may not give the correct picture.[24]

Yet another account of Indian education, observed over time but barely some years before the establishment of the colonial rule in Malabar region of India, gives a fuller and rounded view of the education as it was actually imparted. Paolino Da San Bartolomeo, an Austrian Carmelite missionary and Orientalist, had stayed in Malabar for 13 years from 1776 to 1789. He was an accomplished scholar and his first-hand account of education in Malabar makes a vivid and authentic depiction of education in India. The first of his impressions was that education in India was much simpler and inexpensive in comparison to the schooling in Europe. Students assembled under the shade of the coconut trees and sat in rows. They learnt letters of alphabets by tracing these on sand with their fore fingers. The writing teacher called *Agian* or *Ellutacien* instructed standing before them if they needed greater attention, otherwise sat in front of them cross-legged on a tiger or deer skin or a mat. After narrating this inexpensive

[24] Ibid., 20–21.

method of education in some detail, Bartolomeo makes a remarkable comment,

> This method of teaching writing was introduced into India two hundred years before the birth of Christ, according to the testimony of Magasthenes, and still continues to be practiced. No people, perhaps, on earth have adhered so much to their ancient usages and customs as the Indians.[25]

Bartolomeo's Account

Bartolomeo goes on to describe that a teacher in Malabar got two Panam from each of his pupils for every two months. Some offered rice in certain quantity in lieu of cash. There were other teachers who instructed the students without charging any fees, who were compensated by the overseers of temples or by the chiefs of different castes. After learning the fair skill in writing, they moved to schools called *Eutupalli*, where they wrote on palm leaves. Palm leaves stitched together and fastened between two boards was called *Grantha*. The guru or teacher received the utmost reverence and respect. When he entered the school, all the pupils threw themselves down at full length before him, placed their right hand on their mouth and did not utter a single word until given express permission. Any student showing disrespect or flouting the rules were liable to expulsion from the schools, but the pupils were obedient and hardly acted offensively.[26]

Bartolomeo further mentions the subjects covered at the schools:

> 1st, the principles of writing and accounts: 2nd, the Samscred grammar, which contains the declensions and conjugations; in Malabar it is called *Sidharuba*; but, in Bengal *Sarasvada*, or the art of speaking with elegance: 3rd, the second part of this grammar, which contains the syntax, or the book *Vyagarna*: 4th, the *Amarasinha*, or Brahmanic dictionary.

[25] Fra Paolino Da San Bartolomeo, *A Voyage to the East Indies*, trans. William Johnston (London: Vernor, 1800), 261–262.

[26] Ibid., 262–263.

The fourth subject which he mentions is obviously *Amarakosha* of Amarasimha, a Sanskrit grammarian and poet from ancient India. He also talks of shlokas being taught by the gurus.

> These verses serve not only as examples of the manner in which the words must be combined with each other, but contain, at the same time, most excellent moral maxims, which are thus imprinted in the minds of the young people as if in play; so that, while learning the language, they are taught rules proper for forming their character, and directing their future conduct in life.

Bartolomeo specifies some ideas of morality contained in the slokas, like this one: 'Why have we ceased living in the forests, and associated ourselves in cities and towns, if the object of our doing so be not to enjoy friendship; to do good mutually to each other, and to receive in our habitations the stranger and wanderer?' Others underlined the need of having knowledge, need of having slanderous tongue, marital fidelity, forgiveness and modesty. He also noted that the education was quite wedded to the religious practices. He describes that the sacred enclosures where children were taught invariably had a Lingam. He is obviously referring to Siva temples. But he says that the Lingam was worshipped only by the Sivanites (Shavites) and another sect paid 'divine honour to Fire'. He was perhaps referring to the performances of sacrifices, the havan. He also found two more statues generally placed at the entrance of the schools, those of Ganesha, 'the protector of the sciences and of learned men', and of Sarasvati, 'the goddess of eloquence and history'. Each student while entering the school offered salutations to these deities and recited words in prayer. He commented, 'This is real idolatry; but these practices at any rate prove that the Indians accustom their children early to honour the gods, and to consider them as their protectors and benefactors'.[27]

Other subjects being taught to the Indian youths were poetry, fencing, botany and medicine as one discipline, navigation, the

[27] Ibid., 263–265.

use of the spear on foot, the art of playing a ball, chess, tennis, logic, astrology, law and silence. Bartolomeo lists the subjects in this jumbled order only. Moreover, he also gives the native words for all these disciplines, but the word given for law is *svadhyaya*, which may be a printing error. *Swaydhyaya*, a Sanskrit word, means self-study. *Swaydhyaya* and *mauna* (silence) may be a part of philosophical training of an initiate. Bartolomeo goes on to describe the following:

> Youth destined to be Brahmans, must spend ten years within the precincts of the temple at Trichur, and avoid all intercourse with the female sex. They are obliged also to observe the strictest silence, which continues for five years. This is the first degree of philosophy. It thence appears that Phythagoras must have borrowed his philosophy in part from the Indian Philosophers, or others whose doctrine was similar, for his scholars were subjected to silence for the same number of years.

He noted that surgery, anatomy and geography were not taught, he explained, as the Indians were least interested to leave their beautiful country and the non-killing of animals kept them away for practicing surgery or learning anatomy. Navigation was also learnt only for riverine navigation. The Indians valued physical education and even martial arts, but mainly for physical robustness. Here, another remarkable aspect of education was that all these exercises, arts and sciences were taught by different masters and each of them received similar respect by the learners as mentioned earlier. Twice a year, each teacher received a piece of silk from his pupil, a present called *samanam*, which he used for clothing.[28]

Bartolomeo's account clarifies a great issue with regard to vocational education. He provides the following detail:

> The boys, in the ninth year of their age, are initiated with great ceremony into the calling or occupation of the caste to which their father belongs, and which they can never abandon.... Hence it happens that the Indians do not follow that general and superficial

[28] Ibid., 265–266.

> method of education by which children are treated as if they were all intended for the same condition and for discharging the same duties; but those of each caste are from their infancy formed for what they are to be during their whole lives. A future Brahman, for example, is obliged, from his earliest years, to employ himself in reading and writing, and to be present at the presentation of offerings, to calculate eclipses of the sun and moon; to study the laws and religious practices; to cast nativities; in short to learn everything, which, according to the injunction of the *Veda*, or sacred books of the Indians, it is necessary he should know. The *Vayshya* on the other hand, instruct youth in agriculture; the *Kshetria*, in the science of government and the military arts, the *Shudra*, in mechanics, the *Mucaver*, in fishing; the *Ciana*, in gardening and the *Banyen*, in commerce.

And he praised the arrangement: 'By this establishment the knowledge of a great many things necessary for the public good is not only widely diffused, but transmitted to posterity; who are thereby enabled still farther to improve them, and bring them nearer to perfection'.[29] However, he informs that girls are not allowed to venture out of homes, and he does not talk about their education.

Bartolomeo describes only the educational arrangement of the Hindus of Malabar, which he describes as the Indian education system, and the description duly attests his assumption. The British colonial reports also reflected that educational arrangement throughout the Indian subcontinent had a civilizational core both in curricula and in organization but with obvious regional variations. Bartolomeo had only high praise for the upbringing of the children and educational arrangement for the kids and youths of India. This is remarkable since Bartolomeo was a missionary and had come to India with the missionary purpose only.

As the Company's rule expanded, the traditional educational system of India declined and withered away. A. D. Campbell, collector of Bellary, in his report dated 17 August 1823 accounts the condition of education in the district prior to the establishment of

[29] Ibid., 267–268.

the company's rule and its subsequent destruction. He confirms the effective and economic method of education practised in India and its 'imitation' in England. The report reads as follows:

> The economy with which children are taught to write in the native schools and the system by which the more advanced scholars are caused to teach the less advanced, and at the same time to confirm their knowledge, is certainly admirable, and well deserved the imitation it has received in England.

Campbell then states with anguish that a large number of people are no longer able to avail the advantage of the system as a result of their impoverishment. He explains the causation of mass poverty: English manufactures capturing the Indian markets and thus diminishing the means of the native manufacturing classes, relocation of most of the troops outside the English-held territories resulting in the reduced demands for grains and the drain of capital from India to Europe. The earlier ruling classes liberally funded the education as they prided supporting education, but the English rulers drained money and resources back home. The impact on education was disastrous; the collector records the following:

> The greater part of the middling and lower classes of the people are now unable to defray the expenses incident upon the education of their offspring, while their necessities require the assistance of their children as soon as their tender limbs are capable of the smallest labour.
>
> Of nearly a million souls in this District, not 7,000 are now at school, a population which exhibits but too strongly the result above stated. In many villages where formerly there were large schools, there are now none, and in many others where there were large schools, now only a few children of the most opulent are taught, others being unable from poverty to attend.

'Such is the state in this District of the various schools in which reading writing and arithmetic are taught in the vernacular dialects of the country, as has been always usual in India'.[30]

[30] Sunderlal, *Bharat Mein Angreji Raj*, 1123–1126.

Another factor that Campbell points out is that the government completely stopped aiding education and sciences. He notes, in particular, that 'there is no doubt that in former times, especially under the Hindoo Governments, very large grants, both in money and in land, were issued for the support of learning.'[31]

Elphinstone reported the similar state of education in the Bombay Province in 1824 as reported by Campbell from the Madras Province one year earlier. In fact, the status of education met the same fate throughout the Company's empire in India. Walter Hamilton, a scholar, on the basis of several reports, wrote in 1828 that the literature and sciences were declining among the Indians. The number of scholars was decreasing and those still receiving education study fewer subjects. People had left studying philosophy and sciences, and no studies were being undertaken barring those required for performances of religious rituals and for astrological purposes. The reason he cited for the decline of literature was the disappearances of the royal courts and nobles which patronized learning during earlier times. Sunderlal, after citing different scholars, points to the four factors for the decimation of the robust education system which prevailed in the precolonial India, accessed by both highly and lowly. These were the deindustrialization of the country and the resultant impoverishment of the masses; the destruction of the traditional village panchayats and the closure of the village schools run by them; the end of the native rulers which dispensed grants to educational institutions; and the conscious British policy to keep Indians unlettered so that they could not unite to question the alien rule.[32]

Inclusive Education

Among the factors mentioned here, one factor needs more attention. The precolonial administration was fundamentally a decentralized form of governance. The famed 'village republics' wielded substantial authority locally and controlled and dispensed

[31] Ibid., 1126.
[32] Ibid., 1127–1129.

resources on their own. Dharampal points out that there are voluminous data scattered in the very British records which confirm that the basic expenses such as education and medical care, the local police, the maintenance of irrigation facilities and others had primary claim on revenue. The parents and guardians of the scholars contributed according to their respective means, by paying some fees or by way of presenting gifts to teachers or occasional feeding of the needy scholars towards the maintenance of the system, but it was the share from the revenue which basically supported such an elaborate system of education which catered to all the sections of society, imparted education gratis to many and also cared for the food and lodging of the resident scholars. For example, according to the Bengal–Bihar data of the 1770s and 1780s, the revenues of these areas were divided into various categories in addition to what was called the *Khalsa*, which went to the provincial or higher rulers. The rest of the categories accounted for about 80 per cent of the computed revenue, and two of these categories were termed *Chakeran Zemin* and *Bazee Zemin* in the Bengal and Bihar records of this period. The *Chakeran Zemin* referred to recipients of revenue who were engaged in administrative and accounting activities, while the *Bazee Zemin* referred to those who were in receipt of what were termed religious and charitable allowances. These revenues not only went for the upkeep of religious places but also for facilitating learning, to provide for learned persons, medical practitioners, poets, to jesters, etc. In 1770, almost one-half of the province was held upon free tenure under the *Bazee Zemin* category, and *Bazee Zemin* in many districts of Bengal and Bihar numbered as high as 30,000 to 36,000 which included individuals, groups as well as institutions. This system applied everywhere, be it Punjab or Madras. In fact, it can be safely assumed that about a quarter to one-third of the revenue paying sources (not only land but also sea ports, etc.) were, according to ancient practice, assigned for the requirements of the social and cultural infrastructure until the British overturned it all.[33] Later, the British started founding

[33] Dharampal, *The Beautiful Tree*, 72–81.

and funding educational institutions in India on a limited scale primarily to man the colonial administration and to colonize the Indian minds.

The above records collected for the sole purpose of mapping the indigenous education and the specific description of Bartolomeo clearly demonstrate that, first, the Indian people valued education and learning and had made adequate arrangement for the same. And in fact, every village had a school. Second, there were no exclusionary practices prevalent in the schools of the country as it is made out to be these days. Third, quality and cost-effective education was provided and received by all the sections of society cutting across castes and creeds. The precolonial education was better than the education provided in European countries including England. Specially, the Indian pedagogy, described as the monitorial system, was adopted in England and elsewhere and brought great improvement in education there. Fourth, the education and the other social works were largely financed by the revenues generated through dedicated sources and the rulers too made generous endowments to the institutions and men of learning.

Apart from the above remarkable features, two specific aspects of the indigenous education of India lead to two different traditions of India originating in two different ages of India's past. First, as the records reflect, the texts taught and read throughout the country included the Vedas, the Shastras, the Puranas, the epics, namely the Rāmāyaṇa and the Mahābhārata, the classics by Kalidasa and other texts available in Sanskrit language. This was the continuation of a tradition originating in the very ancient past of the country. And even more remarkably, this tradition formed the backbone of a living ancient civilization. The dedicated institutions for the Sanskrit learning, teaching of Sanskrit religious and utilitarian texts in the general schools and studies of Sanskrit texts in private along with the schools of particular Indian language depending on the region where they were located, and teachings in relevant utilitarian subjects like accounts affirmed the existence of a transcendental civilization culture throughout the country. At the same time, the Persian schools commanded the prime position in the education system to be later replaced by the English education in the country. These schools trained the scholars in the Persian knowledge system, which fed the Islamic empire, courts, administration and diplomacy. While the Arabic was the language of religion and there were Arabic schools too, which mainly taught religious texts to the Muslim scholars, the Persian schools attracted a great number of Hindu learners as well. The Indic education, however, was not in its best form when it was being mapped by the Company administration. What is evident is that two systems of education, Sanskrit and Persian, ran parallel to each other covering the entire subcontinent along with the other regional schools, providing education of the regional language and in the regional language depending on the region where they were located and subjects of local orientation.

Islamic Education and the Decline of Pre-Islamic Education

The traditional indigenous system just before the onset of the colonial rule, which Bartolomeo describes, notwithstanding the fact that they matched the European standards and even excelled theirs, was itself struggling. Bartolomeo spoke unequivocally:

> It, however, cannot be denied that the arts and sciences in India have greatly declined since foreign conquerors expelled the native kings; by which several provinces have been laid entirely waste. Before that period, the different kingdoms were in a flourishing condition; the laws were respected, and justice and civil order prevailed; but, unfortunately, at present everything in many of the provinces must give way to absolute authority and despotic sway.[34]

India's pre-Islamic system of education had lost its pre-eminence with the expansion of Islamic rule in India. It began in the

[34] Bartolomeo, *A Voyage to the East Indies*, 268.

early 11th century, when the Ghaznavids raided the larger part of upper India and annexed areas of Punjab and beyond into their empire. In the next phase, during the closing years of the 12th century, Muhammad of Ghor finally established his rule in India by defeating the Rajput ruler Prithviraj Chauhan in the Second Battle of Tarain in 1192 CE, and thus began the Islamic rule in India expanding over time to cover the larger portion of India for the next six centuries. Delhi and Agra remained the main seats of Islamic empire, and there were other seats of power from where different suzerain and semi-suzerain Muslim dynasties ruled over different times. The Islamic rule eclipsed by the end of the 18th century though it lingered on to be finally replaced by the British colonialists. Nonetheless, it continued in parts of India as native states under the British paramountcy, and finally, along with the Independence, India was partitioned, and its Muslim majority regions were ceded as the Muslim homeland. Though Arabic was the language of the Islam, Persian was the language of the Islamic courts, administration and diplomacy, which connected India to and placed it in the larger Persian world.

The rise of Islamic power caused the decline of the pre-Islamic education in India. The initial military campaigns, which led to the foundation and expansion of the Islamic rule, involved large-scale destruction of the temples and viharas, which served as the educational centres as well. The destruction of holy shrines and places was re-enacted later too. The scholars and institutions of traditional learning mostly lost state patronage which they used to get generously from the earlier rulers. In fact, the Buddhist religion and the education centres could not bear the onslaught and vanished from India altogether. Diana L. Eck noted the following while chronicling the history of Banaras:

> While Vārānasī grew increasingly famous as a Hindu place of pilgrimage, it continued to have a significant Buddhist monastic presence until the twelfth century, when Qutb-ud-din Aibak's armies demolished Sārnāth as well as Vārānasī's great Hindu temples. While the Hindus recovered from the blow, the Buddhist

> tradition, dependent entirely upon his monks, monasteries, and centres of learning, was virtually eliminated.[35]

Despite losing state patronage, the Sanskrit schools and the individual teachers continued to work and teach dharmik scriptures, literature and laws. Besides the apprenticeship, schools kept imparting training for various vocations. These schools run by the priestly families, mostly surviving on contributions from the students, also received aid from the liberal provincial Muslim chiefs and the Hindu chieftains.[36] Historian Abraham Eraly notes that the Hindus adjusted to the Muslim rule, but their prolonged subjection reinforced their phlegmatic conservatism. While the Muslim society treated the Hindus with quite scorn, the state of Muslim culture was not much brighter either, and Muslim scholars were as much sunk in obscurantism as Hindu pundits. During the Islamic rule, the knowledge base of society remained stagnant.[37] In this period, girls and women were deprived of formal education in line with their general social degradation.

The Muslim rulers instead patronized the Islamic education in India in order to propagate their religion, to train the manpower for running their administration as per their norms and to cater to the religious needs of the ever-burgeoning Muslim population in India. Though the Islamic institutions of learning and scholarship in India were no match for the same flourishing in the contemporary Islamic world at places such as Baghdad, Dimashq, Cairo, Cordova, Makkah, Shiraz, Samara and others, many notable centres of Islamic education and learning developed in India under the patronage of the sultans, the chiefs and private persons.[38] Islamic education had its important centres in India;

[35] Diana L. Eck, *Banaras: City of Light* (New Delhi: Penguin, 1983), 57.

[36] Suresh Chandra Ghosh, *History of Education in Medieval India: 1192 A.D.–1757 A.D.* (New Delhi: Originals, 2001), 4–5.

[37] Abraham Eraly, *The Mughal World: Life in India's Last Golden Age* (New Delhi: Penguin Books, 2007), 340–341.

[38] Narendra Nath Law, *Promotion of Learning in India during Muhammadan Rule (By Muhammadans)* (London: Longmans, Green and Co., 1916), vii–viii.

Delhi, the chief seat of the Muslim rule, excelled. Beginning with the slave dynasty, the Muslim rulers founded numerous educational institutions. Nasiruddin established the Madarsa-i-Nasiria in Delhi under the chairmanship of Shiraz. Alauddin Khilji greatly promoted education in Delhi by establishing many madrasas and employing reputed scholars therein, and his patronage made Delhi a famed centre of art and literature. Mohammad Tughlaq and Firoz Tughlaq also supported education in Delhi. Under the Mughals, Delhi only gained as a centre of Islamic education. Humayun founded a centre for the study of geography and astronomy, philosophy, Persian language and grammar. Akbar's foster mother Maham Anga founded a mosque masjid Khairul Manazil which evolved into a madrasa. Jahangir and Shah Jahan also contributed to the expansion of education. Aurangzeb also founded new institutions and aided the old ones, but he directed the education towards orthodoxy.[39]

Agra was another important seat of Islamic learning as Delhi was. Obviously, the rulers had sought to work for its prestige. Sikandar Lodi founded many maktabs and madrasas in Agra and converted it into an important centre of Islamic learning where learners from other countries too came to study. Later Babar and Humayun added to the madarsas in the city. It was during the reign of Akbar that Agra became a major centre of craft, fine arts and culture, and it served like a massive university where scholars from different lands such as Arabia, Persia and Bokhara gathered to pursue their vocation. Near Agra, at Fatehpur Sikri too, Akbar established many schools. Later Mughal emperors added other institutions, and by the time of Aurangzeb, Agra turned out to be a great centre of Islamic education.[40]

Jaunpur of Uttar Pradesh too emerged as an important seat of Islamic education where education was patronized successively by the Turks, Afghans and Mughals. Sher Shah Suri is believed

[39] R. N. Sharma and R. K. Sharma, *History of Education in India* (New Delhi: Atlantic, 2000), 67.

[40] Ibid., 67–68.

to have received his education here. The city supported various types of educational institutions where history, philosophy, war and statecraft were taught. Ibrahim Sharqi had founded a number of madrasas here and managed finances for them. Mughal rulers supported these institutions here. During Mohammad Shah's reign, a number of institutions were established in this city.[41] The city was famous for its handicrafts and fine arts as well.

Bidar located in the north-eastern part of Karnataka was the capital of the Bahmani Sultanate and flourished as an education centre under royal patronage. Mahmud Gawan (1411–1481), a prime minister in the Sultanate, built a great university, the Mahmud Gawan Madrasa. He, himself a linguist and a mathematician, founded the distinguished religious school with carefully chosen scientists, philosophers and religious seers. The library of madrasa consisted of 3,000 manuscripts. The Bahmani sultans were very careful about education, and with a view to spread Islamic education, they established a maktab in every village.[42]

The Islamic rule, culture and education influenced the Indic civilization through all these centuries. There remained areas of perennial frictions and also there emerged avenues of convergences. The latter led to the evolution of a composite culture reflected in India's cuisine, clothing, art, architecture, music, language, literature, philosophy, etc. During the Islamic rule, the Persian language spread to the different corners of the subcontinent as a pan-Indian language in the same manner as English during colonial rule. The functionaries of empire received the dictates from the imperial seats of power, namely Delhi and Agra, in the same language. The Hindus too flocked to acquire the language as it was mandatory to have jobs in the imperial and royal administrations. The Persian schools became widespread as the demand for the learning rose. The learning of the language by a great number of people let Persian tastes, etiquettes and ideas

[41] Ibid., 68.
[42] Ibid.

percolate in the Indic culture and made their mark on the Indian art, literature and manners. The intermingling of languages led to the birth of a new language in India, that is, Urdu.[43] The Islamic education thus evolved to a major component of education in India which attracted pupils as well as scholars of different religious affiliations. The Islamic education holds sway until date. It has full constitutional protection, and the Indian state gives aids and recognition to it.

Ideally, Islam values knowledge. The Quran, the fountain of Islamic education, holds reading and writing as a religious duty, acquiring knowledge as a divine act, source of nobleness, bliss, glory and, finally, the redemption as well. According to the Hadith, the ink of a learner is more blessed than the blood of a martyr. The Islamic system of knowledge covers not only the spiritual and ethical values but also the norms and laws regarding family affairs, running businesses, jurisprudence, governance and science as well. Nonetheless, the crux of Islamic education is to seek redemption through the knowledge of Allah as the Lord, choosing Allah and none other as one's Lord and acting on or undertaking Allah's Lordship throughout one's life.[44] In Islam, faith and knowledge are treated as inseparable, as without knowledge one cannot know God and without God there is no true knowledge. The Quran, as the transmitted words of God, is thus knowledge and par excellence, and the Prophet, to whom the Quran was revealed, is the embodiment of perfect knowledge. As such, Islam postulates that attainment, acceptance and embodiment of the Sunna—Mohammed's works, Hadith, sayings attributed to Mohammed, the Sharia, exegetical law derived from a logical extrapolation of the three aforementioned works, in addition to the Quran—form the bedrock of a proper and fruitful life.[45]

[43] Ghosh, *History of Education in Medieval India*, viii.

[44] Khosrow Bagheri Noaparast, *Islamic Education* (Tehran: Alhoda, 2001), 26.

[45] Eric Hilgendorf, 'Islamic Education: History and Tendency', *Peabody Journal of Education* 78, no. 2 (2003), 64–65.

The Muslim rulers in India established and patronized maktabs, madrasas, libraries and Khanqahs. Roughly, the maktabs imparted primary education and the madrasas imparted higher and specialized education. Khanqahs were the gathering places for sufis, where they shared mystic experiences. In India, most mosques had attached to them at least a maktab, if not a madrasa, as per the Islamic practices. All Muslim boys were required to attend a maktab so that they could learn the relevant portions of the Quran in order to perform their daily ritual prayers. The content of education imparted in the maktabs varied from place to place. However, a Muslim boy beginning to speak is taught to repeat the Kalima, the formal declaration of faith. This is followed by learning of certain prescribed verses from the Quran by heart. At the age of about seven, a Muslim boy started learning the Quran and received instructions in religious precepts and practices. This was the minimum standard of education imparted at a maktab, but at some places reading, writing and some elementary arithmetic were also taught. To this could be added the narration of the legends of the prophets and of the notable Islamic figures and some selections from poetry. However, learning by rote was practiced, and it was observed, among such surviving schools during the British days, that rarely the meaning of what the students were taught to recite was explained to them.[46]

Madrasa is also an Arabic word, which originally meant any type of educational institution. But after the rise of Islam, it came to be associated with the Islamic religion. In India, however, there were no standard courses for the madrasas; they differed from place to place. The report by Adam on education in Bengal (1835–1838) with regard to the madrasas records grammar, rhetoric, logic, law, the external observances and fundamental doctrines of Islam, astronomy (Ptolemy in translation), other branches of natural philosophy and treatises on metaphysics being taught. Music apparently missed from the list of disciplines

[46] F. E. Keay, *Indian Education: An Inquiry into Its Origin, Development and Ideals* (London: Oxford University Press, 1918), 139–140.

as it was not important from the religious perspective. Medicine, not in the list, was taught as Muslim physicians called hakims learnt their medical traditions and practiced in India. Education was formal and scholastic with a strong emphasis on grammar, having as its climax the discussion of dry, abstract and metaphysical trivialities. Science of some kind was taught and so were literature and history. History was quite a popular subject which comprised the works of Muslim historians.[47] As far as arts and crafts were concerned, there was little difference between the training of the Hindu and the Muslim craftsmen. In both the Hindu and the Islamic tradition, mainly the rote learning prevailed in which the teacher passed on to the students their knowledge and traditions.

The Islamic education began for the education of the Muslims who were mainly concentrated in the urban centres, but it had wider influences and clientele. This was despite the uncertain fate of the madrasas which depended for funding on the impulses of the despotic rulers. Many such educational centres were raised and deserted, and some of them repaired over time and closed again. The humble maktabs attached to the mosques functioned rather permanently, and it was here that Persian was taught, and these attracted the Hindus in large numbers as well.[48]

The process of the adoption of Persian had begun in the times of the Lodi rulers who had employed members of the Hindu scribal communities and maintained revenue documents in Persian and Hindavi. Later Afghan ruler, Sher Shah had deployed two *karkuns* (writers), one for Persian and other for Hindavi, at every district. In 1582 CE, Akbar designated Persian as the official language, overarching the different cultural and religious communities of his empire. Now onwards, it was used throughout the empire from the central seat of the imperial order to the remotest outpost in the hinterland. The demand for learning Persian rose rather exponentially. As a few generations passed, by 1700 CE,

[47] Ibid., 140–142.
[48] Ibid., 142–143.

India surpassed even Iran in number of people literate in Persian by seven times. The madrasas mostly located in urban centres and the village maktabs imparted the learning of Persian. For India's scribal castes, the Kayasthas and Khatris, which served in the state administration, learning the language was a practical necessity. From the age of four, children of the Kayastha caste were taught practical skills like accounting (*siyaqi*), which made them to tabulate rent rates and audit revenue accounts. Kayathas serving as land registrars (*qanungo*) and village accountants (*pawari*) were the frontline functionaries of the governance. At the higher levels, they worked as news writers, revenue reporters, petition writers, surveyors and court readers. The knowledge of Persian not only ensured them employment in the imperial administration but also higher status in the society, where felicity in Persian language and manners were markers of higher culture. Madrasas, maktabs and other educational outlets taught classics drawn from the Persian literary canon; among others, they invariably had Sa'di, Firdausi, Nizami, Amir Khusrau, Tusi and Jami in their courses. The influence of Persian was in fact so intense that Shivaji had to commission the compilation of a Persian–Sanskrit glossary, the *Rajavyavaharkośa*, to find Sanskrit equivalents for the Persian lexical items.[49]

Catering to the needs of times, versified bilingual word books called *nisab*s (rudimentary dictionaries) came into existence. Earlier, they explained the Hindavi terms to the Persian-knowing immigrants, but after the mid-16th century, these workbooks did the opposite, explained the Persian words to the Hindavi speakers. Such wordbooks multiplied exponentially in the 18th century as they introduced to the aspiring classes, below the ruling classes, the world of great opportunities and access to courtly cultural norms. The significance of these wordbooks can be understood by the Persian word for dictionary, *farhang*, which also means good breeding, greatness or education. The Mughals had even

[49] Richard M. Eaton, *India in the Persianate Age 1000–1765* (London: Allen Lane, Penguin Random House UK, 2019), 381–385.

loftier goals as they sought to place India at the centre of the wider Persephone world. For this purpose, Akbar commissioned the compilation of a comprehensive Persian dictionary which was known as the *Farhang-i Jahangiri*, as it was finally completed in Jahangir's regime. The dictionary had about 9,000 entries, which consolidating all earlier efforts covered by the Persian language comprehensively.[50]

The Persianate traditions also engaged with the Sanskrit traditions. In order to cement their claim as Indian suzerains, the Mughals appropriated India's pre-Persian culture. From the later decades of Akbar's reign and continuing through those of Jahangir and Shah Jahan, the Brahmana and Jain scholars had a significant presence in the Mughal court serving as astrologers, translators, religious guides and political negotiators, and they inevitably drew the Mughals in their world. Akbar commissioned Vihari Krsnadasa· to write *Parasiprakaśa* which combined a list of parallel words in Persian and Sanskrit and a Sanskrit grammar in Persian. Akbar and Jahangir together ordered about 15 Sanskrit works to be translated into Persian. Of these works were the epics, the Mahābhārata and the Rāmāyaṇa, which Akbar sponsored from the 1580s. However, the overriding concern of the translation was to emphasize epics' political character and to accommodate Indian deities to Persianate sensibilities. In the sciences, however, the knowledge passed between the Persianate and Sanskritic worlds more freely. The 14th-century Indo-Persian scholar Shihab al-Din Natauri assimilated the Ayurvedic knowledge of medicine and Avicennian tradition. As the Avicennian tradition had evolved in the dry Middle Eastern climate, it needed to widen its coverage of the diseases and therapies peculiar to the wetter tropical climate of India. The Indo-Persian physicians and scholars pursued deeply the Sanskrit works on pharmacology and native Indian plants, and both the traditions greatly influenced each other. In the field of astronomy, the Persian works made inroads in the Indic traditions. In 1628, pundit Nityananda translated

[50] Ibid., 382–383.

the tables prepared for Shah Jahan for predicting the location of planets from Persian to Sanskrit. In 1639, he translated another Persian text which however caused fierce dispute amidst its supporters and opponents. Later, Persian notions astronomy caused great ferment in Sanskrit circles.[51]

Islam does not bar women from education, but due to the requirement of purdah they did not get education above the primary level. Affluent families arranged education for the females at home. In India, during the late medieval period, women largely disappeared from public life and were missing from formal educational institutions also. The Muslim royalty and nobility kept their women secluded and under purdah and did not send their daughters to attend schools. The practice percolated down to the ordinary Muslims as well. Nonetheless, the Muslim ruling class arranged education for their girls and women at home. Razia Sultana, who inherited the throne from her father, Shamsuddin Iltutmish, was well-educated and patronized men of letters. Gulbadan Begum, the daughter of Babur, wrote the *Humayun-Nama*, the account of the life of her half-brother, Emperor Humayun. She collected books and maintained a personal library. Ghiyas-ud-din, the ruler of Malwa from 1469 to 1500, had arranged female tutors for the education of the women of his harem. Akbar had the similar arrangement with some rooms set apart for the purpose at Fatehpur Sikri. One of the principal wives of Akbar, Salima Sultan Begum, niece of Humayun and widow of Bairam Khan, was a highly educated woman and wrote poems in Persian.[52] She was known as the Khadija of that era for her wisdom.[53] Maham Anga, Akbar's foster mother; Nur Jahan, the principal wife of Jahangir, the power behind the throne and her niece Mumtaz Mahal, the favourite wife of Shah Jahan; Jahanara Begam, the eldest daughter of Shah Jahan; Zebunnisa

[51] Ibid., 386–389.

[52] Keay, *Indian Education*, 137–138.

[53] Mahua Sarkar, *Visible Histories, Disappearing Women: Producing Muslim Womanhood in Late Colonial Bengal* (Durham and London: Duke University Press, 2008), 73.

Begam, the eldest daughter of Aurangzeb were all well-educated.[54] Names of Zebinda Begum, the fourth daughter of Shah Jahan, and Chand Sultana of Ahmadnagar, may be added to the list of these illustrious ladies, and it is most likely that women of royalty and nobility received some education behind the purdah. As the study of the Quran was incumbent on every faithful, it may be assumed that the Muslim girls were taught by their parents or sent to some private homes to be taught. Educating girls was thus a personal affair, and it can be assumed that as ordinary Muslims could hardly afford a private tutor or even a copy of the Quran; as it was an expensive affair then, girls from ordinary families hardly received any worthwhile education.

Nalanda University: An Institution of Par Excellence

The Indian subcontinent under the different Islamic dynasties had quite a good system of education, but it could not match the genius of Persia and the pre-Islamic system of education in India. Despite that India was not lacking behind with the contemporary European countries. India's pre-Islamic education had two parallel systems, the Vedic and the Shramanic which was best reflected in the Nalanda University functioning until the early years of the Islamic rule when Khalji destroyed it. A Mahavihara, the university taught Vedic learning as well.

The Mahavihara of Nalanda displayed its grandeur even in its ruins located near the town of Bihar Sharif in the state of Bihar. With a modest beginning, the place evolved as a great centre of the Buddhist religion and learning and excelled being so in the contemporary world. Being a well-populated township located near the Magadhan capital of Rajagriha, it emerged as an important religious centre in ancient times. Lord Buddha, Nigrantha Nathputta and Makkhali Gosala frequented Nalanda. Here was held the famous discussion between Lord Mahavira and Makkhali Gosala leading to the foundation of Jainism as a

[54] Keay, *Indian Education*, 138.

separate faith.[55] Ashoka had built a temple and a vihara here. The place also served as the venue for the debate between Nāgārjuna and others in the 2nd century CE. However, the place as a great educational centre started to take shape only in the earlier half of the 5th century. Fa-Hien visited Nalanda in 410 CE, where he said Śāriputra, one of the disciples of the Buddha, was born and reached his parinirvāṇa and found the ancient stupa there, but did not make any reference to any institution of learning.[56] Śakrāditya (415–455 CE) built the first Sangharama, and his son Buddhaguptaraja added another. Tathagataguptaraja and Baladitya (468–472 CE) built more of them.[57]

The Huna King Mihirakula destroyed the University in the course of his campaign against Buddhism and the Gupta King Narasimha Gupta, a great patron of Buddhism, in the early 6th century. The Gupta king after retreating towards the Bay of Bengal not only defeated the Mihirakula but also restored the University and added a Sangharama which was known as 'the college of Baladitya-raja' in the time of Hiuen Tsang. Moreover, he constructed a great vihara of 300 feet high which was greatly admired by Hiuen Tsang. He says that Narasimha Gupta was none other than Baladitya-raja as referred to by Hiuen Tsang. Second time, it was destroyed by Gauda king Sasanka of Eastern Bengal. This time, it was King Harsa (King Harshavardhana of Kannauj, 7th century CE) who after repulsing Sasanka through a successful military campaign not only repaired the damages done to the University but further added to the magnificence and glory of the university. He commissioned another Sangharama which was perhaps the grandest of all as Hiun Tsiang called this one as a 'great' one among all the Sangharamas. The Chinese pilgrim further informs that to the south of this is a vihara of brass (brass plated) built by Siladitya-raja. It is well-known that

[55] Sukumar Dutt, *Buddhist Monks and Monasteries of India* (London: George Allen and Unwin Ltd., 1962), 328.

[56] Hartmut Scharfe, *Education in Ancient India* (Leiden, Boston, Koln: Brill, 2002), 145, 148.

[57] Ibid., 149–150.

Siladitya-raja is the name given to Harsa by the Chinese pilgrim. This vihara was under construction at the time of Hiuen Tsang's stay at the University. Harsa also erected an image of Buddha in the Sangharama built by the founder Śakrāditya and decided to feed 40 priests of the congregation every day to show his gratitude to the founder. And most importantly, Hwui Li, the biographer of Hiuen Tsang, informs that Harsa granted numerous endowments to the university which included the revenues of about 100 villages remitted to the University. About 200 householders in these villages, most probably village heads, day by day supplied several piculs of ordinary rice, several hundred catties in weight of butter and milk, and Hwui Li also makes the point that the students here being so abundantly supplied do not require to ask for the four requisites (clothing, food, bedding and medicine). And this is the source of the perfection of their studies to which they have arrived.[58]

The remarkable thing is that Śakrāditya and his son and successor Buddhagupta were not Buddhists and so were many of the donors to the University. The emblems on their seals depict Lakshmi, Ganesha, Sivalinga and Durga. The university campus was well laid with majestic buildings. The massive buildings of great heights were well-adorned and the campus had been aesthetically landscaped and was well provisioned. Excavations show that not less than 13 monasteries stood there spread over an area of at least one mile in length and half a mile in width.[59] The university flourished until the 12th century CE, enjoying very generous royal patronage from different dynasties. It gravely suffered during the Bakhtiyār Khalji's raids and conquest of the region between 1197 and 1206 CE, but it appears that the University survived the destruction and

[58] H. Heras, 'The Royal Patrons of the University of Nalanda', *Journal of the Bihar and Orissa Research Society, PART I* 14 (1928), 1–23, http://buddhism.lib.ntu.edu.tw/FULLTEXT/JR-ENG/heras.htm.

[59] D. G. Apte, *Universities in Ancient India*, Issue 11 of Education and Psychology Extension Series (Baroda: Faculty of Education and Psychology, Maharaja Sayajirao University of Baroda, 1971), 23–26.

massacre as the Tibetan monk Dharmasvāmin visited Nalanda in 1234 CE and found some buildings intact with some pundits and monks residing there under the leadership of Mahāpaṇiḍta Rāhulaśrībhadra. In the 14th and 15th century, some repairs were made by King Cingalarāja of Bengal and his queen. Soon afterwards, the University was finally shut down[60] or reduced to insignificance.

Nalanda was a seat of higher learning and elite institution. Scholars gathered here from across the subcontinent and from the countries of Mongolia, China, Korea, Tibet and Tokhara. They visited the place not only for going through the courses offered here but also for learning the art of discussion, for having authoritative scholarly learning on any matter of knowledge and for collecting source materials. Alumnus of this institution enjoyed great reputation. Yuan Chwang (Hiuen Tsang) noted, '... foreign students came to the establishment to put an end to their doubts and then became celebrated, and those who stole the name of [of Nalanda Brother] were all treated with respect wherever they went.' However, not everyone was admitted here. Only after a rigorous test of eligibility by the appointed teachers, one was admitted into that hallowed precinct. Yuan Chwang goes on to say that of those from abroad who wished to enter the schools of discussions, the majority, beaten by the difficulties of the problems, withdrew; and those, who were deeply versed in old and modern learning were admitted; only 2 or 3 out of 10 succeeded.[61] Scholars resided on the campus along with the preceptors. Students were not charged for their education. In fact, the Nalanda Mahavihara was very richly endowed. Nonetheless, the students were required to beg, but it had purposes other than sustaining the vihara financially. It was in a way part of the pedagogy, which linked the pupil to society and inculcated in them a sense of commitment to the society and,

[60] Scharfe, *Education in Ancient India*, 150–151.

[61] Thomas Watters, *On Yuan Chwang's Travels in India (Vol. II)*, eds. T. W. Rhys Davids and Stephen W Bushell (London: Royal Asiatic Society, 1905), 165.

on the other hand, it also enforced the idea of the collective social responsibility towards education.[62]

According to Hiuen Tsang, the University accommodated 10,000 monks. He described that there were 1,000 men who could explain 20 collections of Sutras and Shastras; 500 men could explain 30 collections, and perhaps 10 men including the Master of Law could explain 50 collections. Besides these 1,510 great scholars, there were monks of lesser calibre, and the rest were students. It also appears that in Nalanda, a student could be taught by several teachers of different subjects instead of a single teacher as was the practice in the gurukula system.[63] One teacher for every seven or eight students was indeed a great ratio for pedagogy. On an average, 100 lectures or discourses took place on the campus. The university maintained a large collection of manuscripts on different subjects and in different languages. The three library buildings, very appropriately named as Ratnasagara, Ratnodadhi and Ratnaranjaka, housed these valuable manuscripts. Scholars from different places and countries came here for collecting valuable resources. I-tsing is said to have got copied from Nalanda 400 Sanskrit works amounting to 500,000 verses.[64]

The University was headed by a senior bhikshu of competence who administered the institution with the help of two councils, one looking after the academic part, from admissions to commissioning manuscripts, and the other managing finances, logistics and the estates the monastery held. The entire affairs were run on a federated basis as individual teachers and students under the charge of each teacher constituted the federation. Each preceptor worked with autonomy, but all were governed by common norms. The bhikshus were forbidden from accepting gifts in currency or in valuables. They only accepted consumables. However, the royals and the rich commissioned buildings and secured other facilities for them where they could reside and perform their

[62] Apte, *Universities in Ancient India*, 27–29.
[63] Scharfe, *Education in Ancient India*, 151–153.
[64] Apte, *Universities in Ancient India*, 36–37.

religious and academic works comfortably. The great monastery received liberal grants and were endowed with the estates from different rulers over time to maintain itself. Its famous donors were Kumargupta I, Buddhagupta, Tathagatagupta, Baladitya, Vajra, Harsha Vardhana, Purnavarman and Yasovarmadeva. It is mentioned that Yasovarmadeva had donated sums which equalled the total monetary value of the institution. Devapala, king of Bengal of the Pala dynasty, donated five villages for the assembly of venerable bhikkhus and for the upkeep and repair of monasteries. The kings of the far-off Sumatra and Java had also helped this institution.[65]

Though the Nalanda University was devoted to Mahayanism, but subjects studied and taught here covered the domains of knowledge exhaustively spanning the Brahmanical and the Buddhist traditions, sacred and secular, philosophical and practical, sciences and arts. The scholars discussed the religious scriptures of Buddhism, Brahmanism and also the divergent schools of Buddhism. Side by side, the University also trained the learners in secular arts and crafts in a number of fields. Logic or dialectics was a major methodological discipline taught here. Astronomy was another important subject, and the University maintained an observatory and a clepsydra. Tantra was also a popular subject at this university. The Vedas and their six auxiliaries, medicine, grammar, Sankhya, philology, law, philosophy and others were the other courses. The university also had facilities for primary education where young pupils were admitted. They learnt Sanskrit grammar primarily and moved on to learn advanced grammar and other subjects later on.[66]

Hiuen Tsang had spent 16 years in India from 629 to 645 CE, and he had stayed at the Nalanda University for 5 years as its resident scholar. I-tsing, another Chinese scholar following Hiuen Tsang, had studied at Nalanda for 10 long years from 675 to 685 CE. Both these Chinese scholars had the first-hand experience

[65] Ibid., 32–36.
[66] Ibid., 30–31.

of the Indian educational system at its best. On the basis of their observations, Dr Radha Kumud Moorkerji draws the curricula of the University spanning the three stages of education at the university, namely primary, secondary and higher specialized learning. The initiate at the age of 6 was taught the first book known as *Siddam* or *Siddirastu*, which contained the 49 letters of the Sanskrit alphabet and 10,000 syllables and combinations of different vowels and consonants, arranged in 300 slokas. The book was divided into 12 chapters and the child had to finish the book in 6 months. The second book was the Sutra of Panini containing 1,000 slokas, which the student started to learn at the age of 8 and was expected to finish it in 8 months. Next, the students learnt grammar more deeply advancing step by step and had to master the books dealing with the *dhatu*s (Conjugations) and the three *khila*s (Declensions), which they finished at the age of 13. Further, the pupils studied *Kasikavritti*, which I-tsing regarded as the best commentary on Panini. Composed by the learned Jayaditya, it comprised of 18,000 slokas. The young scholars at the age of 15 started studying this commentary and perfected their knowledge of grammar. I-tsing also informs that the Chinese scholars visiting the University had to study this work first, which equipped them for further studies. Finally, as the part of the elementary education, students learnt composition in prose and verse.[67]

After acquiring the knowledge of grammar and composition in their primary education, the students moved to the secondary education, which comprised of the compulsory standardized five subjects or *Vidya*s: (a) *Śabda-vidya* or *Vyakarana* (grammar and lexicography), (b) *Śilpasthanavidya* (knowledge of arts and crafts manual training), (c) *Chikitsavidya* (science of medicine), (d) *Hetuvidya* (logic) and (e) *Adhyatmavidya* (science universal soul or philosophy).[68] The higher studies were meant for specialization

[67] Radha Kumud Mookerji, 'Practical Aspects of Education in Ancient India', *Proceedings of the Indian History Congress* 5 (1941), 127–128.

[68] Ibid., 128.

in any of the disciplines studied at the secondary level depending on the choice of future life a scholar wanted to pursue. But why would the study of medical science, for instance, be compulsory for a person who wanted to pursue philosophy in his life. In fact, I-tsing who had come all the way from China to India to study Buddhism had to study medical science and other subjects taught at the secondary level. And he gives the explanation which is very instructive even for our times:

> medical study compulsory for all students, not excluding even the monks: 'Is it not a sad thing that sickness prevents the pursuit of one's duty and vocation? Is it not beneficial if people can benefit others as well as themselves by the study of Medicine?' In fact, the disciplines taught at the secondary level enabled the students to realise their natural aptitude and interests and pursue their life accordingly after finishing their education.[69]

Utilitarian disciplines of arts and crafts, however, required practical training. How did the University arrange such practical training? The institution ensured this practical training by making its residents to share the works of provisioning the establishment of the University. This says that the University was a living institution and learners lived their learning. The beauty of the functioning of the university was that it combined the training with actual discharge of duties while students were engaged in their academic pursuits. The University functioned as an order, an institution of learning, a centre of training as well as a workplace. Mookerji draws a picture of how the practical training took place in the campus on the basis of the details furnished by the aforesaid Chinese scholars. The university housed around 12,000 residents including 8,500 scholars, 1,510 preceptors and the support staff. Provisioning of lodging, messing and other requirements of such a great number of residents on the campus was a mammoth-logistic exercise, which the University managed on its own being a self-governing establishment.[70]

[69] Ibid., 128–129.
[70] Ibid., 129.

The University was run by the proceeds of permanent land and revenue grants. Here it is remarkable to note that bhikshus were forbidden from holding possessions other than those for their personal use and even that was already prescribed. These articles were eight, namely the three robes (*tichivara*), a girdle, an alms-bowl, a razor, a needle and a water-strainer to clear the water for drinking of any life form or impurities. The *Samgha* or any of its members was not allowed to accept gold or silver, gifts in cash or money in lieu of any good in kind. A bhikshu, for instance, would accept only robes and would never accept a sum equal to the value of robes from a layman. However, the *Samgha* could own property in common as *Arama* or lands and vihara or buildings. Hiuen Tsang gives the figure of 100 villages under the possession of the University and I-tsing noted the greater number of more than 200 villages. The University needed to manage its property well in order to ensure provisioning for the residents, upkeep of the infrastructure and expansion of the University. Hence, the proper management of the estates was equally important in the context of how the University ran its affairs. The University in fact had an agricultural department to take care and augment the produces of the lands under its ownership or revenue rights. The vihara also had a special staff of cultivators who were called *Aramikas*, who took care of *Aramas* or land belonging to the monastery. Again, a monk was not only forbidden from holding land but also from cultivating any land as digging earth or causing it to be dug was an offence as per the doctrine. This injunction, however, did not apply on the brotherhood of monks which could own land, but the Samgha also refrained from farming on its own. The brotherhood received one-sixth of the land produce if they had revenue grant, which was the usual share of the state from the land produce or practiced sharecropping in which the Samgha could claim half of the produce or as circumstances allowed. Monasteries also employed paid servants or hired labour for higher production, but motive was not greater gain but to ensure, as I-tsing points out, 'that the farming is properly done'. The University did not maintain a store of its own nor did treasured bullions for making necessary purchases rather it depended on the daily supplies from its estate. Hiuen Tsang recorded the daily supplies received by the University as rice amounting to 300 maunds of rice and even larger quantities of butter and milk.[71]

The University had built several edifices over time. Hiuen Tsang saw Nalanda enclosed with high walls having single entrance. The buildings of the university were of several storeys 'with richly adorned towers, fairy-like turrets appearing like provided hill-tops and observatories lost in the mists of the morning'. The Nalanda stone inscription of Yasovarman of 8th century CE confirms Hiuen Tsang's description by stating how the row of monasteries (*viharavali*) had its series of summits (*sikhara-sreni*) licking (avalehi) the clouds (*ambudhara*). I-tsing also saw 8 halls and 300 apartments in the monastery. Such a massive residential university with large number residents required elaborate administrative arrangements. These were separate in-charges of lodging, ration and stores. There were different receivers for robes, undergarments and bowls. There were officials supervising distribution of robes and fruits, of dry fruits and of trifles such as needles, pair of scissors, sandals and braces, girdles and filtering cloth. There were *Aramikas*, who looked after agricultural fields, and there were superintendents who monitored the works of *Aramikas*. And there were superintendents of *Sramaneras* to keep them to their duties. The monks thus had to undertake various types of practical works apart from their religious and spiritual preoccupations. And this provided the scholars with the opportunity of learning by doing in secular disciplines. Besides, the bhikshus were deputed to serve as 'building overseers' to take charge of building operations on behalf of a lay-donor constructing a vihara for purposes of the Samgha so that the buildings might be in accordance with the rules of the order as to size, form and object of the various apartments. Such an overseer was called *Navakammika*. The appointment was made by a formal

[71] Ibid., 129–132.

resolution of the order. The bhikshus had to superintend not merely the new constructions but also the repair works.[72]

Besides sharing the responsibilities of running the estates, victuals and logistics, construction of buildings and their repairs, every monk had to practice certain craft. Spinning and weaving was mandatory for every resident. He was obligated 'the use of a loom, and of shuttles, strings, tickets, and all the apparatus belonging to a loom'. The monks had to prepare their own robes and keep them in fit condition with the help of all necessary weaving appliances.[73] The monastery was also a distinguished school of arts and crafts, which set standards for others.

The scholars of Nalanda were authorities in their field and renowned persons of their times. Chinese traveller Hiuen Tsang or Yuan Chwang had studied the doctrines of Bhūtas, Nirgranthas, Kāpālikas, Jūtikas, Sāśnkhyas and Vaiśeshikas along with Buddhism here. When King Harsha organized the great Buddhist assembly at Kannauj, 1,000 scholars of Nalanda had attended the same. Some of the great scholars of this university were Nāgārjuna, Āryadeva, Vasubandhu, Asanga, Sthiramati, Dharmapāla, Shīlabhadra, Śāntideva, Śāntarakshita, Padmasambhava, Kāmaśīla Candrogomin and Buddhakīrti. To illustrate their repute, one can speak about Nāgārjuna, who along with Āryadeva founded the Mahayana Buddhism and propounded the school of philosophy, Mādhyamika. Padmasambhava had gone to Tibet on the invitation of the king there, and he has been deified there like the Buddha himself.[74] Yuan Chwang spoke very eloquently of Dharmapāla, Chandrapāla, Guṇamati, Sthiramati, Prabhamitra, Jinamitra and Jñanchandra, the great masters of Nalanda University, who had authored valuable treatises and were known and valued by their contemporaries. Shīlabhadra was the abbot of the establishment during Yuan Chwang's visit

[72] Ibid., 132–133.
[73] Ibid., 133–134.
[74] Apte, *Universities in Ancient India*, 38–43.

and was his friend and teacher. Dharmapāla had died perhaps in 600 CE and Guṇamati much earlier. Sthiramati, a contemporary of Guṇamati, had written *Introduction to Mahāyānism*, which was translated into Chinese in 400 CE and another of his short metaphysical treatise in 691 CE. Jinamitra had authored a compendium of the Vinaya of the Sarvāstivādins which was translated by I-ching.[75]

The Indic engagement with learning, its educational institutions and knowledge traditions, as the above description indicates, was second to none in the contemporary world. The apologists of the Western imperialism who applied such doctrines as the 'white men's burden' and the West's 'civilizing mission' had in fact propagated to the Indians and to the world that Indians were unlettered and the British brought education to them. However, contrary to their later claims that they brought improvements to India, it was rather India which guided them to improve their education in England in the early years of their rule. In return, the precolonial Indian education was systematically destroyed to suit the colonial needs.

[75] Watters, *On Yuan Chwang's Travels in India (Vol. II)*, 168–169.

9

Methodology of Shastrarth

Siddheshwar Shukla

In the contemporary world, the cultural plurality has become a buzzword in intellectual discourse across disciplines.[1] Besides nation states, the international organizations have also created various platforms to nourish, protect and conserve plurality in the post-modern society. These organizations are working in a highly professional manner, with a vision to create and maintain plurality at regional, national and global levels wherein all cultures will get equal opportunity to flourish.[2] In this quest to achieve the vision, the giant macro theories and development models of modernity have either become obsolete or are being revised and redefined.

There exists another dimension to this discourse, the cultural plurality in India, which has been home to numerous scripts, languages, dialects, tribes, castes, races, wardrobes, headgears, food habits, marriage systems, family systems, dances, ways of worship, deities, gods, goddesses and also various hypotheses on existence, non-existence and forms of the Almighty. Before the

[1] S. L. Doshi, *Modernity, Postmodernity and Neo-Sociological Theories* (New Delhi: Rawat Publications, 2017); Y. Singh, *Modernization of Indian Tradition* (New Delhi: Rawat Publications, 2018).

[2] UN.ORG, *World Day for Cultural Diversity for Dialogue and Development*. https://www.un.org/en/events/culturaldiversityday/; UNESCO (a), *UNESCO Universal Declaration on Cultural Diversity*. http://portal.unesco.org/en/ev.php-URL_ID=13179&URL_DO=DO_TOPIC&URL_SECTION=201.html

onset of the medieval age, this uniqueness of India was spread throughout the entire land between the Himalayas and the Indian Ocean, but it has gradually shrunken and is now largely confined within the territorial boundaries of India, that is, Bharat. How ancient Indians achieved and maintained cultural plurality on this land, which is still a distant dream even for the developed countries of the contemporary world? It would be improper to say that they were blessed by the Almighty. This is because this praise includes a covert allegation of discrimination on the part of the Almighty which seems to be unlikely for He is assumed to love and care all the human beings on the planet Earth without any discrimination on the basis of place of birth, race, colour, caste, creed, etc. Therefore, the root of cultural plurality in India needs to be searched within the practices which were communicated and inherited for generations. Shastrarth is such a practice of intellectual discourse which has its roots in the Rigveda and ran almost parallel to the political history of India. In this journey, like India, the Shastrarth was also known by different terms through ages, but the basic methodology remained almost the same.

The present chapter makes an effort to investigate into the Indian tradition of Shastrarth from the perspective of communication with special focus on its methodology. The study follows a longitudinal research design, and content analysis has been used for data collection. Besides, an in-depth interview of the domain experts was also conducted. Thc study is descriptive in nature in that it describes the concept of Shastrarth from the methodological perspective and its potentials in creating, protecting and conserving a multicultural global society.

Shastrarth: Meaning and Concept

Shastrarth (*ʃa:stra:rθə*) is a Hindi word made up of two Sanskrit words: *Shastra*[3] (*ʃa:strə*) which means a 'discipline or branch of

[3] Explaining this richa of the Rigved, J. J. Wilson (1866) writes '*Shastra* is explained as *shasana* means governing or punishing. The *Amarkosh* (3.3.178.), mentions three meanings of the word *Shastra as per context* – *Shastra* (Discipline of Knowledge), *Granth* (Book) and *Nidesh* (direction/order/guidance).

knowledge' and *Arth* (*ərθə*) refers to meaning of the message (Rigveda. 3.11.3). In Sanskrit language, the word Shastra is derived from two basic sounds or root words, namely *shas* (ʃa:s) and *shans* (ʃəns) which, respectively, mean 'to discipline[4] or to govern'[5] and 'to describe or prescribe' (approving). Thus, from the Indic perspective, the term Shastra includes everything which disciplines, governs or prescribes us something to live a social life. The most popular and most ancient Sanskrit dictionary *Amarkosh* (3.3.178) provides three synonymous of Shastra: Shastra, path or direction (in reference to order of a school of thought or knowledge) and book (*Amarkosh* 3.3.178).

Interestingly, in the 21st century, the term discipline is gaining importance at the place of subject in reference to a branch of knowledge. As the terms interdisciplinary, multidisciplinary and transdisciplinary have come into vogue, it becomes easier to understand the use of the term 'Shastra' in its original sense of discipline as a branch of knowledge. In the Indic education system, the term Shastra has been used for a branch of knowledge or discipline and also as a suffix in the name of the books related to a particular discipline of knowledge.[6] For instance, one of the most popular non-religious book of ancient India, *Arthashastra*, composed by Chankya, has the term '-shastra' as suffix. This is not an exception but a norm for almost all the existing disciplines of knowledge where the medium of instruction was Sanskrit, Hindi or any other language of the Indian subcontinent. Even today, it is used as a suffix in the names of disciplines in Hindi and other Indian languages such as political science (*Rajniti-Shastra*), sociology (*Samaj-Shastra*) and chemistry (*Rasayan-Shastra*).

The first use of the terms Shastra (Rigveda. 8.33.16) and Arth (*ərθə*) is seen in the Rigveda, the first composition of the mankind

[4] Jiyalal Kamboj, *Rigveda Samhita* (Delhi: Vidyanidhi Prakashan, 2013); H. H. Wilson, *Rigveda Samhita* (Delhi: Parimal Publications, 1866).

[5] A. P. Arya and K. L. Joshi, *Rigveda Samhita. H. H. Wilson and Bhashya of Shankaracharya* (Delhi: Parimal Publications, 1998).

[6] A. S. Altekar, *Education in Ancient India* (Benares: The Indian Book Shop, 1934).

on this planet earth which is said to come in textual form between 1500 and 3000 BCE.[7] In the Vedic knowledge system, the word *arth* has been used in three different meanings: wealth, object of the senses and meaning of the message. However, in association with the term 'Shastrarth', the word *arth* is always used in the sense of 'meaning of the message'. Here, the message could be oral, textual or in any other form. The term 'Shastrarth' is not used in the Vedas. Here two phrases, 'vaag-marg' or vaak-marg (path of speech/pronunciation)' have been used to refer to true or real meaning of the message of the discipline in part or totality (Rigveda 10.71). This indicates the prevalence of oral mode of teaching, learning and knowledge dissemination in ancient India before the textual form became popular.

The researcher could trace the most ancient use of Shastrarth in the Swetashwar Upanishad (6.22), which prescribes the highest degree of faith for a learner in his preceptor to realize the implicit knowledge of the message pronounced by the preceptor in his speech or dictation. Thereafter, it has been used in several texts such as *Nitisar* (1.22), Rāmāyaṇa, *Vakyapadiya*, *Yog Vashishth* and *Hitopdesh*. The word 'Shastrarth' has been used both as a noun and as a verb wherein as a verb it is the process to achieve what is indicated in the noun.

Methodology of Shastrarth

Methodology is described as 'the science of finding out.[8] According to Irny and Rose,[9] methodology is the systematic, theoretical analysis of the methods applied to a field of study. It comprises the theoretical analysis of the body of methods and principles associated with a branch of knowledge. Typically,

[7] Altekar, *Education in Ancient India*, 117.

[8] R. Rubin and E. Barbbie, *Methodology of Social Work Research* (New Delhi: Cengage Learning India, 2011), 15.

[9] S. I. Irny and A. A. Rose, 'Designing a Strategic Information Systems Planning Methodology for Malaysian Institutes of Higher Learning (isp-ipta)', *Issues in Information System* 6, no. 1 (2005): 325–331.

it encompasses concepts such as paradigm, theoretical model, phases and quantitative or qualitative techniques.[10] Kothari has defined methodology as 'a way to systematically solve the research problem. It may be understood as a science of studying how research is done scientifically'. He further explains,

> When we talk about research methodology we not only talk about research methods but also consider the logic behind the methods we use in the context of our research study and explain why we are using a particular method or technique and why we are not using others so that research results are capable of being evaluated ither by the researcher himself or by the other.[11]

In its approach, the methodology of Shastrarth is qualitative in nature, as it does not merely emphasize on data collection and analysis but also on active participation of view and counterview to ascertain the true nature of the subject matter. The methodology provides scope for in-depth understanding, flexibility and generalization.[12] However, tools and techniques such as *hetvabhash* (fallacies of reason), *chhal* (quibble), *jaati* (wrong analogy) and *nigra-sthan* (trespassing the Prohibited Zone) are deployed to maintain the objectivity of the research.

The procedure of realizing the real meaning of the message is described in the Rigveda (10.71), but its codification and compilation came much later. However, it should not be misunderstood as absence or less prevalence of the practice. This could be better understood with a contemporary example of Indian Parliament legislating the Flag Code of India in 2002 which comprises a set of rules, practices and conventions to be followed during the display of the national flag. However, under no imagination it could be concluded that the hoisting of the national flag was not in practice before 2002 or those who lived before 2002 were less careful about the dignity of the flag or were engaged in any idea

[10] Ibid.

[11] Kothari, C. R., *Research Methodology: Methods & Techniques* (New Age International Pvt. Ltd., Publishers, 2007), 8.

[12] Rubin and Barbbie, *Methodology of Social Work Research*, 388–399.

of desecrating the national flag. It simply means that by 2002, people were religiously following the instructions of the elders in the matters related to the hoisting of the flag while questions were raised on the conventions and elders were challenged. Therefore, a detailed codification became imminent. The same seems to be true for the development of the methodology of Shastrarth.

In Rigveda, the process of realizing the true meaning of a message has been described through an example of preparing a popular dish of those days that is known as 'sattu' (Rigveda. 10.71.2). Here, it has been emphasized that only those who follow the procedure achieve the meaning (*tatva*) of the speech of preceptors. The dish is still popular among traditional Vedic (Hindu) scholars in Kashi (Varanasi) and the adjoining areas. In fact, all the *richas* of the *sukta* number 71 of 10th mandala of Rigveda describe different approaches of Shastrarth. Since the medium of instruction in the Vedic Age was primarily oral and the number of disciplines were limited, there was no need of codification. With the increase in the number of disciplines[13] and schools of thought, a number of scholars came forward with a set of rules and regulations.

The first successful attempt was made by Medhatithi Gautama (600 BCE), who is considered the founder of a new discipline of scientific enquiry known as *Anvikshiki* (science of enquiry) par excellence.[14] In his book *Nyaya Sutra*, he provided a firm technical, theoretical and methodological dimension to the process of realizing the real meaning of a message. The discipline later became popular as Nyaya after his book *Nyaya Sutra*. Presently, the book contains five chapters, and each chapter has two parts.[15] The scholars are divided on whether the entire book was composed by one person or by multiple authors. However, they agree to point that the first chapter was composed by Medhatithi

[13] Altekar, A. S., *Education in Ancient India* (Benares City, Varanasi: The Indian Book Shop, 1934), 117–158.

[14] Vidya Bhushana, S. C., *A History of Indian Logic* (New Delhi: Shiv Books International, 2005), 17–18.

[15] R. Ghosh, *Nyayadarshana of Gotama (Etd)* (Delhi: New Bharatiya Book Corporation, 2003).

Gautama. The author has no intention to go on with this debate as the scope of the present discussion is limited only to the first chapter of *Nyaya Sutra* because the subsequent chapters are related to core philosophical issues. In the course of criticism and countercriticism, Vatsyayana (400 CE) authored a commentary on *Nyaya Sutra* which is known as *Nyaya Bhashya*. Though the Nyaya School is credited to have provided the most technically sound methodology of critical review to the Indic knowledge system, it is not the only methodology. The philosophical schools and disciplines of knowledge such as Buddhist, Jain, Lokayata, Vedanta, Navya Nyaya (new Nyaya), Ayurveda and Natyashastra (performing arts) developed their own methodologies of critical review with minor variations.[16] Besides, a majority of disciplines such as literature (sahitya), history (purana-itihas), political science (rajniti), diplomacy (*kootniti*), legal studies (*dandaniti*), Sanskrit grammar (*Sanskrit vyakaran*) and public policy (*nitishastra*) adopted the methodology of Nyaya School.[17]

Although the present analyses are primarily based on the methodology of Nyaya School, the main differences of other schools and disciplines have also been accommodated. According to Gautama, 16 devices or categories (*padarth*) are required to achieve the true knowledge or meaning of a message in textual, oral or any other manner. Those 16 devices could be divided into four groups.[18]

1. Presenting a sound argument
2. Identifying demerits in opposition's argument
3. Approaches/models of Shastrarth
4. Ascertainment (*nirnaya*)

[16] Radhavallabh Tripathi, *Vada in Theory and Practice* (Delhi: D. K. Printworld, 2016); Vidya Bhushan.

[17] W. K. Lele, *Methodology of Ancient Indian Sciences* (Varanasi: Chaukhambha Sanskrit Prakashan, 2013); Matilal; Radhavallabh Tripathi, *Vada in Theory and Practice* (Delhi: D. K. Printworld, 2016); Vidya Bhushan.

[18] S. Shukla, *The Relevance of Shastrarth in 21st Century* (Bhopal: Makhanlal Chaturvedi National University of Journalism and Communication, 2019), 158.

Out of the 16 categories of the Nyaya School, 8 are primarily related to the composition of sound arguments. They are *pramaan* (means of valid cognition), *pramey* (subject matter), *samshay* (doubt), *prayojan* (purpose), *drishtant* (instance), *siddhant* (theory), *avayav* (members of syllogism) and *tark* (confutation). Gautama has provided definitions and descriptions of these categories, while Vatsyayana in his commentary has elaborated them with examples. These eight categories are crucial in composition of a view or statement and its presentation. Here, the form of presentation of a view could be oral, textual or performing art. The Nyaya School also prescribes four categories or devices, *hetvabhash*, *chhal*, *jaati and nigrah-sthan*, for critical analysis of the subject matter or message. Gautama has mentioned five kinds of false reasons: erratic, contradictory, equal to the question, equal to the proposition and mistimed. Besides, 3 kinds of *chhal* (quibble), 24 kinds of *jaati* (wrong analogy) and 22 kinds of *nigrah-sthan* (prohibited acts) have been enumerated in Nyaya Sutra. All of them should be avoided while composing a robust argument but applied in critical review to highlight demerits in the subject matter and also during oral *shastrarth* to detect fallacies in opponent's arguments. Thus, it is the responsibility of a scholar to ensure that the message/s composed for dissemination in a society are free from the demerits: fallacies of reason, quibble, wrong analogy and restricted zones. The ancient Indians used to apply the process of the critical review to test the strength, intention, vision behind every message, argument, discipline and vision, which acted as the foundation stone for the tradition of argumentation in India for centuries.[19]

They could be applied in testing the strengths of one's own arguments and also to find out the demerits in counterview or opposition's arguments. Medhatithi Gautama in his composition *Nyaya Sutra* has presented a detailed description of these categories and their subcategories. His intellectual descendants have

[19] Sen, Amartya, *The Argumentative Indian: Writings on Indian History, Culture and Identity*. (Penguin Books, 2006), 3–73.

further strengthened the methodology by applying it in various situations and solving philosophical problems.

Besides presenting a detailed procedure of composition and critical analysis, Gautama has prescribed three approaches or models to realize the real nature of a *padartha* (object) or true meaning of the message for which he used the term *katha* (intellectual discourse). The purpose of conducting a *katha* is to establish the true nature of the object and deconstruct the false view/s contradictory to the true nature of the object. In other words, we can say that the *katha* was conducted to find out and establish the true nature of the message alongside deconstructing the contradicting views about the same. As the modes of discussion in the ancient times were predominantly oral, these approaches have been defined and explained in reference to their oral formats. However, in the course of time, they were also applied in textual and non-verbal modes of communication (see Shastrarth through ages). These approaches could be defined and explained as follows:

1. *Sāmvad* (Dialogue): The *sāmvad* has been described as the most refined and friendly form of Shastrarth since the age of Rigveda. It may be regarded as a holistic communication including all forms of communication: human to human, human to ambience, human to nature, etc; for example, Sage Rigvedic scholar Vishwamitra asking rivers to provide him path (Rigveda 3.33) and the dialogue between the God Kṛṣṇa and Arjuna in Shrimad Bhagavad Gita. In sāmvad, either both the sides are highly receptive to the thoughts of each other or one is the preceptor (guru) or teacher and the other is the knowledge seeker. Here questions are allowed, but they are only aimed at knowing the unknown and for doubt removal and confirmation of the known. These questions should never be aimed at deconstructing the view of the speaker. However, if the speaker misuses his position and engages in deconstructing the true knowledge established by the predecessor scholars (sages), Vatsyayana allows the listeners/audiences to apply all the instruments of *jalp* (debate until decision of the winner) and *vitandaa*

(debate of deconstruction only) to protect the true knowledge (*Nyaya Bhashya* 4.2.47).

2. *Vaad* (Discussion): *Vaad* is the adoption of one of the two opposing sides. What is adopted is analysed in the form of five members of syllogism and defended by the aid of any of the means of right knowledge, while its opposite is assailed by confutation, without deviation from the established principles.[20] The *vaad* should follow all the protocols and be conducted in a highly friendly atmosphere. It is immune from defeat or victory; so, the declaration of the winner is not there. This is because the presenter of the view in *vaad* approach is generally a preceptor/s, while the other side constitutes a group of students, knowledge seekers or a scholar of equal status of the same school of thought. But the scholar of different schools of thought may also engage in *vaad* with a view to understand each other's point of view with open mind provided they follow the protocols of the *vaad*. However, if any person/s from the other side raises an objection, the preceptor may defer the response or discontinue the speech. Besides, the other may also use the 'right to forfeiture' of the *vaad* which ultimately leads to the end of the debate or may convert into *jalp*.

   In textual format, *vaad* involves deconstruction of the *pūrva-paksa* and establishment of the *uttar-paksa* or rejoinder, that is, the view of the presenter.[21] Like oral, the rules of the *vaad* are also applied in the textual format. This tradition could be traced in Buddhist, Jain, Nyaya, Navya Nyaya, and other philosophical and literary traditions. Almost all forms of academic debates (verbal and textual) of present times are perfect examples of *vaad*.

3. *Jalp*: Victory or establishment of one's own view or opinion or school of thought is the main characteristic feature of *jalp* or debate which is also known as intellectual wrangling. Wrangling, which aims at gaining victory, is the defence or attack of a proposition in the manner aforesaid:

[20] Ghosh, *Nyayadarshana of Gotama*, 52.

[21] Tripathi, *Vada in Theory and Practice*, 3.

by quibbles, futilities and other processes which deserve rebuke.[22] The parliamentary and judicial debates which conclude with a decision could be classified as *jalp*.

4. *Vitandaa*: It is a kind of intellectual wrangling which involves mere attack on the opposite view.[23] Almost all the media debates are *vitandaa* as they never reach on any conclusion or decision.

Gautama and Vatsyayana both have described and accepted the importance of all the three approaches, but later scholars have considered *jalp* and *vitandaa* inferior to the *vaad*. This difference of opinion is up to the extent that Matilal has called *vaad* a good debate, *jalp* a bad debate and *vitandaa* a refutation or deconstruction.[24] The strongest rejoinder to such criticism is seen in an article of Panditraj Rajeshwar Shastri Dravid who says that a *vaad* without *jalp* and *vitandaa* was as futile as a man having sex with a eunuch to produce a child.[25]

Finally, *nirnaya* is the final product or conclusion of the Shastrarth or the true nature of the object or real meaning of the message. It has been defined as the removal of doubt, and the determination of a question, by hearing two opposite sides.[26]

Shastrarth Across Disciplines

Charak Samhita, a monumental book on *Ayurved* (Indian Medical System), also provides a methodology for intellectual discourse, knowledge competitions and critical review. (This is not an institute but only translation of Ayurved.) He has used 36 devices for critical review and termed them *tantra-yuktis* (devices of

[22] Ibid., 53.

[23] Ibid., 54.

[24] B. K. Matilal, *The Character of Logic in India* (New York: State University of New York Press, 1998), 55.

[25] Dravid, Dravid, P. R. Shastri, Shastrarth Vicharpaddhti (Methodology of Shasrarth), *Saraswati Sushma (Sanskrit)*, Vol. 55/1–4, 71–76, (Dr. Sampurnanand Sanskrit University, Varanasi, 200–01).

[26] Ghosh, *Nyayadarshana of Gotama*, 48.

discipline). Shushruta, the father/founder of surgery in India, has used 32 *tantra-yuktis*. Kautilya (321–296 BCE), in *Arthashastra*, has approved 32 *tantra-yuktis*.[27] The great Sanskrit grammarian Panini (500–1000 BCE) has also used *tantra-yuktis* for composition.[28]

The most primitive Buddhist text, *Sutta Pitaka*, compiled in the first Buddhist Council (490 BCE) mentions about argumentations and casuistry.[29] It also provides textual samples of the argumentation. The subsequent Buddhist scholars such as Nagarjuna (300 CE), Asanga (405–470 CE), Dhinanga (400–480 CE) and Dharmakirti (600–660 CE) contributed towards developing their own methodology in the course of criticism and counter criticism of Nyayashastra (science of true reasoning) for over a millennium. In this debate, Jain scholars also developed their methodology with minor variations which suited to their philosophical thoughts. The difference between the methodologies of these three major philosophical groups is primarily on the basis of *jaati*, five members of syllogism and type of *pramaan* (means of valid cognition). Nyaya School subscribes four means of cognition or right knowledge, that is, perception, inference, comparison and word, while Buddhists admit only two, that is, perception and inference.[30] Similarly, out of five members of syllogism, that is, proposition, reason, example, application and conclusion, the Buddhists admit only the first three. Buddhist scholars consider only 19 kinds of *jaati* out of which 9 are similar to Gautama's list, but 10 differ that are described in *Upaya-hridaya*. Another Buddhist text, *Tarkashastra*, also mentions 16 kinds of *jaati* out of which 13 are common to Nyayasutra. Jain scholars primarily follow *Tarkashastra* list for *jaati*.[31]

[27] Lele, *Methodology of Ancient Indian Sciences*, 30–32.

[28] Mishra, Madumesh. *Shastrarth Ratnaavali by Mahamahopadhayay Jaidev Mishra* (Edt), (Vani Vilas Prakashan, Varanasi, 2016); Komatineni, Surendra and J.S.R.A. Prasad, The Role of Tantrayuktis in Indian Research Methodology, The *Journal of Sanskrit Academy*, Vol. XXII, December 2021, 155–165. Available online: https://www.researchgate.net/publication/236962888_The_Role_of_Tantrayuktis_in_Indian_Research_Methodology.

[29] Vidya Bhushan, 227.

[30] Ghosh, *Nyayadarshana of Gotama*, 12.

[31] Matilal, *The Character of Logic in India*, 61–62.

However, all these methodologies were specific to their respective disciplines, but the methodology presented by Medhatithi Gautama was adopted by most of the disciplines, and it also has been interdisciplinary and multidisciplinary in its approach through the history.

Objectives of Shastrarth

Though technical presentation of the objectives of the Shastrarth are first seen in the *Nyaya Sutra* of Gautama, the concept has been described in the Rigveda with perfect illustrations in a poetic form. The Rigveda prescribed objectives of the Shastrarth. They are as follows:

1. Removing impurities (falsehood/dogmas) from disciplines or cleansing the disciplines/knowledge and realizing true knowledge or real nature of the subject matter (Rigveda 10.71.2) through friendly discussions (*sakhayah-sakhyani-janate*).
2. *Taam Sapt Rebha Abhi Sam Navante* or knowledge dissemination or communicating into the masses/society (Rigveda 10.71.3).
3. Learning and evaluation (Rigveda 10.71.4,6 and 7).
4. Vaajineshu or knowledge competitions among knowledge seekers (Rigveda 10.71.5) and learned scholars (Rigveda. 10.71.10).
5. Peer review (Rigveda 10.71.8).
6. Group communication used for knowledge dissemination into the society (Rigveda 10.71.11).
7. *Sampriksha* or asking questions and *sāmvad* or dialogue (Rigveda 8.101.5).

Gautama in his *Nyaya Sutra* has accepted *prayojan* among 16 elements of his doctrine to realize the true knowledge. He defines the *prayojan* as 'with an eye to which one proceeds to act'.[32] Thus,

[32] Ghosh, *Nyayadarshana of Gotama*, 33.

he presents a general definition of the term *prayojan* and provides freedom to the scholars to decide the objective of Shastrarth as per the requirement. In the very first formula (Sutra), he mentions Nihshreyash or ultimate truth or supreme felicity as the main objective of katha, the generic term used by Gautama for *vaad*, *jalp* and *vitandaa*. Besides, deconstruction of the counterview or falsehood and establishing the real view or truth has been described as the objective of *vaad* (*Nyaya Sutra*.1.2.1). The ascertainment—removal of doubt, the determination of a question, by hearing two opposite sides—is the final product of all kinds of Shastrarth.[33] In addition to Gautama and Vatsyayana, other scholars have also described *tatva bodh* or *tatva nirnaya* (true knowledge or ascertainment of the real nature of subject matter) as the main objective of Shastrarth.

Nyaya Bhashya, the commentary by Vatsyayana, has mentioned three objectives of an ideal *sāmvad*: *paripak* or confirmation or strengthening of the known knowledge, *samshay-chhedan* or doubt removal and *avigyat-aarthbodh* or to know the unknown knowledge (*Nyaya Bhashya* 4.2.47.). Furthermore, *tatva-adhyavsaaya-sanrakshan* or the protection of true knowledge[34] has also been described as a primary objective of Shastrarth. According to Vatsyayana, a scholar should use *jalp* and *vitandaa* even in *sāmvad* and *vaad* to protect the true knowledge just as a learned gardener uses branches of thorny plants to make a fence to protect the garden. The use of *jalp* and *vitandaa* in *sāmvad* is generally restricted but allowed if the opponent lowers the standard of intellectual discourse.

However, Vatsyayana restricts the use of *jalp* and *vitandaa* in *sāmvad* for vested interests such as laabh (profit), *pujaa* (respect) and *prashiddhi* (fame). Varadraj (1150 CE) in *Tarkik-raksha* has also included 'protection of the knowledge' as a purpose of katha. Jayant Bhatt (10th century CE) has described three objectives of Shastrarth—*Agyat-Gyapan* (to know the unknown),

[33] Ibid., 48.
[34] Ibid., 50.

Gyat-Sthirikaran (Confirming/strengthening the known) and *Samshay-Nirvartan (*Removing the Doubts). Rajeshwar Shastri Dravid has also mentioned the 'protection of the true knowledge' as the main purpose of *vaad*.[35]

Shushruta has said that 'with the assistance of the *tantra-yuktis* is achieved (1) the refutation of the statements made by a wicked disputant and (ii) the establishment of one's own views' (Lele, 2013). It also helps in achieving the accomplishment of the meaning which is expressed, which is not expressed in clear terms (hidden), which are concealed and which are partly expressed.[36] Rajashekhara (880–920 CE) in *Kavyamimamsa* has described *kavyakaar-pariksha* (examination of the poets/authors) and *shastrakaar-pariksha* (examination of scholars) as the objectives of organizing Shastrarth. Besides, the Shastrarth is also used in *Natya Shastra* by Bharat Muni. Thus, the objectives of the Shastrarth could be summarized as follows:

1. Knowing the unknown (learning and research)
2. Education and teaching
3. Evaluation/examination
4. Confirmation of the known
5. Removing the doubts
6. Cleansing knowledge from impurities
7. Protection of the true knowledge
8. Knowledge competitions
9. Peer review
10. Ascertainment of the real nature of subject matter
11. Questioning or asking questions
12. Dialogue
13. Communication: Intrapersonal, international, group communication and mass communication[37]
14. Knowledge dissemination

[35] Dravid, 71.

[36] Lele, *Methodology of Ancient Indian Sciences*, 25–26.

[37] K. J. Kumar, *Mass Communication in India* (Delhi: JAICO Publishing House, 2009), 1–40.

15. Deconstructing the malice statements (*vakya*) intended to pollute the true knowledge
16. Critical investigation

Scope of Shastrarth: Mode, Language and Subject Matter

Like any other discipline, the scope of Shastrarth was gradually diversified in almost all the parameters such as mode, language and subject matter. As the mode of expression in the Vedic period was primarily oral, there is great emphasis on the oral mode (Rigveda 10.71.1-11) of the Shastrarth. Besides, the methodology of realizing the true meaning of the speech or message also emphasizes on the oral mode of communication. Similarly, Mahatma Buddha himself had not authored any book,[38] but his speeches and teachings were first compiled in a textual form in the first 'Buddha Sangit' (council or seminar) in 490 BCE, about 80 years after his demise. In the subsequent years, textual exposition became popular, which followed the methodologies of Shastrarth of their respective schools in critical review of the subject matter and philosophical propositions of the opposite schools of Shastrarth. This could be established with the following three examples.

Textual Shastrarth between Scholars of Buddhist and Nyaya School

Nagarjuna (150–200 CE), a renounced Buddhist scholar, in his book *Madhyamik-Karika* followed the *vitandaa* model of Shastrarth to deconstruct the existing philosophical schools, particularly the Nyaya School which has emerged as the greatest intellectual challenge to the Buddhism. Nagarjuna criticized

[38] B. R. Ambedkar, *Buddha and His Dhamma* (Baile Japan [Digital Publications], 1957). http://www.banaengp.com/book/buddhaandhisdhamma-english.pdf

all but did not present his views or propositions. Vatsyayana (400 CE) in his book *Nyaya Bhashya* not only served a befitting rejoinder to Nagarjuna in his commentary but also explained Gautama's text, which is considered as the reference book in the Nyaya School of philosophy in universities, even today. However, Dhinanga (450–520 CE) in his book *Praman-Samuchchya* criticized Vatsyayana, but he was counter-criticized by Udyotkara (635 CE) in *Nyaya Vartika*. The *Nyaya Vartika* was refuted by Buddhist scholar Dharmakirti (600–660 CE) in his book *Praman-Vartika*. Furthermore, Vachaspati Mishra (841 CE) in his book *Nyaya-Vartika-Tatparaya-Tika* demolished the propositions of Buddhist scholars Dhinanga and Dharmakirti[39] and re-established the propositions of Nyaya and the Vedas. Furthermore, a Buddhist scholar Udayana (984 CE) authored a book called *Nyaya-Vartika-Tatparaya-Tika Parishuddhi* to deconstruct propositions of Vachaspati Mishra. This process of textual Shastrarth through criticism and counter-criticism continued for over a millennium until the prominence of Buddhism in the Indian subcontinent. However, only one book of the authors is mentioned in the examples, but it should not be misunderstood as the only texts of the concerned authors. These authors have written several other books as well. Besides, there have been many more authors of Buddhist, Jain, Nyaya, Mimamsa, Vedanta, Dharmashastra (social systems), etc., who have presented textual criticism and countercriticism of their pre-existing and contemporary authors were also taken up in oral Shastrarth, training and education. Buddhist scholar Shriharsha (12 CE) in his book *Khand-Khandan-Khandya* (Deconstruction of All Views) deconstructed all the previous philosophical opinions without presenting his own view on those issues. He also provided samples of debate in his book and claimed that the debaters just need to learn those samples to defeat the opponents in oral Shastrarth. In the same format, Jayarashi Bhatta (770–830 CE), a known scholar of Charvaka School, in his book *Tattva-upa.plava-simha* (The Lion that

[39] S. Chandra, *A History of Indian Logic* (Delhi: Shiv Books International, 2005), 135–136.

Devours All Categories or the Deconstruction of All Principles) presented a critical review of all the known philosophical positions. Jayarashi Bhatta was an academician and philosopher of the Charvaka School. In his book *Tattvopaplavasiṃha* (*Tattva-upa.plava-simha*)—the Lion that Devours All Categories or the Deconstruction of All Principles. However, in this philosophical battle which started since the age of Buddha, the Nyaya School emerged as the ultimate winner. These multilateral intellectual battles finally give rise to Navya Nyaya which is considered as the modern school of Indian logic founded by the 14th-century scholar Gangesa.[40]

Textual Shastrarth between Scholars of Sanatan Dharma and Arya Samaj

Dayananda Saraswati (1824–1875), the founder of Arya Samaj, is considered a prominent Vedic scholar of the colonial period. He used to travel from one place to the other and challenge the scholars of various philosophical schools of Hinduism, Islamism, Christianism, Buddhism, Jainism, etc., for oral Shastrarth.

Besides hundreds of oral Shastrarth, most of which were recorded and published, his popular book *Satyarth Prakash* provides a critical review to various schools of Hinduism, Islamism and Christianism. Dayananda has followed the *vaad* model in *Satyarth Prakash* wherein besides deconstructing the subject matter, he has also provided his own views on those issues. His contemporary Akhilanand Sharma in his book *Vaidika-Satyarth-Parkash* provided a deconstructed opinion of Dayananda and established an inclusive perspective of Hindu culture from Vedic evidence.

However, Pandit Jwala Prasad in his book *Dayanand Timir Bhaskar* and Thakar Das Jaini in his books *Dayanand Saraswati mukha-chapetika* (A Slap on the Face of Dayananda Saraswati)

[40] Ibid., 115–267.

and *Dyananda: Chhala–kapata-darpana* (A Mirror on Conceit and Deception of Dayananda) deconstructed *Satyarth Parkash*. In the subsequent years, an Arya Samaj scholar Tulsiram in his book *Bhaskar Prakash* presented counter-criticism of Jwala Prasad. Jwala Prasad's brother Baldev Prasad criticized Tulsiram's narrative in his book *Dharma Divakar*, but Tulasiram published his rejoinder in a new book—*Divakar Prakash*.[41]

Textual and Oral Shastrarth in Kenya

With the advancement in communication technology, we see several cases of textual Shastrarth followed by oral Shastrarth in the British colonial period. In such an interesting case, the author could trace a Shastrarth in Kenya, the African nation, in 1927 CE where Hindu population is significant event today.

Before the oral Shastrarth between Pandit Madhavacharya Shastri representing Shri Sanatan Dharma Pratinidhi Sabha Punjab (Lahore) and Balkrishna Sharma, Chairperson, Arya Vidwat Sammelan, Mumbai in Arya Samaj Temple, Nairobi (Kenya), on 14 August 1927, the textual Shastrarth between the Sanatan and Arya Samaj scholars in Nairobi continued for months through letters. The rules of textual Shastrarth were agreed upon through letters including the time of posting the letters and expecting the duration of submitting the questions failing which the rival would be considered as defeated. The scholars of both the sides agreed upon five questions for textual Shastrarth. They are as follows:

1. Are Puranas in accordance to the Vedic knowledge?
2. Are Puranas against the Vedic knowledge?
3. Are the texts composed by Dayananda Saraswati in conformity with the Vedic knowledge?
4. Are the texts composed by Dayananda Saraswati fictions?
5. Does the Vedic knowledge approve idol worship?

[41] Tripathi, *Vada in Theory and Practice*, 319–320.

After textual Shastrarth, an oral Shastrarth was also organized between 2 PM and 5 PM at the Arya Samaj Temple of Nairobi (Kenya) where a Muslim scholar was chosen as the chairperson. The entire event was recorded; Madhavacharya Shastri was declared as the winner and the reports were published in the local newspapers.[42] This Shastrarth was conducted in Hindi language and a book *Shastrarth Panchak* was also published in Hindi, which is available in Bhandarkar Library, Pune, Maharashtra.

There are several samples of oral Shastrarth, but the most popular among them are the Shastrarth between Gargi and Yajnavalkya in the court Emperor Janak (Brihadaranyak Upanishad), the Shastrarth between Addi Shankara and Mandan Mishra (Shankar-Digvijay) and the Shastrarth between Swami Dayananda Saraswati and Pandits of Kashi with the King of Kashi as the chairperson on 16 November 1869 in Anand Bagh at Durga Kund in Varanasi.[43]

In addition to verbal, textual as well as oral Shastrarth, there are also strong evidence of non-verbal Shastrarth. Bharat Muni in his historical text *Natya Shastra* has described the methodology of Shastrarth for Natyashastra discipline with technical terms, concepts and definitions. He has also presented samples of Shastrarth in the Natyashastra with proper questions and counter questions through various positions in Natya (performing arts). In this reference, the following instance is worth to be cited:

> The sons of Bharata, in the shilpakas performed them, presented the life nd deeds of the sages residing in the vicinity of Himalayas by the way of vidambana (caricature) and vyangyakarana (satire). The sages being laughed at in this way, got infuriated and cursed the actors to be expelled from the divine region of the Himalayas and to become shudra.[44]

[42] *Shastrarth Panchak*, Sanatan Dharma Sabha (Nairobi) (Pune: Bhardarkar Oriental Research Institute Library, 1928).

[43] Tripathi, *Vada in Theory and Practice*, 323.

[44] Ibid., 240.

However, after Bharat Muni's intervention through subsequent plays, a compromise was agreed upon in which his sons were spared on the promise that Muni's disciples would travel from north to south and use their knowledge in a more meaningful Natya for the welfare of all. Furthermore, in the methodology of vigrahya sambhasha (*vitandaa*), Charaka has prescribed to ridicule the opponent through the movement of hands and facial expressions.[45]

Language of Shastrarth

Until it was gradually replaced by English during the British colonial period, Sanskrit had been the language of academic and intellectual communication throughout the Indian subcontinent. Therefore, the dominance of Shastrarth in Sanskrit language is obvious. However, Sanskrit was never the only language for Shastrarth. The Buddhist scholars have also followed regional languages such as *Pāli* and *Prākrt* which dominate Buddhist texts.

During the British colonial period, English and Hindi were also used in Shastrarth.

In the modern times, Raja Ram Mohan Roy is considered a prominent face who carried forward the traditional mode of Shastrarth in at least three languages—Persian, Sanskrit and English—besides widening its scope in Dharmashastra and contemporary issues such as Satipratha (burning of widows) and widow remarriage. His book in Persian titled *Tuhfat-ul-Muwahhidin* (A Gift to Monotheists) in 1804 is a criticism to the Islamic Philosophy. Roy's book in English titled *Essay on the Rights of Hindoos over Ancestral Property* is seen as a rejoinder to the 'Code of Gentoo Laws' (1775 CE) and other translations on Hindu law published by the colonial government and backed by the European scholars. Subrahmanya Shastri, a Hindu scholar of Madras, challenged Roy for an oral Shastrarth in *jalp* model on the issue of Satipratha which was organized in December 1816. In

[45] Ibid., 171.

the colonial period, we see a rise of bilingual scholars, primarily Sanskrit and English, which continued until the second half of the 20th century.[46] In the same period, formal Shastrarth in *jalp* model were also conducted in Hindi language.

Above all, Vachaspati Mishra (841 CE) in his *Nyaya-Vartika-Tatparaya-Tika* has directed the *prashnik* (judges other than chairperson) to translate the language in the mother tongue of the debater if he/she is unable to understand.

Subject Matter

Since the age of Rigveda, Shastrarth was conducted in all the disciplines of the respective ages to ascertain the true meaning or real nature of the discipline in part or whole and in verbal or non-verbal medium. The process has been used to realize the true nature or real meaning of the subject matter by deconstructing or eliminating the false arguments and establishing the sound arguments.

The most ancient records in India present a glimpse about four faculties[47] in higher education: the Vedas (Rigveda Samhita, Samaveda Samhita, Yajurveda Samhita and Atharvaveda Samhita), itihas (history), Purana (historical fiction) and Narashansi Grantha (book about great personalities). In the subsequent ages, more and more disciplines were added. As we see in the contemporary education system, the disciplines in the ancient India were also diversified in the course of time. The Vishnu Purana described 18 disciplines which are described into 4 faculties: Vedas (4), Vedang (6), Vidya (4) and Upveda (4). Besides the four Samhitas, the faculty of the Vedas also includes their respective Brahamanas, Aranyakas and Upanishads. The Vedang includes *vyakaran* (Sanskrit grammar), *jyotish* (astrology), *shiksha*

[46] Ramchandra Guha, 'The Rise and Fall of the Bilingual Intellectual', *Economic & Political Weekly* 44, no. 33 (15 August 2009): 36–42.

[47] Altekar, *Education in Ancient India*, 118.

(education), *kalp* (ritual), *nirukta* (etymology), and *chhand* (prosody). There were four disciplines in the faculty of Vidya: Mimamsa, Nyayashastra, Dharmashastra (science of righteousness) and Purana; and four Upveda: Ayurveda (medical science), Dhanurved (military science), Gandhar (performing arts) and Arthashastra.[48] The discipline of Arthashastra is centred around all the subject matters dealt in the famed book of *Arthashastra* of Kautilya or Chanakya who was the professor in the University of Takshashila and the founder of the discipline. It was earlier translated in English as polity or economics, but if we compare Arthashastra with contemporary disciplines, the subject matter of several disciplines such as economics, taxation, social systems, political science, diplomacy, international relations, military science, management, public policy, policy, public heath, logic, creative writing, methodology, content analysis, philosophy, history and human behaviour are present in Arthashastra. In fact, the discipline of Arthashatra is almost similar to the faculty of social sciences and the faculty of humanities in the contemporary higher education system. Shastrarth had been prominently used in all these disciplines for teaching, evaluation and knowledge competitions in the academic institutions. Even today, Shastrarth is organized in Sanskrit-medium universities of India.

All those issues which were earlier considered as untouchable in modern philosophy are now included on the name of metaphysics and spiritual science. However, the Western scholars and their representatives in Indian universities continue to label the philosophical issues taken up in Shastrarth as religious. If a discourse on soul, existence or non-existence of the Almighty and its form is religious, it should then be called religious even in the new brand name of metaphysics. How did the study of the same topics in their new brand names in English or other European language become non-religious? This seems like a classical case of an old wine in a new bottle.

[48] Vedic Heritage. http://vedicheritage.gov.in/

Furthermore, the Indic scholars never shied away in engaging non-Indic disciplines in Shastrarth. Jagannatha Panditaraja, a multidisciplinary scholar, defeated an Islamic scholar in Shastrarth in Jaipur, Rajasthan. He became so popular that Dara Shikoh invited him to the Mughal Court at Agra, and he was appointed as his Sanskrit teacher.[49] He has been referred as *Samarajya Pandit* (scholar of the Empire) in Sanskrit texts.[50] There are several examples of cross-cultural Shastrarth in *vaad*, *jalp* and *vitandaa* format.

An interesting example on Shastrarth in population studies came during Census 1911 during the British colonial period. The British officers decided to create a separate category of non-Hindu for lower caste Hindus, who were facing social discrimination in those days. A Shastrarth was organized in the Town Hall of Varanasi in the Chairmanship of Pandit Pratap Narain Mishra in full public glare. After conclusion of the Shastrarth, the chairman announced the ascertainment:

> A person cannot be expelled from the jurisdiction of Hindu Dharma for being untouchable (born in an untouchable family). He or she is a Hindu up to the same extent a *savarna* (a person born in a non-untouchable family) is. The untouchables are undivided organ of Hindu society. Expelling untouchables from Hindu society is completely wrong, non-practical and gross violation of the Vedic disciplines.[51]

Similarly, Chattami Swamikal (1853–1924), born in a Nambudri Brahaman family (1853–1924), presented a textual disputation to the socio-religious discrimination against lower caste Hindu with citations from the Vedas and Upanishads. He was a contemporary of Swami Narayan (1854–1928), a popular scholar of the Vedanta philosophy in Kerala.

[49] Tripathi, *Vada in Theory and Practice*, 136.

[50] Upadhyaya, Baldev, *Kashi Ki Panditya Parampara* (The Intellectual Tradition of Kashi), (Vishwavidyalaya Prakashan, Varanasi, 1994).

[51] Ibid.

Therefore, it is now clear that in its history of about 4,000 to 5,000 years, all the topics under the Sun were covered in the Shastrarth from academic institutions to kings' courts to temples to public meetings to intellectual meetings in cities and villages.

Protocols of Organizing Shastrarth

In all the phases of history, events of intellectual discourse have been more popular across the population in comparison to their textual and non-verbal formats. Even today, seminars and conferences are many times more popular and attract more eyeballs than their textual presentations. The same also holds water for the Shastrarth. As in the contemporary intellectual discourse, organizing a seminar requires a set of rules and protocols, the same is applied to organizing a Shastrarth.

Though there are three models of Shastrarth, *vaad*, *jalp* and *vitandaa*, organizing a *jalp* is the most challenging. This is because *vaad* is conducted between a teacher or preceptor and his/her disciples, scholars of the same school or two eminent scholars of different schools who are receptive to the ideas of each other and have no intention to win. However, win and defeat is the most important character feature of *jalp*. The declaration of a winner, the ascertainment in a characteristic feature of Shastrarth, differentiates *jalp* from *vaad*, as vaad has been provided immunity from defeat. The *vitandaa*, however, is not accepted as an independent model from the perspective of an event as it is included in the *jalp* and it follows declaration of the winner/s.

The participants of Shastrarth could be an individual or teams, but only two: *vaadi* (proponent) and *prati-vaadi* (respondent). Here an individual/team is a proponent for his/her proposition and an opponent for the rival's proposition and vice versa. The Rigveda prescribes simple guidelines in poetic form for organizing a Shastrarth to cleanse the discipline from intellectual pollution (Rigveda 10.71.2.), knowledge competition or *Vajineshu* (Rigveda 10.71.5) and evaluation or critical review or peer review

(Rigveda 10.71.8) and communication (Rigveda 10.71.12). However, the subsequent scholars have provided protocols on Shastrarth which gradually developed in later Vedic period, Upanishads, Brahamana books, Mahābhārata and other texts. The protocols of Shastrarth could be divided into two parts as discussed below.

Intellectual Component

The intellectual component could be divided into two parts: human resource or persons and rules for conducting Shastrarth. According to scholars, there should be five kinds of persons[52] of intellectual component: *vaadin* (proponent), *prati-vaadin* (respondent), *prashnik* (judge), sabhaya or sabhasad (members of assembly) and *lekhak* (scribe). The work of the scribe is to record the proceedings of the Shastrarth.

Varadraj (1150 CE) in his book *Tarkik-Raksha* has divided all the rules required in Shastrarth into six categories.[53] They are as follows: rules pertaining to determining the subject matter and admissible evidences, rules pertaining to the model of Shastrarth, rules pertaining to the behaviour of the proponent and respondent including ethics, rules pertaining to the selection of the members and chairperson and their ethics, rules pertaining to the determination of restricted zones and agreement on rules of termination of Shastrarth.

The scholars have prescribed selection of three to five judges through a mutual consent between both the parties. These judges through mutual consent would select one among them, preferably the most experienced and eminent as the chairperson. The duty of the chairperson is to pronounce the ascertainment, while the other two judges may interfere in the Shastrarth through counter questions, encouragement, explaining the aphorisms, simplifying the language for the rival wherever necessary and

[52] Dravid, 71; Tripathi, *Vada in Theory and Practice*, 15.
[53] Dravid, 72.

also translating the difficult questions in simple or regional language. The texts also prescribe responsibilities of chairpersons and judges and high standards of ethics in conducting impartial Shastrarth and declaring the winner. In a poetic way, Dravin writes if three or five impartial, non-jealous and unbiased judges are conducting a Shastrarth, it is equivalent to a sacred yajña.[54] Chanakya has prescribed protocols for the government officers if they want to attend a Shastrarth, such as taking permission of the chairperson before entry, not speak to neighbours, should not sit on a seat higher than the chairperson, not to interrupt, etc.[55]

Infrastructural Component

The concept of Sabha and Samiti are first introduced in Shukla Yajurveda (3.35). Furthermore, Atharvaveda describes Sabha and Samiti in a personified way as two daughters of Prajapati, who take care of the people (*Atharvaveda* 7.12.1).

It seems that the conventions were acting as guidelines for infrastructural requirements of Shastrarth, and they were of secondary importance in comparison to the intellectual discourse. Rajashekhara (880–920 CE) in his book *Kavyamimamsa* has standardized and codified the infrastructural requirements for conducting Shastrarth, particularly in the king's court or when a king is present as the chairperson. Rajashekhara has used the term Brahma-Sabha for the venue of Shastrarth. It should have 16 pillars, 4 doors, a platform and a seat for the chairperson. He has also provided seating arrangements for the chairperson, judges, proponent, respondent, members of the assembly and also who should be included as the members (*Kavyamimamsa* 10). Rajashekhara has guided the kings to organize Shastrarth from time to time, grade the scholars and award them with title and *daan* (goods)-*dakshina* (currency). If not the king, besides being an eminent scholar, the chairperson should be the person

[54] Ibid.
[55] *Arthashastra*, Vol. II, 209–210.

who could arrange for *daan-dakshina*. Even today, the businessmen from throughout India in their visit to Varanasi organize *pandit-sabha* (council of the Vedic scholars) and provide them *daan-dakshina*, but the tradition of Shastrarth has now been confined largely to recitation of few Vedic mantras.

Shastrarth through Ages

The scholars of Indic studies such as Satish Chandra Vidyabhushan, E. A. Solomon and V. K. Matilal have classified the history of Shastrarth in philosophical ages such as Buddhist, Jainism, Nyaya, Vedanta and modern logic. However, the recent most historical classification has been presented by Radhavallabh Tripathi,[56] who has divided the history of Shastrarth into four periods: The Age of Revelation (around 3000–500 BCE), the Age of Argument (500–1000 CE), the Age of Diversification (1000–1800 CE) and Modern Age (around 1800 CE onwards).

As discussed earlier, the term Shastrarth came much later. The most primitive term used for intellectual discourse in ancient India was Brahmodaya or rise of true/sacred knowledge. This was generally conducted at the time of *ashwa-medha-yajna*, the process of which is mentioned in Yajurveda. In the Upanishad period, the term *vakovakya* (intellectual discourse) became more popular as Yajnavalkya has also mentioned it as an important discipline in Yajnavalkya Samhita.[57] In this age, different terminologies were used, but the Shastrarth was mainly based on conventions. Sathpatha Brahamanas and Brihadanakya Upanishads describe several Shastrarth in the court of the Emperor Janaka in which, at times, he was also actively involved. However, in this court, Shastrarth between sage Yajnavalkya and female sage Gargi[58] is among the most popular Shastrarth as this was on the topic

[56] Tripathi, *Vada in Theory and Practice*, 40.

[57] Ibid.

[58] E. Roer, *The Brihadaranyak Upanishad* (Calcutta: Society for Resuscitation of Indian Literature, 1909), 213–222.

Brahma Vidya (Nature of the Almighty). However, the *vaad* model of Shastrarth was the most popular format in this age, as except a few Lokayatas, the sages were followers of the Vedic principles. In this period, *samvaad* (dialogue) is the most popular format; while *vaad* and *jalp* are there, *vitandaa* is absent.

The Age of Argument is actually a period of a millennium involving triangular intellectual fight between Nyaya, Buddhist and Jain schools of philosophies, in which various other schools have also intervened from time to time. This age has produced huge amount of textual Shastrarth in terms of theory, methodology as well as subject matter. This period marks the rise and fall of Buddhism in the Indian subcontinent and *jalp* as the most prominent model of Shastrarth. Chanakya has used the term *Anvikshiki* for the discipline of Shastrarth. Chanakya has also called *Anvikshiki* as the 'lamp of all the disciplines' (*Arthashastra* 2.13). The popular Shastrarth of this age are the Shastrarth between the Buddhist monk Nagsena and Indo-Greek King Menander (165–130 BCE) presented in a textual form in Milind-Panho, the Shastrarth of Ashtavakra (550–500 BCE) in the court of King Janaka described in the *Vana Parva* of the Mahābhārata and the Shastrarth of Aadi Shankaracharya (788–820 CE) with Mandan Mishra and his wife Udaya Bharati described in Shankar Digvijay. It was in this age that the great texts such as *Nyaya Sutra*, *Nyaya Bhashya* and *Kama Sutra* came into existence.

The Age of Diversification is, in fact, the Bhakti age in Indian history wherein poetry and epics were composed in regional languages. In this age, we see dominance of regional languages in intellectual discourse, and the tradition of Shastrarth were confined only in educational institutions, religious institutions and royal courts primarily because the arch-rival Buddhism was eliminated in sustained Islamic aggressions. We see saints such as Guru Nanak, Kabir, Tukaram, etc., flourish in this age. Mughal Emperor Akbar had organized a Shastrarth among scholars of all the existing religions and philosophies of his age in about 1655 CE, which was recorded in *Dabistan-e-Mazahib*

(School of Faiths). The English translation of the book was published by David Shea and Anthony Troyer in 1843 from London titled *The Dabistan or School of Manner*. Besides, the European traveller Francois Bernier also had a Shastrarth on idol worship and other issues with pandits of Kashi, which is described in his letter posted to monsieur on 4 October 1667 from Persia during his retuning journey.[59]

The tradition of intellectual discourse was revived after the colonial government silently promoted the mission of religious conversion in the Indian subcontinent. Unlike the Islamic conversion, which was forceful and based on sword, the Christian missionaries followed a model of intellectual discourse which was similar to the *vitandaa* model of Shastrarth. The Indian scholars starting from Raja Ram Mohan Roy, Ishwar Chandra Vidyasagar, Aurobindo Ghosh, Lokmanya Tilak, Sarvepalli Radhakrishnan, Madan Mohan Malaviya, etc., engaged in intellectual discourse with the scholars of the colonial age. In the modern age, the Government Sanskrit College (1792 CE), now Sampurnanand Sanskrit University, emerged as the centre for Indic knowledge system. With the establishment of three universities of the European model in 1857, Calcutta, Mumbai and Madras, the colonial government set up a new system of disciplines in the Indian subcontinent which they referred to as the 'queens' subjects. This model was promoted and replicated in all the universities in the Indian subcontinent until the colonial rule and also in the post-Independence era.

Thus, the Indian discipline of Shastrarth was made to face an unequal competition wherein the entire funding and focus was centred towards the European logic and argumentation, while the indigenous logic was left to die. Solomon[60] formally announced

[59] Bernier, Francois. Superstitions, Strange Customs and Doctrines of Indous or Gentiles of Hindostan, *Travels in the Moughal Empire 1656–1668 A.D.* pp. 342–44, (Oxford University Press, 1891).

[60] E. A. Solomon, *Indian Dialectics* (Ahmedabad: B. J. Institute of Learning and Research, Gujarat Vidya Sabha, 1976), 17.

the death of Shastrarth in 1976, and by the early 1990s, Pandit Baldev Upadhayaya is seen seeking interference of the heavenly powers to save the discipline.[61]

Conclusion and Agenda for Discussion

'The great danger of this is tendency to read, consciously or unconsciously, Western ideas into Indian philosophy' says Professor Satishchandra Chatterjee.[62] In fact, the scholars of modernity have often used the Indic knowledge system as a punching bag. The entire knowledge across the disciplines was confined in a single department of Sanskrit in Calcutta University which only had Sanskrit literature. This problem of Indic knowledge could be better understood in an imaginary university wherein all disciplines which are now taught in English medium are put into a single Department of English. In the later periods, some universities of pre-medieval Indic disciplines were opened which have really made some progress, but they are largely isolated from modern contemporary disciplines. The Western scholars have already declared the death of modernity and transited into the age of post-modernity. However, Indian modernists who developed a habit of mocking eternity of the Vedas as non-scientific are religiously following the eternity of the modernity that was declared dead by its parents in the 20th century.[63]

There are a lot of differences between outdated modern age and the present post-modern age in today's world, but the most important among them are the rise of indigenous culture and breathing space for cultural plurality which was not possible under the bulldozer of modernity armed with macro theories and meta-narratives.[64] The allegation of Shastrarth being a religious

[61] Upadhayay, 123.

[62] S. Chatterjee, *The Nyaya Theory of Knowledge* (New Delhi: Rupa Publications India, 2015), xx.

[63] Doshi, *Modernity, Postmodernity and Neo-Sociological Theories*, ix–x.

[64] Ibid., 167–226.

mode of debate is ill-conceived and fictitious. There is no denying the fact that the topics related to philosophy have been at the core of Shastrarth throughout its history, but the same is true for modernity which provides Master of Philosophy (MPhil) and Doctor of Philosophy (PhD) to the students of nanotechnology, biotechnology and astrology. A number of instances could be cited to expose the double standard of modernity.

The efforts are being made to apply the methodology of Shastrarth in Indic[65] as well as Western disciplines[66] in the 21st century. Besides, the UNESCO has proclaimed to provide opportunities for indigenous cultures in its policy.[67] In its history of over 5,000 years, the practice of Shastrarth in its various forms has ensured a healthy competition between various existing cultures besides providing scope for the creation of new cultural practices, philosophies and visions about all the topics under the Sun. In doing so, it has made immense contribution in protecting unparalleled cultural plurality in India.[68] The practice was never dogmatic but innovated and revived by a serious of great scholars for over five millennia. Besides being popular through various generic names in different periods of history, Shastrarth also had interdisciplinary, multidisciplinary and transdisciplinary perspectives.

As the whole world is looking for a model to ensure cultural plurality, Shastrarth could contribute in achieving the goal. The need of the hour is to develop a new approach on the foundations which could ensure breathing space for the cultures besides providing space for cultural innovations based on a principal of removing fallacies and establishing the noble views.

[65] 'Sanskrit Shastrarth Parishad Starts', *The Times of India*, 24 November 2011.

[66] Shastrarth (Mumbai: Sarla Anil Modi School of Economics, 2017). http://economics.nmims.edu/samsoe-activities/2016-17/shastrarth-2017/

[67] UNESCO (b), *UNESCO Policy on Engaging with Endogenous People.* https://en.unesco.org/indigenous-peoples/policy

[68] Amartya Sen, *The Argumentative Indian: Writings on Indian History, Culture and Identity,* (New Delhi: Penguin Books, 2006), 3–73.

Bibliography

Bayly, C. A. 'Raja Rammohan Roy and Advent of Contributional Liberalism'. In *An Intellectual History of India*, edited by Shruti Kapila and Christopher Bayly, 28. Cambridge: Cambridge University Press, 2010.

Dravid, Panditraj Rajeshwar Shastri. '*Shastrarth Vicharpaddhti* [Methodology of Shastrarth]'. *Saraswati Sushma* 55, no. 1–4 (2000–2001): 71–76.

Maadhavaananad, S. *The Brihadaaranyaka Upanishad*, 3rd ed. Calcutta: Advaita Ashrama, 1950.

Munsi, S. *Kashi Shastrarth (Sanskrit)*. Prayag: Vaidik Granthalaya. http://aryamantavya.in/kashi-debate-of-swami-dayanand/

Upadhyaya, Baldev. *Kashi Ki Panditya Parampara* [The Intellectual Tradition of Kashi]. Varanasi: Vishwavidyalaya Prakashan, 1994.

10

Indic in Southeast Asian Culture

Ritika Joshi

Cultural boundaries of India exceed its geographical boundaries. Many regions in South Asia and Southeast Asia have been vastly influenced by the Indic culture. The cultural influence of ancient India on Southeast Asia has been vast. The regions in Southeast Asia which are most influenced by the Indic culture are the islands of Java, Bali and Sumatra in contemporary Indonesia. This chapter will revolve around ancient India's influence on contemporary Indonesia and the factors which led to the propagation of the ancient Indian culture. At the same time, it is important to analyse the factors which led to the easy adoption of the Indic cultural motifs in Southeast Asia.

The focus is on the islands of Java, Bali and Sumatra, lying more or less contiguously across the ocean, and the period of history under consideration is the one during which frequent contacts with India, primarily motivated by commerce, led to the adoption and absorption of religions such as Hinduism and Buddhism, which shaped all aspects of social and cultural behaviour, permeating the very fabric of Indonesia in an indelible way to the present times. The phenomenon of Indianization, its links with factors such as trade, coastal settlements of Indian traders, movement of Buddhist monks and Brahmana priests are critical.

Contextualization

While there are historical links between India and the islands of Bali, Java and Sumatra, there is also a debate as to how far ancient India influenced Indonesia. Was it merely a derivative culture or did it assimilate elements from Indian culture in its own? Was there any similarity existing already between Indian and Indonesian cultures which led to the easy adoption? Few scholars argue that the emphasis on Indian connections, some of which go back to pre-historic times, is not motivated by a misapprehension of Indonesian cultural autonomy, that is, Indonesian culture is not seen as a derivative but parallel, and the use of Indian paradigms are highlighted in order to understand precisely the multilayered nature of Indonesian cultural reality, of which features of Indian origin or shared with India, adapted, transformed, fused and reinterpreted in a unique way, are only a layer. Monica L. Smith[1] labels it as 'Indianization' from the Indian point of view.

The strength of the Indic tradition lay precisely in offering flexibility and scope for variants and reinterpretations. The question of the so-called Indianization of the Southeast Asian region is still, to a great extent, a controversial matter among historians for it is not an easy task to quantify and separate those elements that in the culture of the Southeast Asian countries can be identified as the straightforward result of Indian influence. The use of the very term Indianization has been challenged repeatedly in order to highlight 'the syncretic rather than purely derivative nature of South East Asian elite cultures'.[2] The impact of Indian culture on Southeast Asia is what is usually described as Indianization, and Coedes defines this as the expansion of an organized culture based on the Indian concepts of kingship, one whose main features were Hindu/Buddhist cults, Puranic

[1] Monica L. Smith, '"Indianization" from the Indian Point of View: Trade and Cultural Contacts with Southeast Asia in the Early First Millennium CE,' *Journal of the Economic and Social History of the Orient* 42, no. 1 (1999): 1-26.

[2] Wisseman, 4.

mythology, the Dharmashastras and the adoption of Sanskrit as an official language.[3]

The view of Indianization as a one-way process impregnates the 20th century writings on Southeast Asian history up to the Second World War. Not many scholars of this period really took into account the proficient seamanship of the Southeast Asian peoples, and even when this was acknowledged, it was still in most instances by lip service. The problem of ascertaining whether Indian influence was only a veneer on the indigenous societies, in spite of which they managed to preserve their original character, or whether the indigenous societies were fully integrated into a society of Indian type cannot easily be solved to this day. Although the data supplied by archaeological research are numerous, much more still has to be known about the so-called 'indigenous societies' as a whole.[4]

It is necessary at this point to emphasize the fact that research highlights the existence of a 'common ancestry'[5] between the peoples of peninsular India and those of Southeast Asia, which goes back to prehistoric times and precedes the wave of Indo-Aryan culture in India itself. Many similarities, therefore, could be traced to that common ancestry. This would also explain, to a great extent, how Indianization was possible, developing as it did in a naturally fertile ground.

The early 20th-century researchers and historians tended to see Indianization as a civilizing mission to barbarian countries. India was described as the 'mother of civilization' with an imperial mission to rival that of Greece and Rome in the West. 'Hindu colonists brought with them the whole framework of their culture and civilization and this was transplanted in its entirety among the people who had not yet emerged from their

[3] G. Coedes, *The Indianized states of South East Asia*, ed. W. F. Vella (Honolulu: English edn, 1968), 15.

[4] Ibid., 16.

[5] I. W. Mabbett, 'Translator's Preface', in *The Devaraja Cult*, ed. H. Kulke (New York: Southeast Asia Program, Department of Far Eastern Studies, Cornell University, 1978), viii.

primitive barbarism'.[6] Southeast Asia was known then as Greater India, thus emphasizing its role as an Indian, if not political, at least cultural, colony.

Soon after the Indian Independence, the 'Greater India Society' and its journal became defunct. This Indo-centric perspective of most Indian scholarly writings was fully endorsed and partly fostered by Western academics, the majority of whom had a background of Sanskrit philological studies and were primarily specialists in Indology. In the second half of the 20th century, greater emphasis was put on studying and on reaching a greater understanding of Southeast Asia in its own right. Indianization came to be viewed as an elitist 'superstructure on the autochthonous substratum,'[7] and an attempt was made at balancing the view of foreign forces shaping the Southeast Asian region.

The factors that historians associate with the process of Indianization are as follows: (a) trade and trading routes (b) Indian coastal settlements (c) movement of Brahmanas and Buddhist monks; and (d) Indian and Indianized local rulers.

There are various historical sources which talk of the India–Southeast Asia connection. Beginning with the Indian sources, the panorama is as follows. The Jatakas offer tales of seamen, and the Rāmāyaṇa is believed to mention Java (Yava). The *Mahaniddesa*, a Pali text placed by Sarkar not later than Ashoka' s reign[8] and by Noıman at the beginning of the 3rd century BC,[9] fares much better because it lists identifiable geographical names. Somewhat imprecise references to places are found in the Puranas.[10] The Tamil work *Cilappatikaram* (circa 5th century AD) mentions a flourishing trade of India, presumably with Yavadvipa, and the second part of the *Pāli* text *Culavamsa* (1186/1333), from

[6] Majumdar, 16.

[7] Coedes, *The Indianized States of South East Asia*, 56.

[8] Sarkar, 22.

[9] K. R. Norman, *Pali Literature Including Canonical Literature in Prakrit and Sanskrit of All Hinayana Schools of Buddhism* (Wiesbaden: Otto Harrassowitz, 1983).

[10] Sarkar, 23.

Ceylon, has clear reference to the relations of the island with Southeast Asia.[11]

The best-known European source for Southeast Asian history is, however, Marco Polo's account of his travels (13th century AD). Perso-Arabic sources span from 9th century to 16th century. With a few notable exceptions, that is, Ibn Battuta, most of these authors never visited the countries described.

Finally, there are the Old Javanese literary sources, the *Nagarakertagama* (1365) and the *Pararaton* (circa 1278/1478). These are fairly late texts, but they contain stray references to earlier periods. Epigraphy is the most important historical source for an assessment of the Indian presence. In India itself, the earliest epigraphic record to mention Indonesia is the Nalanda charter of Balaputradeva, king of Suvarpadvipa, circa 860 AD. It refers to a grant of five villages for the building of a monastery.[12] Other inscriptions dating to the Chola period are found, that is, the grant of Rajaraja I and some later inscriptions relating to Chola naval expeditions.

Sumatran material consists of Old Malay inscriptions from the Palembang region (682–683 AD), followed by the Tamil inscription of Loba Tuwa dated 1088. An inscription linked with the site of Kota Cina in North Eastern Sumatra, one of the first Indian entrepot in this part of the island, possibly a Tamil one,[13] was found in 1826, but subsequently disappeared owing perhaps to the action of local villagers'[14] Balinese epigraphy that goes back to the 10th century AD. One particular inscription is in 'pre-Nagari' script, but in Old Balinese; the second half of the inscription is in Old Javanese script, but in Sanskrit.

[11] Ibid., 25–26.

[12] Ep. Ind. (Epigraphia Indica) XVII, Sastri, H. Krishna, 1923–1924, New Delhi: ASI, 322–324.

[13] E. E. McKinnon, 'Kota Cina Its Context and Meaning in the Trade of South East Asia in the 12th/14th Century' (Unpublished PhD thesis, Cornell University, 1984). https://www.iseas.edu.sg/images/centres/nalanda_sriwijaya_centre/archaeologyunit/sea_ark/edwards_mckinnon_1984.pdf

[14] Ibid., 78–79.

Indic Sites

Starting with the Dieng plateau temples in central Java, the Buddhist temple of Barabudur (8th century AD) together with Candi Mendut and Pawon and the 9th-century AD Hindu temple of Prambanan are a rich source of information on relations with India through their iconography. In East Java, Jalatunda and Belahan are among the earliest remains (10th century AD) followed by the monuments of the Singhasari period and of the Majapahit era (Panataran, Trawulan). Scenes from the Rāmāyaṇa and other Sanskrit and Old Javanese works are depicted on most of these temples; the style of the reliefs is more specifically Javanese.

In Sumatra, Buddhist temples are found in the Batak region (Padang Lawas) as well as at Muara Taku in the Padang Highlands. Of interest are the antiquities of Palembang, thought to have been the centre of the Srivijaya empire. At Kota Cina, the remains of a Hindu Siva temple were excavated in the 1970s, and relevant connected statuary was found in the immediate surroundings of the site.[15]

In Bali, the site of Gilimanuk dated to early AD,[16] excavated by Soejono, has given evidence for Western contacts through the finding of beads. Other notable monumental sites are the Tampaksiring complex of Candis with monastic establishments, the Tirta Empul, the Goa Gajah at Bedulu, the Mother Temple Besakih, the temple of Penulisan and Gunung Kawi in Pejeng. Stutterheim believes that the Hindu–Balinese (in the sense of Indo-Balinese) period of temple art dates back to 700–900 AD.[17]

[15] Ibid., 50–77.

[16] Bronson and Glover (1984: 41), as quoted in I. C. Glover, *Early Trade between India and South East Asia* (Hull: University of Hull Centre for South-East Asian Studies, 1989).

[17] W. Stutterheim, *Indian Influences in Old Balinese Art* (London: The India Society, 1935), 30.

Trade Routes

A pre-existing pattern of internal commercial exchanges was the basis of the development of international trade in Southeast Asia, and through such frequent external contacts, the socio-political conditions of the region underwent considerable changes. Prior to the arrival of foreign merchants, commercial exchanges took place between the hunting population of the highlands and the lowland cultivators as well as between the hinterland populations and the people from the coast.

Trade was seemingly concentrated in the coastal centres with a redistribution of profits that enhanced the hegemony of the rulers. What were the goods exchanged along the international trade routes? They were spices, textiles (cotton and silk), metals (tin among them), stones, drugs and medicinal plants, camphor, beads, coral, opium, woods and cowries; and the volume of trade increased considerably over the centuries. Goods were bartered as evidenced in the Chinese text *Zhu Fan Zhi* dated around 1225 AD, but also exchanged with gold or paid for with money.[18] Currency systems and the weights used in Southeast Asia show definite links with those in use in India.[19]

The history of the Sung dynasty (470–478 AD) refers to the bringing of Indian textiles to Southeast Asia, possibly Sumatra.[20] This is especially important when considering the spread of ikat weaving techniques in Indonesia, possibly of Indian origin, or at least highly influenced by Indian textiles. In particular, double ikat is found in Bali as well as in Odiya (Saktapar) and Gujarat (Patola).

Indianization spanned over a long period, roughly from 3rd to 14th century AD. Therefore, giving rise to a new question: Why did Southeast Asia adopt Indian culture?

[18] Sarkar, 255.

[19] Glover, *Early trade Between India and South East Asia*; ibid., 256–257.

[20] Sarkar, 252, 255.

Trade was indeed an essential factor that motivated the movement of people and ideas, but to say that Indianization was the result of trading activities alone would be a gross understatement. Trade was an incentive to the movement of people, and along the trading routes travelled Buddhist monks, with a proselytising mission, and Brahmana priests, invited by Hinduized monarchs to perform rituals or motivated by a desire to explore new lands and find wealth; the caste injunction of not crossing the sea did not seem to have been a real impediment. Indianization was most of all a movement of ideas.

The whole question of Indianization as an important factor in the process of early state formation in Southeast Asia has been the subject of controversial studies from which opposing models of statecraft and polities have ensued. It is often the case that not enough attention has been paid to the 'endogenous change' as opposed to the 'exogenous causes and agents' in many of these instances, with the result that the role of 'Indianization' is still being overemphasized as 'the prime mover' in the state formation process, rather than only one of the many causes.[21] However, another strand of debate also focuses on the prime role of Indian cultural motifs in state formation. It would be gross negligence to negate the role of Indian cultural motifs.

The ritual nature of kingship in both South Asia and Southeast Asia should not readily be overlooked, as it certainly appears to be one of its multifaceted features. The adoption of a Hindu/Buddhist cosmology acted as a legitimation of the power of the ruler, and this was translated into a complex architectural symbolism whereby cities were built on the model of Mount Meru, the centre of the Universe.[22] The power afforded by such cosmologies was the most effective motivation for the Southeast Asians to become Indianized. It was a process that led to very significant

[21] Wisseman Christie, in David G. Marr and Anthony Crothers Milner, *Southeast Asia in the 9th to 14th Centuries* (Heng Mui Keng Terrace: Institute of Southeast Asian Studies, 1986), 6566.

[22] J. S. Lansing, *The Three Worlds of Bali* (New York: Praeger, 1983), 20.

changes in the very fabric of the societies it touched. It could be said to have been 'wedded' to the pre-existing social organizations whereby no real dichotomy was present. As Kulke points out, the idea of a 'universal Hindu ruler' gave an 'institutional framework' to the pre-existing local political dynamics.[23] The instance of the 'Indianization' of Bali is bound to throw much light on this matter, a proposition put forward by,[24] whereby it is suggested that the 'Balinese civilization was primarily rooted not in the courts but in networks of temples which managed everything from the control of irrigation to the rituals of a Balinese version of the Hindu caste system'.[25] Nonetheless, in this scheme of things, the relationship between temples and kings remains fundamental and is inescapably connected with questions relating to the role of ritual as allied to power. The small island of Bali represents a classical instance of 'Indianization'. Countless inscriptions testify to the efforts that its rulers undertook 'to restructure their societies in light of the new Indic cosmologies and theories of the state',[26] and this process equally touched courts and villages.

It was through the performing arts that Indian culture became accessible to villagers and started spreading, and this is recorded in inscriptions, which often talk of tax incentives to encourage royal performers to take up residence in villages. 'The inscriptions show then that from the earliest moments in the history of Balinese civilisation the arts were not exclusively based in either courts or villages but flourished along an axis between them'.[27] And along this axis, the temple and temple life were central to their development.

Cultural values, beliefs and ideology are more easily transmitted and perpetuated through the medium of performance. The impact that the Rāmāyaṇa and the Mahābhārata epics had on

[23] Kulke in Marr and Milner, *Southeast Asia in the 9th to 14th Centuries*, 7.
[24] Lansing, *The Three Worlds of Bali*, 15–49.
[25] Ibid., 6–7.
[26] Ibid., 26.
[27] Ibid., 30.

the development of the performing arts in India and in Southeast Asia cannot be overemphasized, and this impact is still evident in the living dance dramas of today from all the Southeast Asian regions. If dance and drama still show such a marked Indian matrix in terms of narrative contents, then it is likely that at an early stage this was coupled by formal and technical influence.

It would not be far-fetched to conjecture that among the people that travelled from India to Southeast Asia, there were dancers and musicians. Southeast Asians may have become familiar with Indian styles of dance in the course of their travels to India or through contact with the Indian Shastraic tradition. The true function of the temple in the scheme of things cannot be fully understood without taking performance into account, within India and Southeast Asia both. Going back to the Balinese paradigm, it is unlikely that direct exchanges existed between Balinese and Indian courts; although it should not be excluded in toto that Indians did reach Bali at some time or other. Certainly, the Gilimanuk evidence points to the fact that the island had an involvement in the international trade routes.

The importance of analogies in studying South and Southeast Asian statecraft has been given sharper focus by Kulke's attempt at investigating Khmer notions of statecraft by using an Orissian model.[28] This attempt was welcomed, among others, by Mabbett who thought that its justification was to be found not only in the fact that Indian culture influenced Southeast Asia but also in the common ancestry of all 'monsoon Asia'.

The relationship between ritual and kingship is still a key area of investigation for an understanding of both ancient South and Southeast Asia, and this is also linked to a study of the role of performance. The interconnection of ritual as performance and performance as ritual was noted by Schechner, among others, in his study of the Ram Lila: 'Theatre is a mixture, a braid, of

[28] H. Kulke, *The Devaraja Cult* (New York: Southeast Asia Program, Department of Far Eastern Studies, Cornell University, 1978).

entertainment and ritual. At one moment ritual seems to be the source, at another it is the entertainment that claims primacy. They are a twin-system, tumbling over each other, and vitally interconnected'.[29] Performance, in its widest sense, was one of the ways through which, for instance, the Balinese negara could assert its supremacy as the centre of the world and its performing artists could be the link between the court and the villages.

In this scheme, the role of temples was paramount, as most performances occurred during the festivals and within temple precincts. What Lansing says with reference to Balinese temples may hold true for other Southeast Asian instances; and it certainly occurred in India itself, particularly in those regions such as Odisha and Southern India, where there seems to have been a parallel relationship of kingship with the whole 'temple culture'.

> The very existence of these temples is explainable only in terms of their relationship to the performing arts on the one hand and to Balinese cosmology on the other. The relationship among these elements temples, texts, performances, and cosmology—is essentially circular: temples exist to hold festivals, where they are activated by the performing arts, whose function is to sound the texts of Balinese cosmology, which establish a world view in which temples are essential to the continued functioning of the Middle World (viz. of humans).[30]

This one can be found even in today's India, where temple festivals generate various activities among which performance takes the lion's share; and the role of temples as the link between the world of the gods and that of humans and as the only effective protection from negative forces, personified as evil spirits or demons, is reaffirmed through the processions, plays and ritual re-enactments of the gods' deeds. This is apparent when one witnesses the yearly Ratha Yatra of Lord Jagannath in Puri (Odisha).

[29] R. Schechner, *Performative Circumstances from the Avantgarde to Ramlila* (Calcutta: Seagull Books, 1983), 85.

[30] Lansing, *The Three Worlds of Bali*, 146.

East India and Southeast Asia

There were links between Odisha/Andhra regions of India and Southeast Asia, especially maritime Southeast Asia. The dynamics of Indian influence have to be considered. Odisha has a rich history and has played a remarkable role in the influence towards Indonesia. Odisha has a rich maritime past. Odisha is rich in rivers and seaports and served as the bridge between India and Southeast Asia. The area between southern Kalinga (south Ganjam) and the Tamil region took the lead in mediating the filtering of Indian ideas to those regions lying across the Bay of Bengal.

One of the facts that strikes anyone who becomes involved in a study of Odisha's ancient maritime past is the disappearance of most of its ports and the considerable geographical changes that have taken place over the centuries. In talking about the geography of Odisha, one ought to bear in mind that such significant changes were related to the riverine character of the region, which bore important consequences. These changes can be identified as the drying up of some of the rivers, silting of river mouths, emergence of sand ridges that covered the sea coast and recurring floods. In many instances, such changes were determined by men, more accurately, by the changing patterns of cultivation, with an increase in the so-called shifting cultivation. This involved massive deforestation to keep up with the population growth.[31]

In addition to this and to some extent related to the above,

> The river cycle leading to bifurcation of natural courses arose out of the change of speed owing to the load of soil carried by the rivers.... Loads, coming in increased shape, led to deposits of soil in one branch, with water diverting its course through the other, and ultimately leading to the drying up of the former.[32]

What would point in that direction is that the people of the Mahanadi, in Cuttack, celebrate a festival known as Bali Yatra,

[31] K. Patra, *Ports in Odisha* (Bhubaneshwar: Panchashila, 1988), 202.
[32] Ibid., 204.

'Voyage to Bali', on the day of the Kartika Purnima festival. 'Gathering in thousands on the river bank they worship the ships in solemn manner. Many people take into small boats and sail a little way ahead in direction of the river mouth. Innumerable miniatures are floated with all paraphernalias of real ships'.[33] The celebration of this festival is undoubtedly related to sea voyages, and this would point to the importance that maritime activities held in the life of the Odias.

It is generally recognized that the southernmost portions of modern Ganjam were known as Kalinga, somewhat overlapping with Kongoda (south Tosali), the area north of the Vaitarani river was named Utkala and the area further north bore the name of Odra. All these regions had some role in the maritime activities of the Odia people, but Kalinga had a somewhat greater impact. The *Aryamanjusrimulakalpa* talks of the Sea of Kalinga with reference to the Bay of Bengal, and the islands of the Sea of Kalinga are referred to as Kalingadrisu. This is not evidence that such islands would necessarily be the Indonesian islands as it could well be related, for instance, to Andaman and Nicobar, but it is certainly another important reference to Kalinga's seafaring past.

Three major points have been focused upon in an attempt to evaluate the role that ancient Kalinga played vis-a-vis Southeast Asia. These will be presently reviewed. The Chinese writings of the end of the 1st century AD describe the Indianized state of Funan, roughly located in modern South Vietnam, including parts of modern Cambodia, and talk of its founder as being Kaundinya, Huntian in Chinese, a Brahmana by birth who married a local princess. This seems to be corroborated by a Sanskrit inscription of Campa dated 658 AD in connection with the founding of the capital of Kambuja at Bhavapura, which relates the story of a Naga princess who married a Kaundinya Brahmana, and this has been broadly interpreted as standing for the merging of Indic culture and the indigenous one, notwithstanding controversial views on the origin of the legend.

[33] Ibid.

Later sources from the 4th century relate that another Brahmana, Kaundinya II or Jiao Zhenru in Chinese, came from the state of Pan Pan, located in the Malay peninsula, and took over the kingdom, changing all the laws of the country and making them the same as those of India.[34] It is not possible to be certain of the correctness of equating Huntian and Jiao Zhenru with Kaundinya as there are considerable problems of transcription involved when using Chinese sources. The two Kaundinya, if it was at all their names, point to Indian influence of a sort, but it is impossible to say with any certainty whether this was from India itself or whether it reached through the mediation of an Indianized neighbouring centre. It has been remarked that to this day, there are groups of Kaundinya Brahmanas in the Ganjam district of Odisha. They live relatively close to the sea, in Paralakhemundi, at the feet of the Mahendra mountains. Interpreting the Kaundinya story as indicating that Kaundinya had come from India, a connection can be seen between the Kaundinyas of Funan and the Kaundinya of Paralakhemundi. It has also been noted that the same name Mahendra (as in Mahendragiri of Ganjam) appears in the history of Funan in connection with Parvata (mountain). The History of Southern Jin dynasty (5th century AD) relates that in Funan it is customary to worship Mahesvara who always descends on Mount 'Motan'.

The inscription on the stele of Sdok Kak Thom relates that when Jayavarman II of Cambodia reigned at 'Mahendra parvata', sometime during the first half of the 9th century AD, he installed there a Sivalinga, helped by the Brahmana Hiranyadama.[35] This 'Mahendra Parvata' has been identified with the 'Phnom Kulen', the plateau north of the Angkor plain.[36] The Mahendra Parvata existed before Jayavarman, and this same mountain was the 'Motan' of the History of Southern Ji.[37] It will be remembered

[34] Liang Shu, *The Golden Khersonese*, trans. P. Wheatley (Kuala Lumpur: Oxford University Press, 1961), 48–50.

[35] Coedes, *The Indianized states of South East Asia*, 99.

[36] Ibid., 100.

[37] Wheatley, 124–125.

here that the Mahendragiri hills of Ganjam district are also connected with the worship of Mahesvara as the Lord of the Mountain and King of all Gods.

A possible association of Pan Pan with Kalinga has been suggested[38] in view of the fact that early AD Chinese sources report on the presence of many Brahmanas in this prosperous state and that some ministers bore titles beginning with the Kun lun.[39] Here, the term seems to be used with reference to an ethnic entity, and the prevalent view is that this is a reference to the Malay people. Chinese sources speak of a 'Kun lun writing', of a 'Kun lun language', of 'Kun lun merchants and pirates' and 'Kun lun ships', and it has been pointed out by the Chinese writers that Kun lun and Ku lung are equally correct versions of the same word.[40]

Ku lung may then be Kaling, and this would be Kling which would, therefore, refer to Kalinga, also known as Kling in ancient times.[41] The name Kling is, however, still used to refer to southern Indians in Malaya and Cambodia.[42] The place name Ho Ling is vaguely reminiscent of Kalinga, and it has in fact been suggested that it might be a Chinese transcription of the very name Kalinga.

Palaeographic research would be the key to solve some of these problems. What, however, would require sharper focus is the symbolism of the Mahendra Parvata, which comes across in connection with Odisha, Funan and Central Java. The symbolism of these sites, their association with kingship (and water) and ancestor worship could perhaps tell more about Kalinga and Southeast Asia than the Chinese sources. The temple mountain or the Mount of Lord Mahendra is linked with the fertility and

[38] Sarkar, 175, 212.

[39] Wheatley, *The Golden Khersonese*, Kuala Lumpur, 1961 48–49.

[40] Ibid., 49.

[41] Sarkar, 173.

[42] Wheatley, *The Golden Khersonese*, 192.

prosperity of the kingdom, and it has been connected with the notions of divine kingship. The concept of Devaraja, God-king, was popularized by Coedes in connection with the kings of Angkor, and its Indonesian equivalent was highlighted by the same author.

'The quest for the origins and ramifications of this cult reveals a web of connections spreading out widely across South South East and East Asia' (Herman Kulke, 1978, The Devaraja Cult, New York, 1–2). The Devaraja was not a deified king, but the god Siva (and later Visnu or Buddha) of whom the king was an earthly representative. A linga was consecrated on a mountain by the ruler to guarantee fertility and strength. This occurred in Odisha on Mahendragiri, on the Mahendra Parvata of Funan, which was the basis for the subsequent Angkorian state cult of the royal linga, and in Java where king Sanjaya erected a linga on the Dieng Plateau, invoking prosperity on the land, as shown by the 732 A.D. Canggal inscription.[43] The Mahendra mountains of Ganjam had been regarded as the most sacred religious site of India since ancient times.

In following the debate regarding the Indian origin of Shailendras, it becomes clear that it represents a central point in all discussions on Southeast Asian history, as differences appear to be not a matter of methodology but of ideological perspective. The early history of Central Java is still a controversial matter as evidence is incomplete and great gaps of knowledge still exist. The inscription of Canggal, north of Yogyakarta, dated 732 AD, is the oldest and testifies to the existence of a King Sanjaya who seemed to have subjugated neighbouring principalities as well as consecrating a linga on the Dieng mountain to ensure prosperity.[44] A 907 AD inscription mentions the same name

[43] K. R. Hall, *Maritime Trade and State Development in Early South East Asia* (Honolulu: University of Hawaii Press, 1985), 119.

[44] H. B. Sarkar, *Corpus Javanese Inscriptions*, 2 vols (Calcutta: Firma K. L. Mukhopadhyay, 1972).

Sanjaya as that of a line of kings who referred to themselves as rulers of Mataram.

They were of Shaiva religion, and the splendid temple complex of Lara Jonggrang at Prambanan was erected during their rule. However, the Kalasan inscription of 778 AD refers to Shailendra dynasty, who, were Mahayana Buddhists, built the unparalleled Barabudur. They made an abrupt exit from the Javanese scene in 856 AD.[45] The evidence given by various other inscriptions, such as Kalasan, 778 AD, Ratu Baku plateau, undated, and Karangtengah, 824 AD, allows a partial reconstruction of the history of these two dynasties, who seem to have coexisted and collaborated with the Shailendras being in a position of pre-eminence. After 856 AD, however, it appears that the Shailendras, after fighting the Salva king Rakai Pikatan, moved their seat of power to Sumatra, where they already had established dynastic alliances with Srivijayan kings by means of marriages, while the Shaiva king remained in Central Java and had the Lara Jonggrang temple built immediately following his victory, as shown by an inscription dating from 856 AD found on the Ratu Baka plateau. This sudden change in the dynastic history of Central Java should not be interpreted as a religious war, for there is evidence that Hinduism and Buddhism peacefully coexisted side by side with temples being built near each other. The disappearance of the Shailendras from Java is quite different from the other shift of power that occurred in the island in the 9th century AD whereby East Java acquired more prominence: the move of the Shailendras was entirely determined by a dynastic power struggle, while the shift to East Java of the Mataram kings was dictated by religio-economic reasons.

It was R. C. Majumdar who first formulated the hypothesis that the Shailendras may have had a Kalingan origin and may have been dynastically connected with the Eastern Gangas or

[45] J. G. De Casparis, *Prasasti Indonesia II Selected Inscriptions from the 7th to 9th Century A.D.* (Bandung: Dinas Purbakala Republik Indonesia, 1950); De Casparis.

the Sailodbhavas of Kongoda or even the Sailas of Vindhyas.[46] This he felt was corroborated by the following facts: (a) after the Shailendra rule, Malaysia came to be known as Kling (Kalinga); (b) the Shailendras used a type of Nagari script in their Javanese inscriptions similar to that found in Pala inscriptions of Bihar and Bengal; and (c) royal dynasties with names beginning with Saila, 'mountain' are found among those that ruled Odisha, Bengal and Bihar. Majumdar believed that from Kalinga, the Shailendras first moved to Lower Burma and then to Nalaya and finally Java. Other points raised by Majumdar refer to the Shailendra intercourse with Nalanda in Bihar and more generally with Pila India, proven by inscriptions found at Kelurak in Java, relating to a Bengali Brahmana guru of the Shailendra kings and at Nalanda. Sarkar himself expressed dissatisfaction with the prevalent views on a Southeast Asian origin of the Shailendras and reverted to India, suggesting that the homeland of these rulers was to be found in the Krishna–Godavari delta. 'The Kalingans and the Vidarbhans represented, generally speaking, a Saiva strain in the cultural phenomenon of South East Asia in the pre Sailendra period' (Sarkar 1985: 212).

It may also be worth noting that the city of Puri seems to have been an important centre from a commercial point of view since ancient times, tentatively identified with the Celitalo known from Xuan Zang's accounts and by him described as mushrooming with foreign missions.[47] Such foreign missions were later superseded by the mathas, religious centres mainly concerned with the welfare of pilgrims and representing non-Odia interests, as the Jagannath cult became the focal point of the city's activities and of its surrounding region. The neighbouring port of Pipli, still active under the Muslims well until the coming of the British,[48] points to the important maritime

[46] R. C. Majumdar, *Suvarnadvipa* (Calcutta: Modern Publishing Syndicate, 1937), 225–227.

[47] Patra, *Ports in Odisha*, 11–12.

[48] Ibid., 19.

links of Puri and its region. The mathas played a central role in the economic life of the city of Puri, under a religious garb, in keeping with the changes occurring in connection with the growth of the Jagannath cult, which had become the state religion from the 12th century AD. In this context, the fact that pilgrimage in Puri has been and still is a major source of revenue should not be overlooked. To hypothesize the presence of Indonesian entrepots in the Puri area of Xuan Zang's times would not be too great a flight of fancy, bearing in mind that it was not only the Indians who had merchant ships but that the Indonesians too were quite proficient merchants and seamen. In the context of this chapter, mention should be made of the contacts between the Bengal/Bangladesh areas and Indonesia. These have had a remarkable influence on the manufacture of bronzes, especially in Java, where many bronzes, dated from the 8th to the 9th century AD, can be classed as being of northeastern Indian provenance, Pala style, in particular, or as being heavily indebted to this style when manufactured locally.

The finding of the inscription of Nalanda bearing on the contacts between King Balaputradeva of Suvarnadvipa and King Devapala and of a number of bronzes, in the monastery grounds, initially thought to be of Javanese provenance but subsequently pronounced to be Pala style, gave impetus to further research. It transpired that the contacts between Indonesia and Bengal had been earlier than the date of the Nalanda charter, judging at least from the number of bronzes from Bengal/Bangladesh found in Java, especially from the Chittagong area, from as early as the 8th century. Remarkably no Pala bronzes have been found in Sumatra, despite the dynastic contacts highlighted by the Nalanda charter. Instead, Sumatra is fairly rich in South Indian style bronzes, which would be in accordance with the evidence of South Indian entrepots. Another East Indian centre for bronze manufacture seems to have influenced the style of Javanese bronzes: this is Achutrajpur, near Banapur in Puri district, Odisha. The similarity with the sculptural school of this village has been seen in the Javanese adoption of 'a border of closely set comma-shaped flames around the circular halo',[49] which apparently was distinctive of the Achutrajpur bronzes.

Renewed Bengali influence can also be discerned in much statuary from Singhasari Java, in Sumatran temples and in much terracotta art of Majapahit time: such trends admittedly reappear fairly late in time and cannot too easily be explained. From the above discussion, it is clear that long-established connections between the areas of Odisha/Andhra and the Indonesian islands seem plausible.

Conclusion

Apart from trade links, there was a whole movement of ideas that reached the Indonesian shores via Kalinga and the Kalingans, by this implying a specific mediation which did not exclude contacts with and influences from other parts of India, as shown by the Sumatran contacts with Tamil Nadu and the exchanges of the Indonesian world with the Bengal of Pala–Sena times, but certainly played a significant role in the way 'Indic' models were absorbed by Indonesians. This could be termed as the 'direct influence' for want of a better definition, and it should be reiterated that it 'was' only an influence not a domination underpinned by colonization or massive migration: 'Indic' ideologies served the purpose of legitimizing the power of local Indonesian rulers. Another point emerges from the value of Orissian analogies, as in the instance of the symbolism of the sacred mountain, for an understanding of the Indonesian material, based on affinities stemming from the interaction of Hindu, Buddhist and local tribal cults, the latter reflecting pre-historic and proto-historic common ancestry between the east of India and Southeast Asia. As the historians are sharply divided over the Indianization of Southeast Asia, what remains

[49] P. L. Scheurleer and M. Klokke, *Ancient Indonesian Bronzes* (Leiden: E. J. Brill, 1988), 28.

uncontested is that India did cast an influence so much so that the states were carved out of Indic ideologies. Whether to view it as a 'colonization' or the persuasive power of Indic motifs is open to debate.

Bibliography

Christie, J. W. 'Markets and Trade in Pre-Majapahit Java'. In *Economic Exchange and Social Interaction in South East Asia*, edited by K. Hutterer, 197–212. Ann Arbor: The University of Michigan, Center for South and Southeast Asian Studies, 1977.

Christie, J. W. *Theatre States and Oriental Despotisms: Early South East Asia in the Eyes of the West*. Hull: Centre for South-East Asian Studies, 1985.

Iyer, K. *Bharata Dance Dramas of India and the East*. Bombay: Taraporevala, 1980.

Majumdar, R. C. *India and South East Asia*. Delhi: B. R. Publishing, 1979.

Sarkar, H. B. *Cultural Relations between India and South East Asian Countries*. Delhi: Indian Council for Cultural Relations and Motilal Banarsidass, 1985.

11

Colonial Institutions and Oriental Knowledge Formation

Santoshi Kumari

The discovery of India's past and its Oriental presentation began in the 18th century by the colonial state which took to Indology and antiquary formalized in the knowledge institutions of the Asiatic Society of Bengal (ASB) and of the Archaeological Survey of India (ASI). The ASB was established in Calcutta in 1784 and the ASI in New Delhi in 1861. Under the presidentship of Sir William Jones, the ancient texts were translated into English and were used in writing the history of the land. The ASI, though formally established under the Director General, Sir Alexander Cunningham in 1861, had predecessors of surveyors, explorers and antiquarians who provided ample data to establish a formal institution for explorations and excavations. The textual and archaeological materials were arranged in an orderly fashion to present historical narratives. Both the knowledge institutions, the ASB and the ASI, have been applauded for their contributions in the academia and in the narratives produced by them, and they are still the fulcrum of intellectual discourse. The history produced by these knowledge institutions created an image of the land, both for the Orient and the Occident, which kept evolving and changing due to the discussions influenced by the contemporary political developments.

The nucleus of the narratives in the colonial and the postcolonial phases remained almost static, though they changed their axes. A case in point can be the historical writings in the colonial period which were classified as ancient, medieval and modern. Religion was the variable for the classification. Ancient period was considered as the period of Brahmanas/Hindu, the medieval period with the Islam and the modern period with the coming of British rule. In the modern period, religion was not the variable, but scientific and systematic presentation of each event was emphasized, and the credit was given to the Europeans. In the postcolonial period, the narratives have shifted their focus from the religious affiliation of the periods; the historical narratives within the boundaries of ancient, medieval and modern, however, persist. Most of the ideas in the nucleus form germinated in these knowledge institutions. It is in the context that the present chapter attempts to re-explore the imperial objectives behind the narratives produced in them and relook into the process of cultural colonization of India.

Fencing India's Conquest

The Act of 1784 (Pitt's India Act of 1784) formed a six-member board of Privy Councillors and of Court of Directors 'for the better Government and Security of the Territorial possessions of this kingdom in the East Indies'.[1] The Act enabled the establishment of the Courts:

> That all his Majesty's subjects, as well as the Servants of the said United Company ... declared to be amenable to all courts of Justice (both in India and Great Britain) of competent Jurisdiction to try offences committed in India, for all Acts, Injuries, Wrongs,

[1] P. Mukherji, *Indian Constitutional Documents (1773–1915)* (Calcutta: Wentworth Press, 1915), 9.

Oppressions, Tresspasses, Misdemeanors, Crimes and Offences what so ever by them ... in any of the Lands or Territories of any Native Prince or State or against their Persons or Proper ties or the Persons or Properties of any of their Subjects or People, in the same Manner as if the same had been done or committed within the Territories directly subject to and under the British Government in India.[2]

The collection of revenue and penalizing the offenders had compelled the imperialists to know the proprietorship of the land and to understand the ancient legal texts of India, as they believed that only a just system could give them easy access to the resources of India and smoothen the acceptance of the British rule by the Indians. Edmund Burke, an Anglo-Irish statesman, philosopher and an influential member of parliament (1766–1794) in the House of Commons, was a strong proponent of establishing fair rule of governance according to the norms of the society.[3] He was deeply concerned with the British dominion of India and the corrupt affairs of the East India Company. He firmly believed that the conduct of the East India Company had an adverse impact on the Indian traditions, because of which the Indians were suffering. Therefore, he proposed to establish a 'just' government in the land which should be in coherence with the native laws of India. This would in return fetch high moral foundation for the Crown in a distant land which would be different from the corrupt functions of the East India Company.

To unravel the norms of the land, for the establishment of a just judicial system and collection of revenue, it was important to get educated about the 'distant community' and a foreign land, which in the opinion of Thomas Macaulay was 'the strangest of all political anomalies' and was a state that 'resembled no other in history'.[4] It was not that Englishmen were in dark

[2] Ibid., 24.

[3] The views of Edmund Burke can be studied in A Vindication of Natural Society (London: M. Cooper, 1756).

[4] T. R. Metcalf, *The New Cambridge History: The Ideologies of Raj* (London: CUP, 2008), ix.

about India and its people. Prior to the 18th century, books were written by the Europeans at different intervals of time which had shaped the image of the Orient. These works can be broadly divided into two branches: one which provided a general understanding about the socio-religious and cultural aspect of the distant lands and communities and the other which dealt with the linguistics. The Portuguese, Dutch, French and English, all in their respective capacities, produced work which helped their countrymen to access the Indian trade and markets. To name a few, *Livro* of Duarte Barbosa, Gracia da Orta, Abbé Raynal, Robert Orme, Edward Terry, Ralph Fitch, Thomas Roe, Ovington and Henry Lord produced accounts which illuminated on vegetation, herbs, society, philosophy and religion. These accounts were primarily used by European traders to build a general understanding of India, and the data was used to earn a better share of profit in the business. The missionaries, such as Thomas Steven, Abraham Roger, Roberto de Nobili, Father Paulinus, Father Heinrich Roth and Pere Pons, had produced works on regional languages and had translated a few Sanskrit texts which dealt primarily with the languages and grammar. The missionaries believed that a better conversation with the locals in their native languages will help them pursue their objectives easily and fulfil their aim in the land.

In the 18th century, politics and philosophy of England played a pivotal role in shaping the British administration of India. The French Revolution (1789), the American Revolution (1765–1783) and the Irish Rebellion (1798) had made a deep impact on the philosophical understanding of the state. In the light of such historical developments, England had to bring in novel techniques for ruling India in which the Crown had to make a mark and convert it into a prized possession. The philosophy of governance had to be embedded in the proposal of thinkers like Edmund Burke who emphasized the establishment of just governance and in parliamentarians like Thomas Smith, who emphasized the responsibility of Englishmen to civilize the 'barbaric' nation.

After the Pitt's India Act of 1784, when the revenue collection came under the control of the Privy Councillors, there was an urgent need to know the proprietorship of the land, so that the British administrators could fix the responsibility of land tax collection. The British administrators were ignorant about the agrarian system of India. The Company had adopted different forms of collection of land revenue at different stages which kept on changing almost like a 'rudderless boat' every year from the days when Diwani rights of Bengal were handed over to the Company.[5] The ownership of land in India, to begin with Bengal, was so baffling for the Englishmen that Philip Francis said the following:

> (It) neither resembled the Oriental 'despotism' of an all-powerful monarch who could dispose of his subjects' property at will, nor the feudal order of the European Middle Ages. Rather, he conceived that India possessed an ancient aristocracy, whose title to their estates had always been recognized as hereditary until it was subverted by Bengal's British rulers.[6]

In the medieval Europe, King was the theoretical owner of the land, the landlord owned the land and its production; various categories of peasants tilled the land and in return were paid in agricultural products and forest goods. In India, on the contrary, a complex ownership of land prevailed. The farmers tilled the land/field and had the power to decide the nature of crops to be harvested. He paid a fixed amount of produce to the zamindar as tax. The relationship between the zamindar and the peasant was not as exploitative as in Europe; rather, *jajmani* relationship existed between them. The categorization of peasants was not restricted only to the very profession but was also rooted in the caste system of the Indian society. Similar was the case with the landlords. Perplexed with the complexities involved in the proprietorship of the land and the social milieu of India, the English administrators believed that the key to arrange these complexities into an orderly fashion laid in the textual sources.

[5] R. Guha, *The Rule of Property for Bengal* (Orient Longman, 1963), 13.
[6] Ibid., Chapter 4.

Unlike Europe, land in India is not a simple piece of geographical entity under somebody's ownership. Land has a cultural and emotional value attached to it. Hence, it became inevitable to understand the people of India who shared a bond with land. Europe was divided into class, whereas in India, the society was divided into Varnas, castes, sub-castes, communities and tribes. The complexities of the Indian society were multilayered so much so that the practice and the norms at times coincided, while at some places and in some situations they did not. The foreign texts that were written about the Indian society many a time presented a state of confusion. Therefore, during the days of Lord Wellesley (1798–1805) when the British began to make their way into the Indian countryside, direct observation was emphasized in gathering the information on the Indian society.[7] The British administrators established societies and departments to solve the entangled threads of complexities and dynamics of India and arranged the data in such a fashion which suited the administrative needs. The departments which were primarily concerned with surveys were the Survey of India (1767), the Great Trigonometrical Survey (1802–1852), the Geological Survey of India (GSI; 1851), the ASI (1861), the Botanical Survey of India (1890) and the Linguistic Survey of India (1891).

The Orient and the Occident

The Survey of India defined the boundaries of the British East India Company. It conducted surveys of the land and produced detailed maps. The Great Trigonometrical Survey (1802–1852) was started by the British surveyor Colonel William Lambton in 1802. He surveyed the land from St. Thomas Mount located in Chennai to the foothills of the Himalayas. The GSI was founded in 1851. The department studied the soil, water and rocks and assessed the wealth above and below the land. The ASI was established in 1861 and was responsible for the excavation

[7] Metcalf, *The Ideologies of Raj*, 114.

of historical materials, conservation and preservation of the cultural monuments in India. The Botanical Survey of India was established in 1890 for the survey of plant resources. The first Census of India was conducted in the 1872. The Linguistic Survey of India was established in 1894. It made comprehensive survey of the languages of British India, and recorded 364 languages and dialects.

Land survey was carried out for the agrarian order in which the term 'estate' was coined for the rural areas, which became the units of revenue administration. Estate comprised of villages (*mauza*). Zamindars were given responsibility to assess tax on their estate. The parlance of estate was mahal. The estates had fluid boundaries. The British thought that there were no administrative maps of villages (*mahal*), *pargana* (cluster of villages), *mauzas*, neither was held an assessment of soil and its productivity. Therefore, they felt the need to first organize the rural areas and create data regarding the measurement, crops production, quality of soil, forest products and other flora and fauna which could add to their colonial endeavours with a purpose for better collection of taxes.[8] In the year 1854, John Lawrence wrote about a survey work carried out in Punjab: 'every detail of cultivation, of forest, grove, brushwood, of sterile waste and sand, of hillock and riverine, of pool marsh, and rivulet of road and path, of building habitation, and garden ... (was carried out).'[9]

The village was historicized and naturalized. Cartography was made a natural way of looking at the landscape. Three types of maps were produced by the survey department: the topographical, the *mauza* and the cadastral map.

The Scientific Revolution, a significant historical event which marked the age of modernism, progressiveness and rationality in Europe, had great impact on the functioning of imperialism. The scientific revolution was focused on to recovering the pasts from

[8] N. Bhattacharya, *The Great Agrarian Conquests* (New Delhi: Permanent Black, 2018), 70–71.

[9] Ibid., 75.

the ancient texts. The way world was visualized after the 15th century, that is, after the Scientific Revolution, had fundamentally changed. Now every matter was arranged in order and systematic presentation was paid utmost importance. The objectivity of argument and purpose had to be well defined. Any argument would be classified as progressive only when it followed a scientific method. Facts and figures along with proofs were required, and abstract and complex presentation was better to be shunned off. The Scientific Revolution, Industrialization and Imperialism together created a deep impact in shaping the perspective of imperialists in India. The rural areas were organized into villages, products were catalogued, lands were measured and classified, and then taxes were levied.

The survey of land had simultaneously unravelled the dynamics of the Indian society. The Indian society was classified into Varnas, castes and communities, who were the traditional stakeholders on land and its resources. The hierarchies, complexities and fluid boundaries between the caste and sub-castes were both astounding and incomprehensible for the imperialists. After all, the world where they came from was divided in binaries: rich–pauper, king–subject, master–slave, lord–serf, buyer–seller, town–village and tax collectors–taxpayers. Therefore, the need of the hour was to classify the colonial population. Census was carried out and, with this, slowly and gradually, the data collection shifted from land to man. Anthropological studies were conducted, cultures were recorded and histories of communities became a matter of great interest to British administrators. Colin Mackenzie, Francis Buchanan, H. Elliot, James Kerr, H. Risley and L. S. S. O'Malley are only few to name here who switched their roles from administrators to surveyors and scholars in order to produce data of people and customs of India. This exercise was again an attempt to present a scientific and 'systematic' information on Indian population. This information was used for social engineering, identifying the communities and moulding them to suit the needs of imperialism. Interestingly, every time imperialists made an incessant effort to present the Orient in an orderly fashion, the complexities and dynamics created a hiatus in the presentation. The physical anthropological studies emphasized on racial theory.[10] Systems of castes and tribes were studied, analysed and catalogued. The customs and cultures of the four Varnas which branched out into several castes and sub-castes became a matter of documentation. The profession associated with them came under the ambit of revenue. Their settlements were mapped. But there were a large number of communities which were mobile, and their profession was not well defined. They followed customs which were 'mysterious' and not same as that of people who followed Varnas, so they were documented as thugs, *banjaras*, tribes and forest dwellers.[11] Another section of population was of Muslims, whose religious practices and culture was distinct from Hindus. The Euro-centric lens presented Indian subcontinent as a land of migrations and invasions.[12] The British administrators-cum-scholars credited the foreign attacks as the catalyst of change in Indian history. People from foreign land conquered the northwestern part of India, established their settlements and many a time ruled the land. In due course of time, they were assimilated in the indigenous population through the process of acculturation. Therefore, cultures could not be considered as the criteria to arrange the Indian population. Complexities and dynamism were two variables which were not welcomed in the scientific lens of Europe. Europe legitimized tabulations, binaries, and unilinear development for a clear and systematic understanding. Hence, religion was chosen as the variable on which the society and customs of India could be arranged, which would not only present the data in a scientific way but would also suit the imperial interests to divide and rule the land.

[10] The work of Herbert Risley, *The People of India*, can be read to understand the racial theory attached to castes of the Indian society. His narrative was used to fulfil the imperial interests in the colonial India. Delhi: Asian Educational Services, 1999.

[11] W. H. Sleeman has worked on 'Thugs', which can be read to understand the imperial designs implied in the British India. Report on the Depredations Committed by the Thug Gangs of Upper and Central India, G. H. Huttman, Calcutta, 1840.

[12] The writings of V. A. Smith can be read to get a glimpse of Euro- centric perspective. His work can be read for example, *The Early History of India*, Oxford: Clarendon Press, 1908.

Shaping Data into Knowledge: Inception of ASB

The ASB was the first institution of its kind in the colonial India which exchanged notes from different departments to publish articles in its annual journal *Asiatik Researches*, later known as the *Journal of Asiatic Society of Bengal*. These articles helped in formulating the idea of British India not only for the lay readers who were interested in the Orient but also for the academia. The ASB declared that the primary work was to read and translate the texts of the Indian subcontinent. The contributions of the ASB and Sir William Jones are matters of celebration, especially in the narratives of ancient Indian history. His contributions are applauded in academic circles. He is credited to have discovered the glorious pasts of India which even natives had forgotten. It is only in the recent researches that the imperial inclination of Jones and the ASB are being scrutinized.[13] One cannot deny the role of ASB in shaping up the glorified image of a colony in the West. The vibrancy of the land was quite evident in most of the articles published and books selected for translation. The *Journal of Asiatic Society of Bengal* published articles inspired by anthropological studies, survey reports, languages, customs and religions of India. The society translated sacred texts into English, which educated both the Occident and the Orient about the Indian subcontinent. It was because of such contributions that India was considered as the land of utopia which could provide an alternative model of society for an industrialized West. Nevertheless, one cannot overlook the imperialist designs embedded in the functioning of the ASB and its founder William Jones.

With the Act of 1784, the judiciary had passed in the hands of the crown. The philosophy behind the establishment of judiciary was to check the corruptions of the East India Company and bring in a just system for the colonial subjects. It was believed

[13] *Colonialism and Its Forms of Knowledge* written by Bernard S. Cohn can be read for this purpose. B. S. Cohn, *Colonialism and Its Forms of Knowledge: The British in India* (Princeton: Princeton University Press, 1996).

that native laws should be the basis for ruling the land, which were intact in the textual sources. Therefore, the requirement was to appoint persons who had a knack for learning languages. An employment in the British India was considered as an opportunity to get rid of poverty. The application for the job of a judge in the Supreme Court of Calcutta should be seen in the above light. William Jones, who was a linguist of repute, had command over several languages and had translated *Tarikh-i-Nadiri*, a Persian text, which was well received in the west, could not break the chains of poverty. William Jones had therefore put in his application for the appointment of judge in the Supreme Court of Calcutta from 1780. But every time his application was turned down by Lord Thurlow.[14] French ruler Louis XVI commented that he knew French of his people better than himself.[15] Hence, this time Lord Thurlow's opinion was superseded by the recommendation of the Crown, who was well aware of the imperialist requirement and the suitability of Jones as judge.

William Jones boarded Crocodile, the warship, in 1783 and sailed for five months to reach India. While in the voyage, he penned down his thoughts. Few glimpses in the writings elucidate that Jones was well aware of his imperialist position. However, his later writings where he praised Sanskrit language and textual sources of India as a reservoir of ancient wisdom indicate that he was intellectually honest, and imperialism could not dent his academic integrity.

He identified 16 areas of interest which he desired to study. Some of them were the segregation of laws in terms of religion, Hindus and Mohammedans, geography of India, best mode of rule in Bengal, medicinal practices, natural products, issues of morality, trade and commerce of India, administration of

[14] O. P. Kejriwal, *The Asiatic Society of Bengal and the Discovery of India's Past 1784–1838* (Calcutta, 1988), 33.

[15] Lord Teignmouth, *Memoirs of the Life, Writings and Correspondence of Sir William Jones* (London, 1804), 42.

Marathas and Mughals, best accounts of Tibet and Kashmir,[16] which had direct bearings on British rule in India, and the other areas of interest indirectly fulfilled the imperial needs. In the 18th century, India had many regional kingdoms. Nizam-ul Mulk was ruling in Hyderabad and had organized the administration efficiently. Murshid Kuli Khan and Alivardi Khan had established independent kingdom in Bengal. Saadat khan was the ruler of Awadh. He had succeeded in suppressing lawlessness and disciplining the big zamindars who had refused to pay taxes. Mysore was under the rule of Haidar Ali. Tipu Sultan was another ruler from this state who was known for modernizing his army with the help of French and had exhibited instances for maintaining communal harmony in the state.[17] Down south, we had the kingdom of Travancore, whose King Martanda Varma was considered as the leading statesman of the 18th century. The Rajputana states had took advantage of the growing weakness of Mughal power and had virtually freed themselves. The most outstanding Rajput ruler of the 18th century was Raja Sawai Jai Singh of Amber. However, William Jones chose Marathas over all the above-listed kingdoms not only because it dominated a considerable portion of India but also because it openly declared its religious affiliation as the *hindavi swarajya*, that is, the rule of the Hindus, which suited the imperial interest to divide the country on religious lines.

The region of Bengal had its own importance in 1784. It was the first province where the British administration was established under the jurisdiction of British Parliament and sway of Crown; it was also one of the richest provinces in the 18th century, well connected with rivers and coasts. It was the hub of fine textiles and boat-manufacturing units and hence was lucrative for trade and commerce. A political control over this province would have ensured maximum revenue in the pockets of imperialists.

[16] Ibid., 228.

[17] Tipu Sultan had funded for the construction of an image of Sharda, a Hindu deity, in the Shringeri Temple in 1791, which was ransacked in a loot.

Anglo-Russian Question and the Role of Knowledge Institutions

The imperial interest of Russia in India and its impact on the policies of British India have not received enough attention in academic discourses. Russian imperialism was continuously expanding in the region of Eurasia. William Jones was quite aware of the geostrategic location of the Indian subcontinent. He wrote, 'When I was at sea ... on inspecting the observations of the day, that India lay before us and Persia on the left whilst a breeze from Arabia blew. It gave me inexpressible pleasure to find ... almost encircled by the vast regions of Asia.'[18]

Kashmir and Tibet were the regions which connected India with Eurasia. There was a threat for contestation of power from Russia. Russia was interested in the Indian market.[19] Therefore, the land routes of the northwest had to be secured, and thence travelogues and exploration reports of the surveyors enjoyed ample space in the knowledge-making process of ASB. It is not surprising that Jones wanted to gather information through the accounts of Kashmir and Tibet. England was a naval power. The peninsular part of India is surrounded with Indian Ocean which easily connected it with the rest of the imperial markets. Any imperial threat could be countered by the naval supremacy of England. A well-defended boundary in the northern-most part of India would mean the supremacy of British imperialism over a colony which was well connected in the age of imperialism. The other listed themes in the diary of William Jones had direct or indirect economic potential for British imperialism. A better understanding about them gave better control over economic and cultural exploitation.

[18] Asiatic Researches, 1884, Vol. 1, Calcutta: Brojondro Lall Doss, ix–x.

[19] Rohan, 'Russian Expansion and the English Challenge in Central Asia: A Historical Perspective', *Journal of Social Science and Linguistics* 5, no. 1 (2015): 132–143.

Sanskritized Wisdom at ASB: The Politics of Translations

William Jones has been appreciated in almost all the academic writings for being proficient in Sanskrit and his love for this language. His command over the language, no doubt, turned out to be of great help for the Orient and the academic circle which until date depends largely upon the translations carried out in the ASB for rewriting history. William's journey of learning Sanskrit in India is not devoid of imperial inclination. Jones had a list of 12 languages which he desired to learn in his lifetime. The list had Greek, Latin, Italian, French, Spanish, Portuguese, Hebrew, Arabic, Persian, Turkish, German and English.[20] Sanskrit was not even in the list. Nevertheless, later William Jones worked hard to establish Sanskrit as a branch of Indo-European language which had composed the ancient wisdom of the Orient. He contributed to the standardization of diacritics and believed that it was more scientific than Greek language. The reason should be assessed in the light of the changing imperial interest in India. In the 17th century, the West considered Sanskrit as the language of gentoos, moors and heathens.[21] The ignorance about the language was well recorded in the *History of Hindostan* by Alexander Dow in 1792. It was reflected in the imperial interest of his time where he writes:

> Excuses may be formed for our ignorance concerning the learning, religion and Philosophy of the Brahmins.... Literary inquires are by no means a capital object to many of our adventures in Asia. The few who have a turn for researches of that kind are discouraged by the very great difficulty in acquiring that language, in which the learning of the Hindus is contained.[22]

In the late 18th century, command over Sanskrit language meant receiving the key to decode the ancient knowledge which was recorded in the texts of India and was long forgotten by the

[20] Teignmouth, *Memoirs of the Life*, 192.

[21] Cohn, *Colonialism and Its Forms of Knowledge*, 25.

[22] Alexander Dow, *The History of Hindostan: From the Earliest Account of Time to the Death of Akbar* (London: John Murray, 1792).

natives too. Warren Hastings, the first Governor General of India, realized the linguistic limitation of the British officers and especially the judges. Thence, he encouraged the British officers to learn the language. Jones initially took help of the pandits and the maulvis to interpret the laws for judgments, but very soon realized that the pandits manipulated him. At those junctures of his life, he felt the need to learn the language and take complete charge of declaring a judgment, which is a clear indication of his humane and rationale being. He made an incessant effort to find a committed teacher who would help him master the language. His search ended in Nadiya.[23] Jones used few texts to discharge his duties as judge. His repeated use of certain texts and the selection of few law books by the ASB standardized them as the books of law for the land, wherein the legal system of the land was not concentrated in one or two books. Communities settled in different regions had their own set of laws, not necessarily recorded in the texts. People who followed the texts for judgments did not have single texts. The complexity and dynamism of the legal texts followed footsteps of the diversity of land. Plethora of laws books were written in a given point of time which had advised dharma for the ruler and people. The *Nitis*, the *Dharmashastras* and the *Smritis* are considered to be the books on legal system of India. Only to name a few, the *Kamandakiya Nitisastra*, *Gautama Smriti*, *Baudhayana Smriti*, *Apastamba Smriti* and *Vasishtha Smriti* are some of the legal texts which deal with civil and criminal laws along with the inputs on economy, polity and religion. The chronology of the texts has been arranged by the scholars from 600 BCE onwards.

The rigidity in the *Varnasramadharma*[24] was not a constant feature of the Indian society. There was certain amount of flexibility exercised in the social hierarchy of caste and sub-castes which depended upon the politico-religious culture of the region in a given age. Hence, there was never one form of legal system

[23] Ibid., 68–69.

[24] *Varnasramadharma* is the moral code of conduct (dharma) prescribed to each Varna, that is, Brahmana, Kshatriya, Vaishya and Shudra.

which was applied uniformly throughout the country. For instance, marriage laws were prohibited among the *sapindas*[25] and were punishable in the Brahmanical fold of society. It is not applied uniformly across the country. The definition of *sapindas* changes in law books. It also, therefore, changes in its implementation. Marriages in the maternal *sapindas* are allowed in the southern part of India, but not in the northern part. *Sapindas* in the *Yajnavalkya Smriti* is considered up to five ascending and descending generations on maternal side and seven generations in the paternal side, whereas the other lawgivers differ in the number of generations.[26] Similarly, *Apastamba Dharmashastra* does not give proprietorship to wife after the death of her husband, but *Gautama Dharmashastra* does.[27]

Interestingly, all the texts are normative in their narration, which holds true even for the Manusmriti, which was popularized as the legal text for Hindu population of India during the colonial period. Therefore, the instruction and implementation of norms will always be doubtful. For example, in reference to polygamous marriage, the *Vasishtha Dharmasutra* states that a Brahmana can marry three women, Kshatriya can marry two women, and Vaisya and Shudra can marry only one. If one goes by the legal text and believes that this was uniformly followed and any deviation from the rule was a punishable crime in India, then one should read the Buddhist text, the *Digha Nikaya*, which refers to the story of Mahagovinda who when desires to renounce the world offers his 40 wives to another man. Similarly, in the Vinaya Pitaka, a man from the Lichchavi[28] clan consulted other members of his community to kill his wife for committing adultery.[29] The ASB, in its exercise of translating the texts, was popularizing some

[25] *Sapindas* are blood relatives.

[26] U. Singh, *A History of Ancient and Early Medieval India* (Delhi: Pearson, 2009), 298.

[27] Ibid., 299.

[28] Lichchavi was a clan which followed republic form of government and not the monarchy. Their capital was located in Vaishali, present-day Muzaffarpur district of Bihar.

[29] Singh, *A History of Ancient and Early Medieval India*, 298.

and leaving out on others. This kind of knowledge production legitimized certain texts as the rule of the land and ripped apart the spirit of diverse legal ethos. In corollary, this exercise of make-believe created binaries in the legal system of India that there were two sets of legal books: one for Hindus and the other for Muslims. The diversity and flexibility of legal practices followed in ancient India lost ground in the attempt of scientifically ordering the country.

The anthropological studies, census and the articles published in the *Journal of Asiatic Society of Bengal* played a pivotal role in arranging the Indian society in two phalanges: Hindus and Muslims. The cultural complexity of the Indian population was breathtaking for the Europeans who had witnessed binaries in their histories. One common thread which ran in the non-Muslim population of the country was the idol worship and the ritualistic religious practices. Therefore, to present the demographic study, the imperialists chose religion as a criterion for arrangement of data which reduced the complexities of the Indian society into numericals of castes and sub-castes. Brahmanas were referred to as the heads of the Brahmanical society and learners of the Sanskrit texts in the travelogues and in the foreign accounts of the medieval period. Thence, the society was bifurcated into two religions: Hindus, where the Brahmans were at the highest pedestal, and the Muslims, who had established their rule in the country from the early medieval period. The writings of imperialist scholars like Orme give a glimpse of the imperialist communalism sown in the 18th century where Muslims were considered as violent, despotic and masculine and Hindus as indolent, passive and effeminate.[30]

Indian Pluralism and ASB

After the revolt of 1857, the British administrators had realized that the key to rule India was to break the communal harmony and continuously increase the gap between the Hindus and the

[30] Metcalf, *The Ideologies of Raj*, 133.

Muslims. In order to fulfil the imperial interest of establishing an unchallenged British rule in the Indian subcontinent, the knowledge produced in the ASB and the imperial history presented Hinduism as a static universal doctrine, whereas the academic discourse on the religions of ancient India had successfully proved that Hinduism had evolved and encompassed various doctrines and philosophies. If the religion of ancient India has to be traced primarily from the textual sources, then the roots had to be from the four Vedas: Rigveda, Yajurveda, Samaveda and Atharvaveda. The first three Vedas are considered to be the religion of the Aryans, and the last Veda recorded the religious practice of the non-Aryans, as it did not concentrate on the Brahmanical rituals but on superstition and magico-rituals.

By the coming of the 6th century BCE, the Brahmanical rituals had reached their full orthodoxy. In the early Vedic period, Indra, Varuna, Agni and Soma were the chief deities. They were replaced by Prajapati, Siva and Vishnu in the later Vedic period. The philosophy of religion at this point in time was more concentrated on *yajña* and *daan* and material prosperity was desired. Interestingly, in the 6th century BCE, when *Varnasramadharma* had become rigid and gifts, sacrifices and religious paraphernalia were elaborate, the philosophy of Upanishads germinated. The Upanishads and *Aranyakas* emphasized not on rituals but also on the discourses and process of liberation, karma and spirituality. Two forms of philosophy branched out in India: *Astika* (one who accepted the Vedic authority) and the *Nastika* (the one who rejected it). *Purva Mimamsa*, *Uttara Mimamsa*, *Nyaya*, *Vaisheshika*, *Samkhya* and Yoga are the examples of the former. Charvaka or Lokayata philosophy are the examples of the latter. The deities worshiped were not only restricted to the sacred texts of Hindus. The archaeological evidences of sculptures of *Yakshas*, *Yakshis*, *Nagas* and female figurines which looked like goddess of fertility were worshiped too. The religion was not always practised in terms of offerings made to gods and temples, but certain rituals which were related merely to *daan*/(gift) on certain auspicious days or ritual bathing were also an integral part. In the days of Bhagavad Gita and Puranas, elements of devotion seeped in. Submission of oneself became significant more than rituals, temples and statutes. In the 200 BCE, sectarianism, Shaivism, Vaishnavism and Shaktism gained prominence. In 300–600 CE, Puranas and Smritis became important. *Vratas*, tirthas and various self-disciplining rites became significant. In the southern part of India, composite gods were worshiped, for example, Hari-Hara (Vishnu and Siva). The ancient India witnessed the renunciatory religions along with the Brahmanical religions, in which Buddhism and Jainism were the most famous religions. The assimilation of Buddha and Jain tirthankaras into the Brahmanical pantheon of gods started from 600 CE. The elements of syncretism through the mythologies of avatars started shaping up the religion. The religion of Tantra, where yogic practices, sexual rites, attainment of supernatural power and liberation were desired, developed in the same period. Tantric sect of Pancharatra, Sahajiya, Kapalika, Kalamukhas and Nathas developed in the early medieval period. In the southern part of India, deities such as Subramaniyam and Ganapati were popular. Female deities, mostly as the consort of the male deities, were worshiped. There were exceptions like Pattini, who was an extremely popular goddess in the coastal areas. In the early medieval period, a great deal of philosophical writings emerged which can be understood under the terms of Advaitavada, Dvaitavada and so on and so forth. Another sect of Dashnamis came in the early medieval period which emphasized on the culture of *Mathas*. The Kṛṣṇa cult was another popular cult which developed from the Vaishnava theology. The Alvars and the Nayanar sects of South India drew inspiration from the Vaishnavism and the Shaivism, but there are fine differences in the philosophies of these sects. Similar is the case with Shaiva Siddhanta, Kashmir Shaivism and Virashaiva traditions. The Shakta cult inspired many female deities' sects: the Sapta Matrikas, Yoginis, Viraja, Stambheswari and Kamakhya.

The above-listed names of sects and cults are mere glimpse of religious diversities prevalent in India, which had not stopped evolving until the coming of the British administrators. In the 14th–15th century, devotional songs and saints became important in developing sects, to name a few, Kabir Panth and Ravidas Panth were popular. The only commonality among these religious sects was that the followers worshiped one or the other deity most of the time, and offering rituals and gifts were a common practice. The British administrators-turned-scholars, alien to these religious culture of India, clubbed them together and presented a data of Hinduism, which for them was juxtaposed to the Mohammedans of the country. The ordering of the data into two religious branches followed the British understanding of a society which had to be arranged in binaries. Sir Edwin Arnold wrote *The Light of Asia* in the 1879 and popularized Buddha and Buddhism in religious discourse. The historicity of the Buddha became a quest for the Europeans. The ASB and the English Indologists became interested in the textual sources of Buddhism. The history of religious movement and renunciations were emphasized in the writings of the ASB. The surveyors and explorers who were the precursors of the archaeologists in India started locating the historical sites of Buddhism. The texts of Chinese travellers were considered as the guidebook to locate the monuments and statues of Buddhism. Sir Alexander Cunningham, the first Director General of the ASI, established in 1861, paid utmost attention in locating the art materials and inscriptions related to Buddhism. The archaeological reports produced in ASI became a treasure for historians not only in the colonial period but even after Independence. However, the knowledge produced in this institution was not devoid of imperial interests. The data produced in the ASI reports was used to further divide the country on the lines of religions. Buddhism was presented as a religion of protest against the Brahmanism. The narrative of decline of Brahmanism, age of Buddhism and revivalism of Brahmanism was propounded by the scholars. The unilinear development of religions, the story of contest and rivalry among the religions of India became common lines of narration in the British writings to divide the country and fulfil the imperial interests.

Colonial Institutions' Hegemony

William Jones invited membership to all who loved Oriental knowledge, but in practice the natives were not allowed to become the members of the ASB. The natives were inducted in the Society only when not enough interest was exhibited by Englishmen and there was a financial crunch which affected the survival of the Society. Dr H. H. Wilson proposed names of some natives in January 1829 who were then elected as the members of the Society. In 1876, the members of the Society rose up to 285. The membership fees was reduced to ₹9. R. L. Mitra, the first native to become the president of the Society, writes that by this time not many Europeans had the interest and time for the society. Many European men would not devote their time to literary and scientific pursuits. 'Such pursuits require leisure and ease of circumstances, early literary training and an affluent retired life'.[31] Therefore, natives had to be inducted as members despite their defective education in early life and less interest in the researches.

The authors of knowledge institutions have always been praised for their narratives, and it is believed that the funding of the institution was either through the British government or through the membership fees. But it is worthy of notice that the first biggest donation to the ASB came from the King of Oudh worth ₹20,000 in 1828 which was supplemented by another ₹5,000 by his prime minister in the time of financial crisis.[32]

The establishment of ASB was inspired by the Royal Asiatic Society of England wherein the spirit, that is, quest for knowledge, was intact but the quality was shaped by the imperial interests. It becomes evident from the composition of the members of both the societies. In England, the professors of colleges, ministers of religion and educated men of independent means and retired from business were the active members, whereas in ASB every

[31] R. L. Mitra, *Centenary Review of the Asiatic Society of Bengal from 1784 to 1883*, Part 1 (Calcutta, 1885), 8–9.

[32] Ibid., 71.

individual was an employee of the Crown working in the capacity of a judge or an esquire. These employees could devote very few hours for Oriental knowledge that had no immediate connection with the imperial business.[33] The statement of Mr Edward Blyth, who was selected as a Curator of museum in the Society, informs that not every time competent men were brought in the ASB. In 1841, he wrote,

> It is in the Mineral department, unfortunately, that I am at present less qualified'... and with the liberal encouragement and support I may reckon upon receiving ... I shall soon render myself competent to discharge that portion of my duty which relates to the efficient management of the museum.[34]

William Jones was a man of scholarship; though under the shadow of imperialism, he worked and intended to collect knowledge about the Orient in the ASB. After the demise of Jones, the sincerity of the institution was undermined. The weekly meetings of ASB were converted into monthly meetings, and within six months, meetings were held once in three months. Now the Society was used for private meetings on the second and fourth Wednesdays of every month. Private meetings were held at 7.30 PM at the dinner table of the Englishmen in India. The seriousness of the conduct of curating Oriental knowledge was by now reduced to dinner table discussions.[35]

The Society published *Asiatic Researches*, a yearly journal started in 1788. The essays were purely based on scientific themes. James Prinsep in 1832 changed the name to the *Journal of the Asiatic Society of Bengal* and its orientation for publications. This time, the articles were essentially literary. It came out with additional advantage of free postage because the government considered that Dr Buchanan-Hamilton's Statistics of Bengal would be published in the appendix of the journal. Essays

[33] Ibid., 17–18.
[34] Ibid., 41.
[35] Ibid., 19.

on ethnographic study of marginal populations; reports on the region of northwest frontiers and on Indo-Greek connections; and articles on historical themes were selected for publications. The knowledge produced in this journal was quite a sensation in the West, and the demand was so high that a pirated edition was brought out in England in 1798. A French translation of the journal was brought out in Paris under the title of *Recherches Asiatiques*. These published essays were used to suffice the imperial designs. For instance, the satisfactory management of the coal mines in Raniganj and the reports of Dr Helfer and other scientific officers invited attention of the British government to the mineral resources, and a resolution was adopted in 1835 to establish a museum of economic geology.[36]

The British government funded strategically the Society and its work. It was not until 1835 that a systematic attempt was made for the publication of Oriental works. Whenever, due to political and financial compulsions, the government abandoned the works of the ASB, the natives came to rescue. For instance, the government had put a stop to printing of translated works of the Mahābhārata; the *Rajatarangini*; the 'Naishadha'; the *Sausruta*; the *Sariravidya*; the *Fatawa Alamgiri*; the *Inaya*; the *Khazanat ul-Ilm*; the *Jawame ul-ilm ul-Riazi*, the *Anis ul-Musharrahin* and a treatise in Arabic, as it would cost ₹20,000. R. L. Mitra writes that the native public most warmly took up the cause. The pandits and the maulvis who had been employed by the government to edit the works volunteered their service free of charge, and Nawab Tauhar Jang of Chitpur undertook to defray the entire cost of printing the *Share ul-Islam*.

The ASB started translating the Vedas in 1847, and not from the year of its establishment in 1784. The translation of the Vedas was not a smooth process. It went through abandonment and revival of the project. Under the chief editorship of Dr Roer and a team of pandits, the Vedas were to be translated in the monthly serial, *Bibliotheca Indica*. This project was abandoned

[36] Ibid., 10–195.

after the Court of Directors made an arrangement with Max Muller, and later even this arrangement was called off.[37] The Indian scholars such as Jaynarayan Tarkapanchanan (translated 19 texts), Bharatchandra Siromani (translated 16 texts), Maheswarachandra Nayantara (translated 19 texts), Pandit Satyavrata Samasrami (translated 44 texts) and Dr Rajendra Lal Mitra (translated 83 texts) contributed more than the English Indologists, but they failed to receive due credit for translating the works. Similar was the case with Pandit Radhakrishna of Lahore. In the year 1867, he urged the adoption of a comprehensive scheme that should bring to the light the treasures of Sanskrit lore buried in the private libraries in India. The government took it warmly. Mr Whitely Stokes, Dr Buhler from Bombay, Dr Kielhorn from Puna and Mr Burnell from Madras were entrusted with the management of the undertaking. All of them went in the annals of history, but Radhakrishna lost his sheen, the one who proposed the collection.[38]

The choice of texts for translation was influenced by imperial interest. Until the text was important enough to carry forward the administration of the British government, it was never considered in the project. This becomes evident from the statement of the court:

> Great impulse given to publications in Mohammedan literature and the Arabic language. Out of the 38 nos. of *Bibliotheca Indica* issued in 1854, 27 of them are Arabic only 10 are Sanskrit and one is English ... referring to the Mohammedan works, we observe that they have no relation whatever to India ... but they embrace to a very large extent abstruse Mohammedan theology and Sufyism ... works utterly worthless for the illustration of the past or present condition of India and of little utility to European scholars ... when we authorized the appropriation of a special grant to the encouragement of Indian literature we had in view especially the literature of Hindus.[39]

[37] ASB Proceedings, Calcutta: Baptist Mission Press, May 1806, 59–62.
[38] ASB Proceedings, Calcutta: Park Street, August 1856, 59–68.
[39] Ibid., 60.

William Jones and ASB interpreted the historical themes of India according to the imperial needs. During 1784–1856, the British parliament along with the Crown wanted to establish British rule in India with a difference, where it wanted to portray a just image and downsize the corrupt practices implemented by the EIC. The Mughal dynasty was in the last phase; regional kingdoms which were ruling the land mostly were engrossed in enmity and there was tussle for power between the zamindars and the rulers. Hence, the British government had the desire to present itself as a good alternative for better governance. Therefore, the need was to create a conducive intellectual environment for the smooth transition of power, which could have been best dealt with by exhibiting similarities between the West and East. William Jones drew parallels between a large number of classical gods and the goddess of the West with those of Indian mythologies, for instance, Janus–Ganesha; Saturn–Manu or Satyavrata; Jupiter–Indra; Hermes–Narada; and Ceres–Lakshmi.[40] In 1786, Jones in a lecture on Indo-European languages, conducted in ASB, told that there are six ancient languages: Sanskrit, Latin, Greek, Gothic, Celtic and Old Persian. They all are so similar in roots that it seems that all of them descended from a common language.[41] Brahmanas were considered as the custodian of Vedic knowledge. Jones wrote that the Brahmanas of Tirhut migrated from Egypt and hence are called Misra. This had an echo in 1851 in the presidential address made by John Pickering in the American Oriental Society:

> Whether Egypt communicated its knowledge of the arts and the sciences to India, or the rivers, or whether they interchanged their philosophy and the arts with each other, has long been a subject of debate among the learned, and which now hardly admits of being satisfactorily settled.... That there was an intercourse between the two countries in ancient times, seems to be beyond dispute.[42]

[40] *As Res.*, London: J. Swan Son, 1885, Calcutta, 221.

[41] *As Res.*, 1788, Calcutta: Park Street, 431.

[42] G. A. Barton, 'Tiamat', *Journal of the American Oriental Society* 15 (1893): 6.

The historical connection of India with ancient Egypt had an imperial design. Ancient Egypt was a part of Greco-Roman empire which shares historical connections with Europe. It was believed that the interconnection of the histories would justify the British rule in India.

It was not only the ASB which influenced the course of narratives in the history of India. The ASI was playing key role in dividing the country on the basis of religion, and this time not between Hindus and Muslims, but between Brahmanism and Buddhism. Cunningham recorded the excavation reports of sites that were primarily referred to in Hiuen Tsang's account. Places which provided inscriptions were of utmost importance to him. Thence, historical sites devoid of inscription many a time were left out from the records, and the history of such sites was either never recorded or was pushed towards modern dates. For instance, the narrative of the ASI report on Gaya informs that the region was a Buddhist site, but the evidence of the Barabar caves exhibits both the statues of Buddhism and Brahmanism hailing from the same period. The narrative of Cunningham influenced the later writings, and the academia produced number of researches which established Buddhism as the religion of the region. The region along with Buddhism had Brahmanical and Ajivika presence.[43] The ASB selected data for the publications which suited the imperial needs of establishing the identity and historicity of religions. Amardeva (one of the nine jewels from the court of Vikramaditya) came to Bodh Gaya for prayer and then visited Vishnupad Temple. The visit of Amardeva was recorded in an inscription which was reported by Wilmot but could not find place in the publication.[44] As a result, Gaya was celebrated as the land of Buddhism in the academic

[43] Gaya has Vishnupad Temple and the Phalgu river where death ritual of *sraddha* is performed. In the Barabar caves, statues of Siva, Parvati and Buddha have been found. One of the caves was dedicated by King Dasaratha to the Ajivikas. The Ajivikas are one of the heterodox sect which emerged along with the 62 sects in India around 600 BCE, in which Buddhism and Jainism became popular.

[44] Kejriwal, *The Asiatic Society of Bengal and the Discovery of India's Past 1784–1838*, 45–46.

writings, and the history of Vishnupad Temple was pushed to the days of Gaya mahatmya, an interpolation of Vayu Purana. P. V. Kane dates the text not prior to 1400 CE.

Conclusion

The knowledge institutions of colonial India presented an understanding of India which was highly influenced by the history of Europe. The narratives manufactured in them classified populations not just in Varnas and castes, but labelled them with adjectives such as brave, docile, thief, aggressive, mysterious, knowledge custodian and so on and so forth. The make-believe exercise resulted in selecting only few books as the book of laws which ruled the land, whereas in practice it was otherwise. The religious practices were never so cohesive as presented in the narratives. The land always experienced composite culture and had space for every sect, cult and renunciator, but the narratives made an attempt to write the history in the parlance of emergence, downfall and revivals. The impact of narratives is not restricted to the colonial period. The moulds still persist in the academic discourses, and the real challenge is to break the mould, choose new sources and compare with the evidence recorded in the narratives of these knowledge institutions and rewrite the history of India.

Bibliography

Alam, Muzaffar. *The Crisis of Empire in Mughal North India, Awadh and the Punjab: 1707–1748*. New Delhi: Oxford University Press, 1986.

Alam, Muzaffar. 'Trade, State Policy and Regional Change: Aspects of Mughal-Uzbek Commercial Relations, c. 1550–1750'. *Journal of the Economic and Social History of the Orient* 37, no. 3 (1994): 202–227.

Ashton, S. R. *British Policy towards the Indian States, 1905–39*. London: Curzon Press, 1982.

Asiatic Society and Monthly Journal 21 (1826). London: W. M. H. Allen & Co.

Banerji, Arup. *Old Routes: North Indian Nomads and Bankers in Afghan, Uzbek and Russian Lands: Three Essays Collective*. New Delhi: Three Essays Collectives, 2011.

Bearce, G. D. *British Attitudes towards India, 1784–1858*. London: Oxford University Press, 1961.
Bird, James. *The Journal of the Royal Asiatic Society of Great Britain and Ireland* 1, no. 1 (1834) London: Cambridge University Press.
Braudel, Fernand. *Civilization and Capitalism 15th–18th Century: The Wheels of Commerce*, Vol. 2. Translated by Sian Reynolds. New York: Harper & Row, 1982.
Cannon, Garland. *The Life and Mind of Oriental Jones: Sir William Jones, the Father of Modern Linguistics*. London: Cambridge University Press, 1999.
Majeed, Javed. *Ungoverned Imaginings*. Oxford: Clarendon Press, 1992.
Mill, James, and H. H. Wilson. *History of British India*. London: J. Madden, 1840–1846.
Mukherjee, S. N. *Sir William Jones: A Study in the Eighteenth Century British Attitudes to India*. London: Cambridge University Press, 1968.
Panniker, K. M. *The Geographical Factors in Indian History*. Bombay: Bhartiya Vidya Bhawan, 1959.
Rohan. 'The Indian Merchant Diaspora and the Cross-Cultural Trade in Central Asia from Sixteenth to the Early Nineteenth Century' (MPhil dissertation, New Delhi, JNU, 2013).

Conclusion

Himanshu Roy

Indic thought was in constant flux in the precolonial past. The new settlements, constant inflow of bullion, the new trade routes, the trading centres in the hinterlands, the changing elite and the administration, and the booming trade kept the social mobility dynamic, propelling the changes in social thought. The colonial description of India as unchanging was a deliberate design. The British and the other European trading companies were in India for more than a century. They had witnessed its dynamism in the 17th and 18th centuries and had come for its wealth. Once they seized the state power, their attitude towards India changed. Now, the colonial India was to have a new history. From the 'land of desire', 'treasures of nature' and 'treasure of wisdom', as Hegel had termed India,[1] it became an 'unchanging' civilization; its history became 'fables' and its most knowledgeable section, the Brahmans, became 'immoral', murderers, cheats and robbers; Hindus, the residents of Hindustan, were called 'cunning'. Hegel, a friend of William Jones, had stated that 'Hindus have no history' and that 'they are incapable of writing history' or India had lost conscience in respect to truth. This was the new history, a change that had begun to emerge from the last decade of the

[1] C. Hegel, *Philosophy of History*, trans. J. Sibree (New York: Colonial Press, 1900), 139–167.

18th century. It was Hegel who had also written that 'from the most ancient times downwards, all nations have directed their wishes and longings to gaining access to the treasures of this land of marvels'.[2] After 1757, 'their wishes and longings' had fructified. The defeat of Siraj, the Nawab of Bengal, in the Battle of Plassey, by the British East India Company, led to the loot of the whole treasury by Robert Clive from Murshidabad; and it was carted away to Calcutta and then to London. It was 232 million pounds, of which 22 million pounds was pocketed away by Clive alone.[3] Before it, the Company had already misused the *farman* of trade in India by not paying the taxes to the treasury. Their loot had reduced the Indian society to penury and illiteracy. This loot was not on the agenda of the public discourse; rather, the issue was the social condition to which India was reduced as a result of the loot under their rule. Bengal was the richest province in the 1750s, but it was reduced to droughts and deaths shortly after their takeover. And in the absence of social funding, schools and the health centres were being closed, leading to illiteracy and poor health. It was the beginning of the decline of India as the economic and social power; the land of desire and wisdom had changed to penury and illiteracy.

Before the 1750s, 'the Asian merchants (India and China) had far more capital compared to those of the European.' Marco Polo and Ibn Battuta had stated in their travelogues that Chinese spices trade was far larger in volume than the Europeans.[4] Even its ocean-going ships were far larger in size than the Europeans. But the European historians after their military and political conquest just distorted the past through their 'skilful' interpretations of selective archival documents. It was a newly manufactured history required to suit their newly acquired power to rule over the new subjects. This dynamism of precolonial Asian trade brought in diverse technologies and ideas that constantly enriched our social thought. It simultaneously brought in bullion that filtered

[2] Ibid.

[3] William Dalrymple, *The Anarchy*. London: Bloomsbury, 2019, 133.

[4] Aniruddha Ray, *The Sultanate of Delhi, 1206–1526*. New Delhi: Manohar, 2011, 315.

downwards and expanded into rural hinterlands which kept the skilled labour engaged and socially mobile in the production process at different locations and at diverse centres. The link of this prosperity, as mentioned above, was the trade which connected the rural–urban and the coastal–hinterland population.[5] It expanded the requirement of the labour which were supplied either from outside the country or from different tribes which were not yet part of the mainstream social structure. The professional engagements provided them with constant earnings which kept their social participation in the community intact. It obstructed major social ruptures. The best demonstration of the social participation is recorded in the memoirs of different travellers. Al-Biruni, for example, writing in the 11th century mentioned about Diwali celebration: 'People bathe, dress festively, and make presents to each other ... till noon. In the night they light a great number of lamps in every place.'[6] There were equally important other festivals such as Holi, Basant Panchami and Shivratri which are still celebrated. The rituals of marriage or the forms and manners of organizing the marriage are also similar. These indicate a long civilizational continuity of culture despite the impact of different non-Indic religions which arrived thousands of years ago from outside. Even the change of ruling elite coming from non-Indic religions was not able to dent it much. The regional variations in forms and modes of religion did exist, but the commonalities of the basics of Indic religions maintained the unity. It transcended the variations which also provided democratic space of autonomy to the community and freedom of individuality to subjects.

The cultural variations were glaringly visible in the dialects, scripts and languages which were vernacular. Sanskrit and Arabic-Persian were mostly written and spoken by the academics

[5] For details, see Ranabir Chakrabarti, 'Relationships and Interactions in the Economic Sphere', in *History of Science, Philosophy and Culture in Indian Civilisation*, Vol. II, Part 5, ed. D. P. Chattopadhyaya (Delhi: Pearson Longman, 2009), 145–152.

[6] Al Biruni, cited in D. P. Chattopadhyaya, ed., *History of Science, Philosophy and Culture in Indian Civilisation*, Vol. II, Part 5. Delhi: Pearson Longman, 2009, 281.

or were used in the edicts of administration. The diverse music, dance and architecture reflected the localities of the regions and were expressed mostly in vernacular. It was determined, to an extent, by topography, weather and technologies of the time. Even the gender relation was influenced by these elements which, in turn, is part of the popular culture. Yet there was a running theme of commonalities in them which is reflected in the worship of gods, males and females, which were common—Brahma, Vishnu and Mahesh and their wives—across the Indic lands. The commonality is also visible in the social forms of protests which was inclusive and democratic and is reflected in the Bhakti movement. From Tamil Nadu to Kashmir and from Gujrat to Manipur, women and Dalit saints were the popular representatives, who became their icons in due course. It was a communitarian movement manifested through folk songs and dance on the hymns of gods, laced with social issues and composed by the saints. It created a new social discourse, moderated the old and generated democratic space for individual and social co-optation and mobility.[7] Many of the issues related to social marginals became acute. It was the result of the colonial rule which disrupted its economy and social structure. In precolonial India, these were on the margin. The volume of trade and the arrival of bullion benefited all in different proportion or lessened the severity of the malaise on the victims where it existed. The contemporary discourse of the feminists and of the Dalit activists claiming about their constituencies to be victims for centuries, even in precolonial India, is highly contentious and not universal, neither it is supported by sociological facts. Contrary to it, the literary works of female and Dalit poets and of the foreign residents posit an altogether different picture. In the Marathi Abhanga literature, which has been contributed by series of women saints, there is no reference to the idea of patriarchy. The reference rather is of humiliation, if one reads the Abhanga of Sayrabai or Janabai, which is also visible in the inscription found in the Tamil countryside near Pondicherry. The inscription is of Rajaraja period of the 11th century CE which mentions

[7] For details, see ibid., 239.

about keeping away a small number of residents of a village from its community work. But had there been an absolute caste dominance or patriarchy, as the contemporary discourse suggests, there would not have been 60 female saints from the Lingayata community alone, that too in the medieval times,[8] and many of them were from the 'lower' castes. Similarly, there were series of women saints in Maharashtra who composed Abhanga reflecting their education. Foreign travellers residing in India such as Paolino Da Bartolomeo, an Austrian Carmelite missionary who had stayed in India from 1776 to 1789 in the Malabar region of Kerala, or French traveller Berneir, who had stayed in the court of Aurangzeb, had their interesting observations. The most comprehensive with graphic details, however, is given by the British in their early surveys of Indic society in the late 18th and early 19th centuries. Bartolomeo wrote the following:

> [E]ducation with them (Indians) is an early and an important business in every family. Many of their women are taught to read and write. The Brahmans are generally the school masters, but any of the respectable castes, may, and often do, practice teaching.... It is to these elementary schools that the labouring classes in India owe their education.[9]

This in like manner was partly available for labour in Europe and was imitated from India. Approximately 250 years early, in 1623, it was the same mode of education in India. Peter Della Valle's letter reflects it.[10] British colonial surveys also substantiate it with more graphic details which reflected of universal elementary education for all, funded collectively by the villages.[11] As the colonial rule deepened its roots, the social funding of the indigenous schools in every village dried up, and the English schools

[8] A. K. Ramanujan, 'Talking to God in the Mother Tongue', *India International Centre Quarterly* 19 (November 1992): 55.

[9] Paolino Da Bartolomeo, in Dharampal, *The Beautiful Tree* (New Delhi: Biblia Impex, 1983), 259.

[10] Ibid., 259–260.

[11] For details, see ibid.

being too expensive, most of the poor students remained out of schools expanding the illiteracy in India. In combination with the economic loot, the labour was placed in the worst position. It created and deepened the caste and gender segregation among them to minimize the competition over the resources.

Earlier, 'the annual exchequer receipts of Jahangir did not amount more than 5% of the computed revenue of his empire, and that of Aurangzeb ... did not ever exceed 20%'[12] as major claim over the revenue of villages was on local education, health, irrigation, religious centre and policing.[13] The inscriptions and revenue records from Bengal and Tamil Nadu reflect it. More importantly, the village functioned like a democratic collective either through committees or through general assemblies. The general assemblies nominated or elected the committees as per the requirements of the works. Many times, the local revenue officials were part of it who used to maintain records of the revenue collection and expenditures. In case of any misappropriation of fund or any deviation from the plan of works, the assembly used to penalize the culprit.[14] The assembly or the committees were inclusive of its social composition. The exclusion of gender and castes is not visible in the records; leather tanners, one or two families in the villages, were seemed to be kept away from the desilting process of the irrigation tank.[15] The records mention about inter-caste marriages and pampering of the local crafts to check their migrations. As discussed earlier, the booming trade always provided employment to the skilled labour who were also rewarded for their skills to keep their migrations in check. It also speaks against the stereotypical colonial and postcolonial discourse on caste and gender exclusion as Sanatan (perennial) problem of the Indic society. Contextualized in the backdrop of a

[12] Ibid., 66.

[13] Ibid., 67–68.

[14] S. JeyaSeela Stephen, *Pondicherry under the French*. New Delhi: Primus, 2018, 22.

[15] Ibid.

medieval society, 500 years ago, a Tamilian, an Odia, a Malabari or a Gujarati speaking Arabic or European languages to sale their goods to the traders of Denmark, Portugal, Holland, France, Arabs and Britain must have generated cosmopolitan impact on the Indians; or these traders visiting the coastal areas or hinterland, interacting with Indians to purchase their textiles, spices and other things of their requirements, must have generated economic prosperity for the peasants and craftsmen. The agents, *dubhasiya* (the interlocutors) and the traders were the other beneficiaries. Both the trade and the culture in sync with universal elementary education and skill must have checked the social exclusionary process which later emerged and solidified during the colonial rule in the absence of benefits of booming trade.

The trade and prosperity also had their manifestation visible in the religious pilgrimages of different sections best recorded in the biographical sketches of saints. Sankardeo, for example, from Assam had travelled in the 16th century to different parts of India, for years, or Tulsidas had travelled to Chitrakoot, Benares and Ayodhya in the 16th century, and there were many other such examples as Mirabai, Ravidas and Guru Nanak. Interestingly, these saints and pilgrims were from all the sections that reflected their economic and social freedom. There was, however, wide economic gap between the elite, the economic and political, and the subaltern, which was widely noted by the foreign travellers. This manifested in the power relations in the society, more in the rural hinterlands where social mobility and opportunities were lesser. Many of the castes which are considered as 'lower' in contemporary times had different professional works and social status. Barbers and gardeners (*nai* and *mali*, respectively) were professional doctors with different expertise. The leather tanners, who had unclean social status, were in far better economic position than in the colonial time. Their professional indispensability put them in a strong negotiable position. Similar was the economic position of the *dom* (the profession which handled the dead bodies). These professions, which lost their economically negotiable positions after the arrival of colonial capitalism, sunk in lower economic and social status. Brahmana, which meant researcher, teacher, academic, higher studies, a profession which was followed by different people interested in research and study, was reduced to a hereditary caste, and its professional ethics was termed as dominant caste values; it became a slur. Upadhyaya, Acharya and Mukhopadhyay were professional designations of academics which were occupied by different gender and castes. British colonialism made it a symbol of Brahmana caste, and of social dominance. Brahmana, the academic, was declared as cheat and murderer; he was made an object of derision. What the political Islam was not able to do in 1,000 years of its rule, the British could successfully do it in 190 years of its rule. It succeeded in destroying the indigenous knowledge tradition of research, and of academic leadership which was cosmopolitan to rule over India. The political Islam could only dent it marginally. The only similarity between the two, British and Muslims, was that both were backward in economy in comparison to India when they had seized the state power. While the British took less than 100 years to colonize the whole of India, the political Islam took more than 400 years to expand itself after its arrival.[16] The role of technologies in expediting the process of dominance played a critical difference. While the political Islam brought in paper, which was easy to handle, the British brought in the printing press, which disseminated their ideas in the manner of carpet bombing. Both were intolerant to radical dissension. Even Dara Shikoh's view on Vedantic Hinduism was termed as fidelity, a threat to Islam.[17]

The changes that were actuated by the colonial rule had a disastrous impact on the precolonial society. The British interpreted this disaster, created by them, as perennial existing in India for centuries. Subsequently, the postcolonial historian continued as the history of Indic civilization. The social crisis by the Raj led to the emergence of two themes of discourse and programme of

[16] Vasudha Dalmia and Munish D. Fauruqui, *Religious Interactions in Mughal India*. Oxford: Oxford University Press, 2014, xiii.
[17] Ibid., 31, 55, 67.

action initiated by the social reformers: women and Dalit emancipation. It was felt that they were oppressed for centuries. The second aspect of their activism was to demand from the colonial state modern universal education. Both the issues, the closure of the schools and the death of the traditional crafts, which had given the universal elementary education and employment to the craftsmen, were the result of the colonial rule. The precolonial India had universal women participation in the agriculture, business and crafts. Among the elite, however, it was problematic. The textual interpretations of some of the Smritis on the women issues in the colonial and postcolonial times are blinkers. The texts which argue about the women property rights are rarely discussed. Similarly, it has been rarely discussed that the labour, the craftsmen and the peasants had universal elementary education in their mother tongues. The closure of these schools under the Raj has rarely been explained. One of the most prominent and discussed themes in the Indic history was *Nyaya* which reflects the academic and societal sensitivity towards universal justice. Ideological contest through Shastrarth was one of the methods to propagate one's views. Bhakti was the other method to convey one's ideas. It was equally a protest of the subaltern for *Nyaya*. It also reflected cultural nationalism premised on the similarities and commonalities of religion and godliness which has been existing for centuries. The arrival of new technologies during the colonial regime boosted it with better national bonding. The territorial nationalism, however, in its present form emerged in the 19th century, boosted by the 1857 revolt and assisted by modern capitalism and technology.

Indic civilization had a long tradition of public sphere and civil society. One of its forms was the village assemblies and their different committees which were the institutions of grassroots democracy that managed their affairs collectively. The perception of India, however, was of a nation of traders who were docile, feminine, subservient and unfit for military battles, who could be conquered easily, who lacked democratic institutions, etc., and whose Indic civilization was an unchanging hydraulic society which had been ruled in history by different invaders whose primary function was revenue collection and water management. A reading of Marx's writings on India portrays this image.[18] It was bluntly wrong which was premised on the British parliamentary reports fed by officers of the Raj. It was also argued that the colonial rule actuated the only social revolution in Hindustan which is, again, a highly contentious proposition. The Raj destroyed the 'land of desire' and 'treasure of wisdom'. It colonized the mind and destroyed the trade dominance of the Indic civilization. The sovereign Indian nation developing the fruits of modern technology, capitalism and democracy would have been a far better option.

The British had learnt about the inexpensive universal elementary education from India and had applied it in their own country to the great advantage of their citizens. India, as a sovereign nation, would have surely learnt of new technologies and modern republicanism from other countries, as it had learnt many things in the past, in the march of civilization. That is how it was the treasures of wisdom.

[18] Karl Marx and F. Engels, *On Colonialism* (Moscow: Progress Publishers, 1959), 36–41.

About the Editor and Contributors

Editor

Himanshu Roy is a Professor of Political Science, DDU College, University of Delhi, and Former Atal Bihari Vajpayee Senior Fellow, Nehru Memorial Museum and Library, Teen Murti House, New Delhi. His publications include *Peasant in Marxism* (2006), *Secularism and Its Colonial Legacy in India* (2009), *State Politics in India* (editor, 2017), *Indian Political System* (editor, 2018), *Indian Political Thought* (editor, 2011), *Patel: Political Ideas and Policies* (editor, SAGE, 2018), *Political Thought in Indic Civilization* (editor, SAGE, 2021) and *A History of Colonial India* (editor, 2021).

Contributors

Sonali Chitalkar is an Assistant Professor of Political Science, Miranda House, University of Delhi. Her publications include *Delhi Riot 2020: The Untold Story* (co-author, 2020) and 'Colonial Education' (in Himanshu Roy and Jawaid Alam edited *A History of Colonial India*, 1st ed., December 2021).

Kaustubh Gaurh is a Research Scholar, Centre for Historical Studies, JNU, New Delhi.

Niraj Kumar Jha is an Associate Professor of Political Science, M. L. B. College, Jiwaji University, Gwalior. His recent publications include 'Interpreting Colonial and Nationalism' (in Himanshu Roy and Jawaid Alam edited *A History of Colonial India*, 1st ed., 2021).

Ritika Joshi is an Assistant Professor of History, Hindu College, University of Delhi.

Shankar Kumar is an Associate Professor of History, Hindu College, University of Delhi. His publications include Frank Concise Social Sciences (co-author, 2005) and Indian History and Culture (co-editor, 2014).

Santoshi Kumari is an Associate Professor of History, Lakshmibai College, University of Delhi.

Abhishek Parashar is an Assistant Professor of History, Aryabhatta College, University of Delhi.

Siddheshwar Shukla is a Former Fellow, Makhanlal Chaturvedi National University of Journalism and Communication (MCNUJC), Bhopal.

Dinesh Kumar Singh is an Associate Professor of Political Science, K. R. G. Autonomous P. G. College, Jiwaji University, Gwalior. His recent publications include 'Social Movements in Colonial India' (in Himanshu Roy and Jawaid Alam edited *A History of Colonial India*, 1st ed., 2021).

Sri Prakash Singh is a Professor of Political Science, University of Delhi. His publications include *Dr. Ambedkar on Minorities* (2005), *Dr Ambedkar: Alpsankhyak Prashna Evam Samvaidhanic Pravdhan* (2015), *Chakravarti Rajagopalachari: Vyaktitva, Krititva evam Vichar* (2015), *Politics for a New India: A Nationalistic Perspective* (2018) and *Cultural Nationalism: The Indian Perspective*, Vols 1 and 2 (2015).

Ruchi Tyagi is a Professor of Political Science, Kalindi College, University of Delhi. Her recent publications include *Constitutional Democracy and Government in India* (2012), *Adhunik Bharat Ka Rajnitik Chintan: Ek Vimarsh* (editor, 2015) and *Glocalization and Federal Governance in India: Understanding the Emerging* (editor, 2019).

Index